50 YEARS ON THE STREET

William Roache has become a true British acting icon, having spent five decades playing Ken Barlow in *Coronation Street*. He is the only remaining original member of the cast and the longest-serving actor in a British, indeed world, TV series.

50 YEARS ON THE STREET

MY LIFE WITH KEN BARLOW

WILLIAM ROACHE MBE

**MAINSTREAM
PUBLISHING**

EDINBURGH AND LONDON

This edition, 2011

First published in Great Britain in 2010 by
MAINSTREAM PUBLISHING COMPANY
(EDINBURGH) LTD
7 Albany Street
Edinburgh EH1 3UG

ISBN 9781845967215

A catalogue record for this book is available
from the British Library

Typeset in Adobe Caslon and Sabon

Printed in Great Britain by
CPI Cox and Wyman Reading RG1 8EX

1 3 5 7 9 10 8 6 4 2

To Sara, for 37 years of love and devotion.

ACKNOWLEDGEMENTS

I have to start by saying thanks to Tony Warren, the man who created *Coronation Street* all of those years ago. Without him, none of us would be working on such a wonderful programme, and my life would have been very different. Not only did Tony write the show, he also laid the foundations for what the programme is. I also want to acknowledge the *Street*'s very first producer, Harry Elton, and also Harry Kershaw. Both were father figures who nurtured the programme in those early days.

I also have to thank the succession of managing directors at Granada, all of the producers and directors of the show over the years who have been so supportive, and the cast members I have been fortunate enough to work with during the past five decades. I also want to thank all the technicians and crew who work so hard on the programme, the wardrobe and make-up departments, and the second assistant directors who somehow manage to sort our lives out with great professionalism and with a minimum amount of fuss. I must also thank the press office for both protecting us from the media and for projecting us within it, and my special thanks go to both Alison Sinclair and Janice Troup. My thanks also go to Dominic Khouri for his invaluable help with facts and figures concerning the show, to Helen Nugent, and to Daran Little for his many works of reference over the years regarding the programme.

I would also like to thank John Hayes, Matt Hayes, Victoria Marconetto and all those at Champions UK for their support and work in getting this project off the ground, to Rick Mayston at Getty Images, and to Bill Campbell and Karyn Millar at Mainstream Publishing. My thanks must also go to Paul O'Grady for providing the foreword to this book and for being a friend to both me and the *Street*.

Finally, I would like to say a special thanks to Kevin Brennan, who collaborated with me in writing this book, and to his wife, Lynda, and children, James and Rachel, for giving him the time and support he needed. Kevin was a delight to be with and actually managed to enlighten me and open my eyes when it came to talking about my years on the programme. It was a joy to work with him.

CONTENTS

FOREWORD

The first time I met Bill Roache was when I was hosting the TV comedy game show *Blankety Blank*. I was told that Bill was going to be appearing on the programme and I just couldn't believe it. I'd been a fan of *Coronation Street* for as long as I could remember, and Bill's character, Ken Barlow, had been in my front room twice a week ever since I started watching the show. It almost felt like he was family. The worrying thing when you actually meet someone who you've known through watching them on television is that they might disappoint you. I've met plenty of people in show business who have turned out to be monsters, but not Bill. I was a bag of nerves when I met him – I couldn't have felt more jittery if I had been meeting Elvis – but he put me at my ease immediately and I really liked him. There are so many sides to Bill Roache. He's spiritual, very kind and very funny. He's also a very good actor who has made Ken Barlow one of the iconic British soap characters.

It's incredible to think that *Coronation Street* has now been on our screens for more than 50 years, and even more remarkable that Bill has been playing Ken for all of those years. Of course, Bill and Ken are very different characters: Ken is quite dogmatic, whereas Bill is pragmatic; Bill had a long and happy marriage to his lovely wife Sara until her sudden death in 2009, while Ken is off if there's a whiff of a petticoat! One thing is for sure, Ken Barlow is a pivotal character in the show and without him *Coronation Street* just wouldn't be the same. The programme has

11

always been able to adapt and move with the times, which has been the secret of its longevity. It constantly reinvents itself and brings in new characters, but in the middle of all of that is the rock of the show: Bill Roache.

I think they have done and can do so much with Ken Barlow, and I'm sure there's still a lot of mileage yet to come in the character. It's no coincidence that the character of Ken Barlow has been around for so long and has been involved in some classic scenes and storylines during the course of the programme. I can still remember that Ken, Deirdre and Mike Baldwin saga and the scene in the hallway of the Barlows' house. It was one of those stories on the show where the whole country seemed to come to a standstill as they watched the programme. Of course we know that the *Street* is fiction, but there is a lot of realism in Corrie, and it's the acting that grips us and keeps us watching five times a week.

I've always thought that Ken Barlow is a great character: you can hang anything on him, and that's down to Bill, because he's such a good actor, and the writers of the show. It's a great combination and it works really well. Bill must be one of the most recognisable faces in Britain, but despite that he's managed to remain a very private bloke who never pushes himself forward and is quite happy to let other people take centre stage. He's very self-effacing, and that's rare in our game, because it can very often be a case of dog-eat-dog. He's been a guest on my chat show a couple of times, and I've always really enjoyed him being on the programme; he's so easy-going and genuine, something that I'm sure comes across to the viewer.

I can't believe that he is now 79 years old: he looks and sounds like someone in their 50s! He never seems to age, and I'm sure that comes from within. He's got a fabulous head of hair and is a good-looking man. I don't know what his secret is, but I wish I did. With me, it's completely the opposite. I get up in the morning, look in the mirror and think, 'What happened in the night?' It's clear that even after 50 years Bill is a man who loves his work; he genuinely enjoys it.

I'm sure there are some people who think that life as a soap star is easy. They sit in their dressing-room and wait for a knock on the door to call them onto the set, spend ten minutes acting and then go back and rest, while at the same time earning loads of money – but that just isn't the case. It's really hard, difficult work and it can be quite gruelling at times, with long days and lots of scripts to learn. I've always said that I really admire soap stars because I know just how hard they have to work, and because of the exposure they get, a lot of their private life becomes public. Bill has always found time to talk, and with fans he's always able to say something nice and make them feel good about themselves, which I know he gets a lot of pleasure from. I think Bill's a bit like me in the sense that he always tries to see the best in someone, and is happy to see other people's successes.

He's left his stamp on British television history and has managed to give us one of the greatest soap characters of all time. I admire the man and feel better for knowing that there's a Bill Roache in the world. He's one of the good guys.

Paul O'Grady

PREFACE

It is astonishing to think that last year marked the 50th anniversary of *Coronation Street*, and I was both proud and pleased that it also provided a personal landmark for me.

I was lucky enough to be one of the original cast members in the first-ever episode of the show, when it was broadcast on 9 December 1960, and here I am some fifty years later still playing the role of Ken Barlow in what has become one of Britain's most popular television programmes. It is a role I have enjoyed immensely, and the fact that I am still playing it would suggest Ken is a character the public have enjoyed seeing on their screens throughout those years.

Each time the show has celebrated a particular anniversary so, too, have I, but this, understandably, has always become somewhat lost in the grand scheme of things, so I am delighted to now have the opportunity to write about my career on the *Street*. This book is a celebration of my own time with the show and a chance for me to write about some of the characters, storylines and moments that have been of significance to me during those years. It is not a detailed history of the programme, but rather a personal look at something that has played such a big part in my life as an actor.

I feel very proud to have had such a long association with the show, and also very lucky to have done a job that I absolutely love for such a long period of time. For an actor to be in work continuously for 50 years is quite unusual in itself, and for the work to have been on a programme that has remained at the top of the television ratings throughout that time is amazing, and I consider myself very fortunate to be part of such a wonderful show.

The programme's great strength has always been that it is character based, and there has been a succession of notable characters who have captured the imagination of the viewers and been taken to the hearts of *Coronation Street* fans. Having been on our screens for more than 50 years, the terms of reference for the show are wide, and this is what keeps it alive.

If I'm honest, I really don't know where the time has gone. I have always taken my involvement with the show on a day-to-day, story-by-story and year-to-year basis. The current storyline has always been the most important, and I have always just tried to get on with my work and perform to the best of my ability. When you suddenly lift your head up and think about all that has gone on and how the programme has changed since that very first episode, it is really quite mind-boggling.

This book has given me the opportunity to do just that. I have looked back trying to give an insight and a real flavour of what it has been like for me during the past five decades, not just in a professional sense, but also in my life off-screen. It is about both Bill Roache, the actor, and Ken Barlow, the character I have become so closely associated with. I believe that if you love a television programme, and thankfully plenty of people seem to love the *Street*, then it is nice to know what makes it tick, what the actors and those associated with the show are like and what goes on behind the scenes. I have attempted to do this with a very personal perspective, but one that I also hope gives a genuine insight into *Coronation Street*.

I have explored just what it is like to play Ken and how I feel about him, and I have also looked at some of the storylines he has been involved in. Many people might assume that playing the same character for such a long period of time can be restricting or repetitive, but nothing could be further from the truth. There is huge variety in playing someone like Ken, and the wonderful thing for me as an actor is that I have been able to portray him throughout so many phases of his life. When *Coronation*

PREFACE

Street first started, Ken Barlow was very much the young blood of the programme, fresh out of university and with his whole life stretching before him. In the years that have followed, the viewers have been able to share his life and all the trials and tribulations associated with it. There have been some marvellous moments over the years, but this book is not just about me and my experiences of playing Ken Barlow; it is also about the programme itself and how it has changed and evolved organically, from those early black-and-white episodes right up to the present time, with the show now being seen in glorious HD. It is incredible to think of the span of the programme and the changes that have occurred in British society during that time.

I think the show has always been able to move with the times, but although the programme has changed tremendously, it has done so in a gradual way. There have never been great leaps in one direction or another, and as such, I think it has been a great source of comfort to viewers and different generations. The programme has been a favourite with the nation for a very long time and given great pleasure to those who have watched it.

It has certainly been a huge part of my own life, and this book gives me the chance to share my time on the *Street* with you.

1

HOLD ONTO THE WALLS

I had been in *Coronation Street* since the first episode of the programme was broadcast, in 1960, but as I made my familiar way to Granada Studios in Manchester that day in 1983, I was filled with an emotion I had never experienced before during my 23 years with the show. I was nervous, which is never a bad thing for an actor just before he is due to give a performance, but I was also apprehensive and angry. I also knew the reason for my anger would drive me towards a course of action that would be completely out of character.

Having played Ken Barlow for such a long period of time, I felt I had a pretty good understanding of the character: his likes and dislikes, what drove him, the sort of person he was and the way he would react faced with certain circumstances. Ken had become a well-established figure in *Coronation Street* since first being seen when the programme hit the screens, and I had been lucky enough to have been given some very strong storylines to perform, scripts I could really get my teeth into, the sort of thing all actors love to be involved in, and for that I was very grateful. I had never been the sort of actor who was precious about his work; instead, I always realised how lucky I was to be involved in such a popular television drama serial, which was avidly watched by millions of people each week. The acting, production and direction were of the highest order, and that also applied to the show's scripts. The writers we had working on the programme were superb. They had a real feel for the show and the characters. They were able to produce great storylines and terrific dialogue, all of which made the job of acting on the show such a pleasant and rewarding experience.

Like any of the characters, Ken had had his ups and downs on the programme. At times there had been some heavy storylines, while there were other periods where perhaps he had not been as involved in some episodes. That was all part of acting on the *Street*, and everyone accepted that. There was no way all the characters could be heavily involved in all the stories all the time, but I always felt that one of the main reasons for the show's success had been the richly drawn characters that had been created for all of us. The programme was character based and that had always been one of its great strengths in my opinion. The viewers had got to know those characters over a long period of time and accepted them for what they were. When Ken appeared on their television sets each week, they pretty well knew what they were getting. They had seen him grow from his days as a fresh-faced university graduate, shared in the marriage and death of his two wives and the birth of his twins, and been witness to his many relationships with the opposite sex. They had also seen him wed for a third time, in 1981, when he and Deirdre Langton were married, and it was a storyline involving that relationship that had caused me to feel uncomfortable as I made my way to the studios.

For some reason, I got the impression following the wedding that the writers were trying to turn Ken into a bit of a nerdy character. It was as if they didn't really know where to take him in relation to the rest of the programme. I was fighting it and actually went to see the producer about the situation and the fact that I wasn't happy about it. It was not the sort of thing I ever really did, but at the same time I felt strongly that Ken seemed to be floating in a nebulous state. It wasn't good for the character and it wasn't good for me, because I started to lose confidence. I can never be sure, but I think that as a result of me letting my feelings be known, it was decided that Ken would begin to be involved in much stronger stuff on the programme.

The result was the creation of what was to turn out to be one of the most memorable storylines in the history of *Coronation Street*: when Deirdre began to secretly start seeing Mike Baldwin behind Ken's back. It was an idea that offered great scope for the writers, and as actors the dramatic possibilities of the Ken–Mike–Deirdre relationship gave Anne Kirkbride, Johnny Briggs and myself the chance to really get our teeth into some meaty on-screen situations.

The whole episode had started in a slow-burning way, in a scene where Ken and Deirdre were due to go to the pictures together to see a film, but as she prepared to get ready for their night out, he suddenly announced that there was a documentary on the television that he wanted to see. The upshot of this was that Deirdre decided to go to the cinema on her own and on the way back popped in to see Baldwin. He offered her a sympathetic ear, and it was clear that all was not well with Deirdre's marriage to Ken. She felt as though he took her for granted, and it wasn't long before Mike Baldwin seized on Deirdre's unhappiness to begin an affair with her, providing the emotional and physical excitement that poor old Ken was clearly unable to offer. The affair between the two went on without Ken knowing about it, but then it was decided that as part of the storyline he would find out and things would come to a head. It was this particular part of the story that I had a problem with when I was given my script for what was to be the moment of high drama. I knew I had to do something. It was very much a gut feeling on my part as I read and reread what had been written; every time I looked at the words and at what was supposed to happen I knew it was wrong, and I realised I couldn't go along with the script.

It wasn't a case of me being precious; it was simply the fact that I knew the script that had been written for Ken just didn't ring true. That may sound like an odd expression to use, considering I'm talking about a work of fiction, but in a highly dramatic scene there has to be realism, otherwise it doesn't work. When people have rows and are faced by certain situations, they react. The script I had been given called for a scene in the Barlows' hall with Ken, having found out about Deirdre and Mike, challenging her about the fact that she was having this affair. Mike was then supposed to knock on the door and ask Deirdre whether everything was all right, leaving Ken to just stand there while the two of them had a conversation

– I was absolutely incensed. So when the day arrived when we had to shoot the scene, I knew I had to do something about it, and that was why I walked through the gates of Granada Studios with that mixture of nervousness and anger running through me.

I went to my dressing-room to prepare, putting on the clothes that had been left for me hanging in a small closet by a member of the wardrobe department, before going to make-up. I actually felt that I couldn't talk to Johnny that day. Very rarely does something you have to do as an actor permeate you in that sort of way, but when I was learning my lines the night before, engrossed in the script, I actually started to feel that I didn't want to talk to him or Annie, because I didn't want it to affect what I was going to do, so I withdrew from both of them. I went back to my room and waited to be called on-set and knew that as soon as I walked into the studio I would have to say something. The director for that particular episode was Brian Mills, who was very good and someone I liked and respected.

He had decided to shoot all the scenes involving the three of us on one day. Normally the scenes were done in an order. There would be a bit of the Barlows, then something in the Rovers Return, perhaps a bit more of the Barlows, then the corner shop and maybe a scene involving other people from the street, but on that particular day all we did were scenes involving Ken, Deirdre and Mike. It was quite an intense way of doing things but, at the same time, a very good idea, because it meant we were able to concentrate on the very strong storyline and do the various scenes all in one day, without getting involved in anything else. When it came to the scene in the Barlows' hall, I let my feelings be known.

'Sorry,' I told Brian. 'I can't do that.'

'Do what?' he asked.

'I cannot just stand there while the guy who's having an affair with my wife chats to her and asks what's going on,' I insisted.

'Well, what do you want to do?' Brian said.

'I want to hit him!' I told him.

Brian explained that wouldn't be possible because there was no continuity in the scene – it all had to be filmed from the inside, and there was no outside shooting planned for it – so instead we agreed that Ken would go to hit Mike and then let Deirdre intervene.

When you do a scene the usual procedure is for you to slowly go through it beforehand, speaking the words but not putting any energy into it, while the cameras and the boom microphone are sorted out. We did all of that and then had a gentle run-through of what was going to happen before finally getting ready to do the take. I'm a very easy-going guy. I don't lose my temper and I don't throw tantrums, but on that day I don't think anyone would have changed what I was going to do.

Poor Annie wasn't prepared for what happened to her next and actually burst into tears because of the ferocity of my performance. She was shaken up by it, and when it came to the moment for Mike Baldwin to knock at the door she got an even bigger shock. After Baldwin asked why Deirdre had put the phone down when he'd called earlier, I slammed the door shut with my left hand and then slammed poor Annie against the door itself, leaving her shaken and shocked. She then made her way into the Barlows' living room, sobbing her heart out, and Brian left the cameras rolling, capturing her genuine distress at what had gone on during the course of our scene.

Some people later said that Ken had assaulted Deirdre, because the whole thing looked so ferocious when it was finally broadcast some weeks later. Anne was brilliant throughout the scene, and the fact that we worked so well together definitely helped. She was crying and upset as we did the scene, but the words were there, she was able to carry on, and it added to the dramatic impact of what we did. It was amazing, and I really felt as though I'd been through the mangle because of all the emotion that we had experienced. I'd shouted, I'd screamed, Annie was sobbing and the whole thing had been very physical as I'd slammed her against the door. You feel quite strange after a scene like that and your emotions are raw, but we knew as actors that we'd done something good and made the whole thing work.

In the theatre, it's not good to let your emotions rip like that. You let them rip at rehearsal, but then because you have to recreate them for the theatre, onstage every night, you do it so often that you reach a point where you can perform and actually be thinking about something else. You can't really do that in *Coronation Street*, because you have to display an emotion for the camera and really get a feel for it. What you see is what you get: anger is anger, tears are tears, and I think you have to give of yourself much more than you would normally do. You may have gone over the lines in your head and you're ready to do a take, but it's only when you get out there in front of the cameras that your performance can really come to life. I always feel that when you get a beautifully written row with a line that caps everything off and the scene rises to a crescendo, it's almost as if it's a musical score and your emotions are actually flowing out. It's very cathartic and can really be quite enjoyable. Everybody was surprised at the amount of emotion that powered into the story, and the whole thing really hit the pulse of the nation when it was broadcast.

The atmosphere in the studio after we'd finished was electric, and I knew it was a bit special. It was a moment that really stunned the studio for a while and there was actually a silence, and then Brian Mills came down and congratulated us.

'That was brilliant,' he said. 'Well done.'

From my own point of view the whole thing felt very satisfying, in the sense that I felt I'd managed to add something to what had originally been planned. I hadn't felt comfortable with the scene to begin with and knew that Ken couldn't just stand there limply without reacting, and I think there was also something within me that had been frustrated with the way Ken's character was beginning to look so lame in some of the episodes that had gone before.

All of that came welling up in that scene and I think the end result was better because of it, and Brian did a great job with his direction. He decided to shoot the whole thing from above our heads, with the camera looking down at the hall, and that really helped add to the sense of claustrophobia, with Ken confronting Deirdre and her really having nowhere to go. The set was very well constructed and for the first time ever we had four walls; in previous physical scenes during past episodes, they'd actually had to have people holding onto the walls of a set because they would shake if someone was pushed against them. If we'd had those walls when Ken slammed Deirdre against the door, I think the whole thing might have come crashing down! I'm not sure the physical nature of that particular scene had happened before in *Coronation Street*, I certainly couldn't remember any, and the nice thing was that it involved three major characters from the programme. There was a lot of power and energy in the moment, and although it didn't last that long the effect it had on the nation and on the way 'soaps' were treated after it was quite amazing.

The whole Ken, Deirdre and Mike saga captivated the public when it was broadcast, prompting national newspaper articles, debates on television and opinions from people like marriage-guidance counsellors. When Deirdre decided to stop seeing Mike and stay with Ken after that turbulent confrontation, the *Daily Mail* smartly hired the scoreboard at Old Trafford on the night the episode was broadcast and flashed the message that the couple were not splitting up to 56,000 football fans, amid thunderous cheers from the crowd!

The storyline was described as the most volatile and explosive in the programme's history up to that point. It really was that big a deal and it split the nation, with some people believing Deirdre should stay and others thinking she should give Ken the boot and run off with Mike Baldwin. Johnny, Anne and I were also named TV Personalities of the Year in the Pye Colour Television Awards in 1983. Those feelings I'd had when I arrived at Granada that day helped me when it came to doing my scenes, and the big confrontation was something I think we all enjoyed, even if Annie did end up in tears. When people asked me about it I used to say, 'I haven't enjoyed myself so much since my first wife in the *Street*, Val, died!'

Moments like that are special because acting is such an imprecise science, but for some reason it is a profession I was always drawn to, even though my entire background pointed towards me either spending my life sitting in a doctor's surgery or making a career in the military, rather than spending 50 years as a character in Britain's longest-running soap.

2

CIVVY STREET

There is no way that anything in my background suggested I was destined to be an actor; in fact, quite the opposite was true. Both my father and grandfather were doctors, and within my family there had also been a history of military service. I was born in 1932, and my childhood was spent at the family home in Ilkeston, Derbyshire, with my parents and older sister, Beryl. I think it was always assumed that I would probably follow in the footsteps of my father and grandfather by becoming a doctor, and there was certainly no hint in those early years that I would one day become an actor. At the age of seven I was sent away to Rydal, a boarding school in Colwyn Bay, North Wales, while Beryl went to Penrhos girls' school, which was also in Colwyn Bay.

My first real taste of the stage came when I was at Rydal and joined the school's Dramatic Society; we did several productions, including *Macbeth*, with me playing the role of Lady Macbeth. Although there was no hint of anything theatrical on my father's side, my mother was heavily involved with the Ilkeston Town Women's Guild, directing productions for them, and she was delighted when I got involved in some of the school productions, even going so far as to hand me notes suggesting how I might improve my performance! Despite enjoying the acting and having a real passion for watching films, by the time it came to me ending my schooldays, it still looked very much as though I was going to follow my father into the medical profession, but although I did well in biology in my final year in the sixth form, my physics and chemistry results were not up to scratch. It meant that my results were not good enough to get me a place at St Bartholomew's in London to study medicine, and with the prospect of National Service looming it was probably assumed that I would try to get the necessary qualifications after I came out of the military.

I registered for the army while I was still at school in Wales, which meant I would join one of the Welsh regiments for my two years of National Service, and I eventually joined the Royal Welch Fusiliers in January 1952. I didn't really know what to expect from the army, but I was aware that the Korean War was still going on and the Fusiliers had men serving out there. After six weeks of basic training, it looked as though we would be posted to Brecon in South Wales for advanced training before heading off for Korea. One morning as we were about to have a kit inspection, the corporal in charge of us came in and started asking everyone if they had passed their School Certificate. Most hadn't, but when he got to me I told him that I had a Higher Certificate in Botany and Zoology. Because of this I later found myself singled out, along with a couple of other lads, for what was called the Potential Leaders platoon. In effect, the army had decided that we were possible candidates to become officers, and after less than three months in the army I found myself promoted to the rank of lance corporal and, later, after a period of training and assessment, I was eventually recommended for officer cadet training. After a further four months of training, I became a fully commissioned officer with the rank of second lieutenant. Our passing-out parade took place in December 1952 and we were due to then have some Christmas leave, but before that we had to find out exactly where and when we would be posted after the holiday period. With the Welch Fusiliers battalions serving in Korea, it didn't seem to take much working out where I would be going after the Christmas festivities, but when I went into the main hall to look at a large chart showing all of us exactly where we would be off to, I could hardly believe my eyes.

Written on the chart were the words: 'Second Lieutenant W.P. Roache. Posting. 2nd Battalion, Royal Welch Fusiliers. Caribbean.' I had no idea what it meant, only that I was expecting to be sent to Korea and I was going somewhere else, and after asking exactly where that would be, I was delighted to find out that I would be stationed in Kingston, Jamaica.

I had just less than a year in Jamaica and had a thoroughly enjoyable time there; the island was beautiful and I made some good friends before being sent back to England to attend a three-inch-mortar course before the battalion took up residence at an old army camp in Chiseldon in Wiltshire. The course was to have a long-lasting effect on the rest of my life.

As part of the training we were split up into mortar teams, each consisting of three men. The mortar round was propelled by explosives, which were ignited when the actual bomb reached the bottom of the barrel. Unfortunately, on one particular occasion ours didn't go off. When that happened you were supposed to raise the barrel slightly and then shake it gently, but instead of doing that one of the men in my team pulled the mortar upright and then really shook the thing. The result was that the bomb went straight up in the air, and because I was standing quite close to the mouth of the mortar I quite literally got the full blast, and as a consequence I could hardly hear a thing for about three weeks. It also had far greater repercussions for me: to this day I am 50 per cent deaf because of that incident. Looking back now, I should probably have done something about it, but instead I just got on with things, as most people did back then, and never formally reported it. I'd have probably had an army disability pension today if I had!

After finishing the course I went back to Chiseldon and had the chance to meet the Queen, who visited the regiment to present new colours, and I had to carry the old ones on parade before some of us had lunch with her. It was the second time I had met her, because she called in at Kingston while I was stationed there as part of a Commonwealth tour. Little did I know it at the time, but years later I would meet her again in very different circumstances when I helped show her around the newly built *Coronation Street* set at Granada Studios in Manchester.

My battalion then went to Dortmund in Germany to carry out some combined exercises with other NATO forces. It was very hard, serious, strict stuff, and I have to confess that I didn't really like it very much at all. Add to this the fact that it was all being done in the grey of winter, and after my stint in the Caribbean it all seemed very dreary, but I soon got the chance to see some sunshine again when I volunteered to join a little-known outfit that operated in the Persian Gulf, which somehow seemed a lot more appealing to me. It was called the Trucial Oman Scouts, which was basically a small Arab force of British officers who had the job of keeping the peace between seven sheikhdoms in the Persian Gulf. It turned out to be a great experience, and soon after my arrival I found out that I had been given a promotion. My commanding officer, a guy called Colonel Johnson, greeted me with the words, 'Welcome, Captain Roache.' I was a bit taken aback by this, because when I'd left England I was still very much a lieutenant. He explained that they didn't have any officers under the rank of captain and so that was that, I had been promoted with immediate effect, and I took over as the commanding officer of a squadron of one hundred and forty Arabs, not one of whom could speak any English. I began to wonder what I had let myself in for, but in fact the whole experience turned out to be a good one for me, and I really enjoyed my two years in the Gulf. It was a rewarding experience and I led an almost biblical existence while I was there, which made my reintroduction into civilian life quite difficult to deal with.

It was very much a world apart in many ways, because the existence I had there was so different to anything I would have had back in England. I very soon began to enjoy my time there and loved the tranquillity of the desert. We were based on the edge of the Rub' al-Khali, and in translation that means 'the empty quarter', which gives some indication of just what it was like. I would go out into this area and just sit and think for hours at a time, and found the whole experience extremely peaceful and relaxing. I was in the wilderness and it had a very calming effect on me. The lifestyle was very simple. I was in charge of 140 men, and because there wasn't much else to do each night, I used to enjoy sitting around in the evening and chatting to them. The food was pretty basic, as was the living accommodation. We would eat mainly rice flavoured with basil and ghee. There was the occasional meat dish when one of the men caught something that could be cooked. This ranged from things like goats to a jerboa, which is quite like a rat. I remember on one occasion being given a live jerboa, which I'm sure they thought I would kill and eat, but it was a rather sweet little character and there was no way I was ever going to kill it, and instead made a cage and kept it as a pet, which the men must have thought extremely odd. Some time later another one of the men brought me an owl with an injured wing, which I kept in my tent as I nursed it back to full health. It actually used to sit on the desk in my tent while I worked, and I got quite attached to it. Unfortunately, the owl also got attached to the jerboa, so much so that it managed to get into the cage one day and eat the little thing!

I also had a desert fox with an injured paw, which had been caught in a trap. I nursed the little creature, and after its wound began to heal we became quite good friends. I even made a collar and lead for it, and we would go off on little walks. One night it managed to get itself tangled in one of the tent ropes and started choking. I heard all the noise and quickly ran over to untangle it, but the fox was in a real panic and in its fright managed to bite the tip of my nose, causing quite a deep gash. I managed to stick some penicillin powder on it and then added plasters, making the best of a bad job. As well as being the commander of the squadron I also doubled as its doctor, but never once thought I would have to be giving treatment to myself. My nose started to heal, but then a couple of days later I was pouring out some water and suddenly my hair started to stand on end. I immediately thought I had hydrophobia, which is a fear of water and the first sign of rabies. I telephoned the colonel and told him what had happened, and he said a doctor would be sent out to examine me, but it would take four days for him to get there. So for the next few days I genuinely thought that I had contracted rabies from the fox, and I was about to experience a terribly painful death as a consequence. When the doctor arrived, he looked at the wound and said that I'd done a good job, and then went on to say that I had nothing to fear, because we were in such an isolated place that none of the foxes could possibly be carrying rabies. It was such a relief, and I soon got back to the slow and peaceful existence of life in the desert.

Although the life was basic it was without any real pressure, and there was always a feeling that if I didn't want to do something, then I didn't have to. It was quite a special place, and if we wanted to travel between Sharjah and Dubai, it would mean negotiating sand dunes and mudflats. These days there are huge motorways, and the region has changed an awful lot since my time there, mainly due to the fact that shortly after I left, oil was discovered there. I still look back with a lot of affection when I recall the time I had in the region, but because it was so different to anything else I had ever experienced, I suppose it was no surprise that once I returned home the pace of life and simply being in quite heavily populated areas was quite difficult to become accustomed to once more.

I had done my National Service and then decided to stay on and volunteer for the posting to the Trucial Oman Scouts. I loved the experience I had there, but at the same time it also brought home the fact that it wasn't the way I wanted to spend my life. I could probably have stayed in the army and ended up in charge of a battalion or a brigade, but it just wasn't for me as a career. It would have seemed like a dead end, and I didn't want that. I've mentioned the fact that I acted at school and I had a real love of the cinema. I toyed with the idea of becoming an actor when I was younger, but somehow never really had the confidence. But despite my time in the army and the fact that my background still suggested I was destined for a life far removed from the theatre, I found myself drawn towards the thought that I should try my hand at acting. However, there was still the practical matter of having to earn a living once I left the army, and after taking some time off, I began working for a company specialising in oriental carpets, who thought that my time in the Gulf and knowledge of the area could be useful to them. I lived in a small bedsit in Earls Court, with the idea being that I would learn about the business and at the same time attend the Berlitz School of Languages to learn Persian. I can't honestly say that it was the sort of job that excited me, but it enabled me to live in London, and by this time

I had also decided that I definitely wanted to be an actor.

I'm sure if I had gone to acting school when I was younger it just wouldn't have worked, because of the shyness I have already mentioned, but having had time in the army I came out feeling much more confident about myself and with a determination to have a proper crack at trying to become an actor. The real trouble was deciding how I would go about it. I gave up my job with the carpet manufacturers so that I could concentrate on acting. Living in London was pretty lonely, and I would visit my parents at weekends, but I knew that if I was going to become an actor, I stood a better chance of breaking into the profession if I based myself in the capital. I didn't have any connections with or contacts in the acting world, so I began to write to the director of every film I ever went to see. I got a lot of replies that basically told me they would let me know if they had anything for me, which was a polite way of saying there was no chance; then there were others who were a bit more sympathetic, but at the same time basically saying there were a lot of very good actors out of work and that it was a really tough profession to break into.

Then one day I received a telegram from a director called Brian Desmond Hurst, who invited me to go along to see him at his mews house in Belgravia. He was a very well-known director and a big man with a big personality. When I arrived at his home it seemed very grand, with lots of expensive-looking paintings and statues. At the far end of the room I was shown into was Brian Desmond Hurst, sitting in a huge chair behind an antique desk. I'd sent him my usual letter, and when we met he asked me to tell him more about myself, which I did. He then picked up the phone, said something about me to whoever was at the other end and then handed it to me.

'William Roache?' asked whoever was on the other end of the line.

'Yes,' I replied.

'You'll be playing the part of an anaesthetist,' said the voice. 'It starts shooting at Shepperton Studios on Monday. Will £40 a day be OK?'

'Yes,' I said, hardly believing my luck.

'It's probably three or four days' work,' he added. 'You are a member of Equity, aren't you?'

I wasn't but instinctively said yes, and in those days you couldn't work unless you were a member of the actors' union. I was in a bit of a daze and wasn't quite sure how I was going to get over the problem, when Hurst brought me back down to earth by telling me he'd like to go to bed with me.

'Don't worry,' he added, 'I never force myself on anybody.'

He went on to tell me he held an 'open house' at his place and I was welcome to come along. In fact, I did just that at a later date, and they were very good parties – you just had to make sure you weren't the last one to leave! So I'd got a film part, lied about being in Equity and been propositioned, all in the space of a few moments. The problem with not being a member of Equity worried me, so when the contract for my part in the film arrived I went round to their offices. I was convinced I'd never get my card after owning up to the official there, but instead he told me to fill in some forms, get someone to second me and then I would become a member of Equity. It was that simple, and then I went on to take part in my first-ever film, which was called *Behind the Mask* and starred Michael Redgrave and Tony Britton. The mask referred to the sort worn by a surgeon. I played a young doctor and had two lines, but my professional acting career was up and running. I will always be grateful to Brian Desmond Hurst for that first break, but I came to learn that you never mentioned that he'd given you your breakthrough, because people assumed you'd got it for the wrong reasons.

Having taken part in my first film, I was then able to meet other actors who were kind enough to give me some tips about the profession and offer advice about the way I should go about getting more work in the industry. This included buying a magazine called *Contacts*, which had the names and contact numbers of all agents, casting directors, television companies and film companies. I started to send off letters to anyone I thought might be of use, and some weeks it was literally up to the 100 mark, but my persistence slowly began to pay off. I was rewarded with some small parts in TV shows like *Ivanhoe* and films such as *The Queen's Guards*. I knew I had to spend time learning my craft and thought that the proper place to do this would be in the theatre, and so I began writing to various theatrical companies. I also went along to any West End auditions that I heard about and read for them. Another thing I did in order to give myself the best possible chance, having started acting later than many others, was to have some private lessons from a well-known actress at that time named Ellen Pollock. It was all part of my plan to give myself the best opportunity I could of succeeding, and I was very determined that I would stick with it. I had been drawn to the profession and somehow knew that it was right for me.

One of the theatrical companies I had contacted was St James's Management, which was run by Laurence Olivier. I didn't have an address for the company but knew he was appearing in *The Entertainer* at the Palace Theatre, and so I sent a letter directly to him there. I was amazed when I got a note from Olivier himself, telling me to 'come to the stage door at 7.10 and I will see you for a few minutes'. I got there ten minutes before he had asked me to, but by 7.10 there was no sign of the great man and I just assumed that he'd forgotten, but then about five minutes later he walked straight up to me.

'Mr Roache?' he asked. 'Do come in.'

He then proceeded to show me to his dressing-room and gave me a gin and tonic while he got ready for his performance that night. We chatted about all sorts of things, including the fact that he was shortly going off to Hollywood to make *The Prince and the Showgirl* with Marilyn Monroe, and then he asked what he could do for me. I told him that I'd come into the acting profession late and that some other actors I'd spoken to had actually said that I should get out of it altogether and find a more secure profession. I said that I thought a word of advice from him would be worth a hundred from anybody else.

'Don't give up,' he said. 'I had two years myself that were absolutely terrible, with nothing happening at all. It was really dreadful, but if it's in you, keep at it.'

He told me to contact him after he came back from America and to remind him of our conversation that night, and he would see what he could do for me. He shook my hand, wished me luck and left me feeling determined to carry on. I was also absolutely thrilled that someone like him should take the time and trouble to speak to me, offer encouragement in the way that he had done and at the same time do so while putting me completely at my ease. It is something I have come to realise over the years: truly great people will always find time for you and be kind. I didn't actually get in touch with Olivier as he had suggested, because I didn't want to appear to be a sycophant, but our paths did cross again many years later and he also went on to become a big fan of *Coronation Street*.

The meeting also convinced me of the fact that I needed to move into the world of theatre if I was going to progress as an actor. Having small parts in films and on TV was not really going to do me much good, particularly as the rest of the time was spent hanging around hoping something else would come along. I decided to get an agent and went to the offices of someone called Daphne Scorer. She didn't run a big-time agency, but I thought she might be able to help me move onto the next rung of the ladder, although in order to do so I'm afraid I told her a pack of lies about how I had been in repertory theatre in Colwyn Bay. In fact, the closest I'd got to the stage was watching that particular company from the audience when I was at Rydal School. I managed to bluff my way through it and even gave her the names of some of the actors I'd seen. I believe that if something is meant to be it will happen, and two days after going to see Daphne I got a call from her, asking me to come to see a producer called Norris Staton, who was putting on a twelve-week summer season in Clacton-on-Sea with a company called the Unicorn Players and was looking for a juvenile lead. At the meeting, I just sat there while she told him what a great young actor I was and then about all the plays I'd been in at Colwyn Bay. The result was that I was offered the job, and we shook hands and signed the contract on the spot. So a 12-week season in the theatre beckoned, and as soon as I had actually signed on the dotted line, I began to panic. I knew nothing about acting in the theatre and was about to be thrust into a world that would see me acting alongside some very experienced professional actors. With me, acting was something I was inextricably drawn towards – once I'd left the army there was really nothing else I wanted to do – and yet I was frightened of it. I didn't know if I would be any good, I didn't know whether I would succeed, but at the same time it was something I just had to do. Ignorance was bliss for me, in the sense that I didn't really have a clue what I was doing in those early days, only that I wanted to act, and once I had been given a taste of it in films and TV, I knew the next step had to be the theatre, and that's why I was pleased and scared about the prospect of getting the job in Clacton.

It was very tough for me during the first few weeks, because I really didn't know what I was doing and wasn't even familiar with theatre 'vocabulary' such as using terms like 'upstage' and 'downstage'. I'd talked my way into a professional theatre company when the only real stage work I'd done was at school, but I very soon began to realise that I was now in a place where I could begin to learn my craft. It was a bit nerve-wracking but at the same time enjoyable, because I was learning a tremendous amount as we did one play a week. I was also relieved to discover that, in general, actors were not the arrogant extroverts I thought they would be. In fact, most were pretty shy, and I still believe that the majority of actors are incredibly sensitive. I was also lucky to have a man called Donald Masters as our director, and although the first few weeks were difficult, I began to find my stage feet, and by the end of it all had learned an awful lot. It was a great experience, and I was soon to get another.

After my experience in Clacton I knew it was important to continue my acting education, and I wrote to Nottingham Rep, which had a very good reputation and was quite a prestigious company to be involved with. I got a reply from them, offering me a job as an assistant stage manager, which involved doing things like shifting scenery and sweeping the stage, but it also gave me the chance to take on some small parts with them. It was very different from my time in Clacton, because it was far more serious, with some classical plays being performed and also some very good actors in the company, including a young Donald

Sutherland, who was just beginning his career at the time. There were two other assistant stage managers with the company: one was a man called Norman Florence, and the other was someone who went on to have an extremely successful career on stage, screen and television – his name was Brian Blessed, and we became very good friends.

Nottingham provided me with seven months' work, but I knew I had to make sure I continued to learn and gain more theatre experience, and my next move certainly did that. I applied for an audition with Oldham Rep, another company with a very good reputation. Brian helped coach me with the piece I was going to do for the audition and I was offered the position of juvenile lead, but unlike my time at Clacton, the experience I had subsequently gained made me feel much more confident about joining Oldham, and I knew I could handle the job. I was with them for twelve months, and during that time I only had one play off. We did one play a week, and by the end of my time with them I was exhausted, but what a wonderful experience it was, rehearsing during the day, performing a play in the evening and then learning lines each night. It was very hard work, but it was absolutely perfect for me, and by the end of it I knew I had well and truly served my apprenticeship. As an actor you never stop learning, but by the time I had finished at Oldham Rep, I was certain that I could handle anything thrown at me. I was no longer the young aspiring actor who had very much been on the outside looking in; instead, I felt I had got the sort of grounding I needed and could legitimately feel confident of taking on whatever roles were out there.

3

PLAY OF THE WEEK

While I was in Oldham, Granada Television in Manchester went on the air. It was good timing for me, because I was able to start getting some work with them playing some small parts in three drama series – *Skyport*, *Biggles* and *Knight Errant* – but once I'd finished my time in Oldham, I decided the best thing for me and my career would be to base myself in London. I got a small flat in Primrose Hill, and I also got myself an agent, Terry Owen, of the Lom Agency. I managed to pick up some small roles in films, and one day he called to say that Granada had been on and wanted to see me about the possibility of playing the lead role in a play called *Marking Time*. It was about a young army private soldier who was stationed in Germany, having an affair with a German girl. It was going to be part of the *Play of the Week* series, and as such it was a hugely prestigious thing to be involved in. I knew it was a great opportunity for me, and when I got the part I realised that when it was shown the audience would be big and playing the lead could really lift my acting career to a different level. These plays were a very big thing in those days and the drama was of the highest quality, so to be involved was very exciting for me. I went up to Manchester and did the play before returning to London to wait for it to be broadcast, hoping for the sort of positive reaction and reviews that could give my career a real boost.

I did a couple of small film parts while I waited for the big moment, and then one day Terry phoned and said that Granada had called again, but this time they were interested in me for a possible role in a serial they were planning, which was going to be called *Florizel Street*. He thought it was probably some sort of comedy, but whatever it was I told him that I wasn't interested. I had my flat in London, I was getting acting parts and it all looked very rosy, so I thought staying in London would give me the best chance of furthering my career.

'I don't want to go back up there,' I told him. 'I'm settled in London.'

Terry explained that there was nothing imminently on the horizon, so I might as well go up there and see what happened. In the end I agreed and went to Granada in a very relaxed mood. They asked me to read something in a Lancashire accent, and so I picked up a copy of the *Daily Telegraph* and began to read a report about an MP who had flicked ink pellets at a political opponent. It's funny, but I think that when you really don't want something and are not trying desperately to get it, the whole thing works in your favour, because you're much more relaxed and that can help you. It certainly did that day, because soon afterwards my agent rang again and said that they wanted me to go up to Granada and make a pilot episode. Once again I was reluctant to get involved with the project, but Terry persuaded me that it would be a good thing for me to do. He said it was only three days' work and I would be paid for doing it, so I agreed and went up for the pilot, playing a university student called Ken Barlow. Apparently Granada made two pilots, using many of the same actors, and in the second one the part of Ken was played by Philip Lowrie, who later went on to play Dennis Tanner.

When my agent rang again to tell me they had decided to make a serial, I was still more concerned with trying to find out a date for the transmission of *Marking Time*.

'They want you for the serial,' he said, and then quickly went on to say that it was only going to run for thirteen episodes and it would involve six weeks' work. He also said that *Marking Time* would probably be broadcast right in the middle of it. 'What a great shop window,' he added. 'You'll be on television twice a week in this serial and then right in the middle of it you're the lead in *Play of the Week*.'

I could see the logic in what he was saying and agreed to do it. Those six weeks have now stretched into more than fifty years, and the programme is still going strong. The title of the programme was, of course, changed to *Coronation Street* and the rest, as they say, is history. Certainly nobody could have known way back then what an impact it would have, and they could never have envisaged a programme that would go on and on and at the same time remain so popular with the public. Several generations have watched *Coronation Street* during the past 50 years, and its popularity and appeal have never waned.

The show was created by Tony Warren, who deserves an awful lot of credit for giving birth to something that has become a British institution. I think the story of how the whole thing came about is fascinating, and there's no doubt that Tony's persistence and belief in the idea that he came up with helped drive the project on. There were also some other people at Granada back then who had faith in the programme and made sure that it reached the television screens of the nation. When Tony got the idea for what was to become *Coronation Street*, he was just 23 years old and looked even younger. He was working as a scriptwriter for Granada and produced episodes for things like the *Biggles* series that I mentioned earlier. The story goes that Tony wanted to write something on a subject that he really knew about and was given 24 hours by a producer named Harry Elton to go away and come up with something. Tony returned with the idea for a show about a northern street, with a pub at one end and an off-licence at the other. In between were terraced houses, and the characters who lived in those homes were the people who would form the main players in the programme. It was an idea that apparently had been around in Tony's head for some time, but the opportunity to go away and write specifically for something that Granada could produce galvanised the thoughts he had been toying with, and from that came the idea for *Florizel Street*. Many people thought that whoever had created the programme must have been brought up in a similar street. That wasn't true of Tony, but he did know all about streets like that because his grandmother lived on one, and he clearly must have had a great ear and a good eye to be able to observe and then create the sorts of characters who were to populate *Coronation Street*.

Harry Elton liked what he saw when Tony delivered his script, and then told him to write a second episode and a memo talking about the street and the characters that were going to be part of it. I think some of the characters were slightly different to the ones who eventually became part of the programme, but it was all essentially there. Harry Kershaw was brought in alongside Tony to work as script editor, and Stuart Latham, who was also known as Harry, was asked to produce two pilot episodes. Margaret Morris and her assistant, Jose Scott, were in charge of casting the twenty-two characters who were to appear in the first two episodes. Apparently, as part of its licence to broadcast in the north-west of England, Granada was supposed to provide work for people in the north. Partly as a consequence of this, and also the fact that Tony's brainchild was set very firmly in the Manchester area, just about any actor from the north whom they knew about was considered for audition.

Years later I found out that my route into the *Street* had been slightly different, because while I had been up at Granada playing the young army private in *Marking Time*, Tony Warren had seen me and said to Jose Scott, 'That is Ken Barlow.' It was an observation that was to have tremendous consequences for me, even though I later seemed to do everything not to get the part, with my initial reluctance to even go up and speak to them when my agent had phoned me. It just goes to show that some things are meant to be, and I certainly have no complaints about the fact that I agreed to make the journey to Manchester.

Not everybody was keen on the pilot episodes that were produced, with some of the company's directors and executives quite cool on the project, but Harry Elton then got pretty much everyone who worked at the studios to watch the two programmes one day and asked them to fill in a questionnaire. People seemed to either love it or hate it; the reaction was very passionate either way, and because of that the executives were persuaded to go for the project. In the late summer of 1960, the real planning for the launch of the show began, and by the end of November they had all the actors they needed for the show to be broadcast the following month. By that time Florizel Street had become Coronation Street, and the off-licence had become a grocer's shop, at the insistence of Granada chairman Cecil Bernstein, who along with his brother, Sidney, ran the company. Today, in the corridor outside my dressing-room at Granada, there are many pictures of the various actors who have appeared in the programme over the years, and there is one right next to my door that shows the cast from the very first episode of *Coronation Street*. We posed for that picture at the start of our first week on the show, not knowing how it would go. None of us really knew each other, but we had been assembled specifically to help breathe life into Tony Warren's creation, and after a lot of hard work and rehearsal the first-ever episode of *Coronation Street* hit the screens on Friday, 9 December 1960.

That first week was a nervous time for all of us, but one of the things that struck me very early on was a feeling that we were all in it together and we all desperately wanted the programme to succeed and do well. We rehearsed the first and second episodes for two and a half days, and then on the Wednesday afternoon we did something that was called a producer's run. This was when we did a run-through in front of the producer, the director, the writer and all the technicians. On the Thursday and Friday there were camera rehearsals, and then the first episode went out live, and the second, which was going to be shown on the following Wednesday evening, was going to be recorded almost immediately after, with just a short break for something to eat. Live TV drama was not an unusual thing, and even the recording was live, in a sense, because there wasn't the technology and flexibility there is now. A guy called Derek Bennett directed the first-ever episode of the show, and he had a real feel for the *Street* and what it was all about. I think we all felt we were in on something that was a bit different, and although we hardly knew each other, we very quickly became a team. We were literally working very closely together, particularly when we were rehearsing. You each had a chair in a room and we'd all sit around in a circle. The only real prop was a table and some chairs, and when it came to doing your bit it was done in full view of everyone else, which made it a pretty nervous time for everyone, because you were being watched by all of your new colleagues. On the Friday afternoon after we had run-through the two episodes, we were all given notes on our performance by Derek, and once again this was done in front of everyone else, which was a little daunting, but on the other hand it also helped foster a very good spirit amongst everyone right from the very start.

That evening when the time came for our live 7 p.m. broadcast everyone was very nervous, but at the same time extremely excited. We had run and run our lines so that in theory we were word perfect, but despite all the rehearsing you're still apprehensive. Of course, there's nothing you can do about it because the show has to be broadcast, and you do it hoping that you don't fall flat on your face, both figuratively and in a very practical sense. The sets we had then were nothing like we have now, and they all sort of joined each other. I could put my hand out in the Barlow house and virtually touch the set of the Rovers. This meant that you had to be very careful about unwittingly encroaching on another set, and about things like casting shadows. Once you did your scene you had to freeze and not move or make a sound, because all of this was being done live. Television in those days was a very different thing, and in many ways it was still in its infancy in this country, while Granada was very much a small company catering just for the north-west of England. It was one of a number of local television companies that operated under the umbrella of ITV, and when that first show was broadcast not all the other regions showed it. In fact, it wasn't until later the next year that the programme was shown throughout the ITV network, and we also moved to being shown at 7.30 p.m. on Mondays and Wednesdays.

At the time of that first programme, television very much reflected what was happening in the theatre and in films. There were plays by people like John Osborne, method acting was something that had come to the fore with film stars like Marlon Brando in the 1950s, lots of the drama was of a very gritty nature, and things like *Play of the Week* were a part of that. Tony Warren was right at the cutting edge of this new, realistic style of drama, and when *Coronation Street* emerged we were treated with colossal respect. There was no such thing as a 'soap'; we were categorised as a drama serial, which was very much of the day and of the time. The reaction in the press was a little mixed: some papers didn't like it, while others had completely the opposite view and loved what they saw as this new, realistic working-class drama. When I first went up to Granada I did so thinking that I was only going to be appearing for a maximum of six weeks, but I soon realised that, despite my initial reluctance, I was involved in something that was very good indeed. Even so, there were no real clues back then as to just how popular the show would become. Now I feel very proud and privileged to have been in at the start of something that has since become such a familiar and successful part of television in this country.

4

HELLO AGAIN, UNCLE ALBERT

The cast for that first-ever episode of *Coronation Street* had been assembled after some six hundred auditions had taken place, and we came from various acting backgrounds and none of us really knew each other, but I did notice one familiar and very distinctive face when we all assembled at Granada Studios in December 1960. At the age of 64, when most men would have been thinking about retiring, Jack Howarth was just about to embark on a new phase in what was already a long and distinguished acting career. Our paths had crossed about 20 years before and the meeting had had nothing to do with acting or the theatre. I was just seven years old and had been sent to board at Rydal. The school were obviously aware that being away from home when you're that young can be a pretty daunting experience, so they operated a system whereby all new arrivals were handed over to one of the senior boys, who then showed them the ropes and basically looked after them. The boy who was to look after me was called John, and the first time I saw him he was being dropped off at the school by his father, a short, squat man with a kind face, who carried an impressive-looking ivory-topped cane. I later found out that John's father was called Jack Howarth and he ran a repertory theatre company in Colwyn Bay. When Jack arrived with his son that day he could see I was a little apprehensive about my new surroundings, so he tried to break the ice and put me at my ease by asking where I was from.

'England,' I replied, knowing I was a long way from home and that Rydal was in Wales.

When we met again all those years later we both laughed, remembering that day, and it had been kind of him to try to make me feel better about leaving home for school at a place that had seemed so far away from Derbyshire. It was a pleasant surprise to see him again and strange to think that I was now going to be working with him professionally on a new television show. He had formed his repertory company five years before we first met at Rydal, and just like the character of Albert Tatlock, who he went on to play in *Coronation Street*, Jack was a veteran of the First World War and had served in the Lancashire Fusiliers. Like so many of the people who had been assembled as characters for the first episode, he had a great acting pedigree. He was born in Rochdale and was the son of a comedian, and so I suppose he was always destined to be involved in the theatre or show business in some way or other. He had apparently gone to school with Gracie Fields and began as a child actor at the age of 12, progressing to play juvenile leads before serving with the Fusiliers in France during the First World War. After that he toured in repertory and then set up his own company in Colwyn Bay, which was when our paths had first crossed. His acting hadn't just been confined to the theatre, because Jack had also successfully played film cameos, such as the part of clogmaker Tubby in *Hobson's Choice*, which starred Charles Laughton. When he joined the *Street*, Jack had just spent some 14 years in the very popular radio show *Mrs Dale's Diary*, playing the part of Mr Maggs. Having briefly met him all those years ago, I would never have predicted that the characters of Ken Barlow and Albert were to go on and have quite a strong relationship in *Coronation Street*, which was something that started in the very first episode of the programme. Jack was a lovely actor and also a very emotional man. If you complimented him on his acting, he would well up with tears.

I remember him giving me two pieces of advice during those early days on the *Street*: the first was never to put my hands in my pockets and the other was not to shout during the course of a scene. The first one I could understand, because in the theatre actors learn not to do something like putting their hands in their pockets; the second bit of advice I disagreed with, because I think there are times on television when it works very well. He also used to love telling jokes, but the trouble was that he could never quite get them right. We used to delight in telling him a joke, knowing full well that by the time he came to retell it, the joke would have been changed and lost its meaning. We once told him a joke about a pirate ship being stopped by a Naval ship.

'Where are your buccaneers?' shouts the Navy man.

'Either side of my head!' replies the pirate.

A simple little joke that should produce a laugh, but when Jack tried to retell it later that day the Navy man's line had changed to, 'Where are your pirates?'

Jack also used to like taking cakes and pastries from the tea trolley when it came around, and then he would often stick one or two of them in his jacket pocket to take back to eat in his hotel room. I think it was Neville Buswell, who arrived in the mid-1960s to play Ray Langton, who found out about this and one day slapped his hand across one of Jack's pockets and severely squashed the cream bun he had inside it! The ivory-topped cane that I had noticed and been impressed by when I'd first met Jack at Rydal was still in evidence when he worked on *Coronation Street*, and every day he would turn up for work with it. He was very professional, and his years in the theatre had obviously given him the sort of experience and training that he was able to use to great effect once he joined the show.

That was very much the case with other members of the cast as well: we'd got there by different routes, but we had all been in the theatre, which was essential preparation for what we were all about to embark on. Theatre is essential for learning things like the timing of a laugh and holding a pause. It's a lovely feeling when you're onstage and you get just the sort of reaction from the audience that you wanted. You can only really know if things like that work if you are performing in front of a live audience, and so that's why having that sort of experience was so essential, but I have to say that having done both, I preferred the intimacy of films and television work. Theatre can be physically much harder, sometimes crudely so for me. I like to be totally immersed in the truth of what I'm doing and I believe you can only really do that into the camera, although one of the great rules of television is that you always have to ignore the camera. If you show any awareness of a camera position while you're acting, the whole thing just looks wrong. That is the case today and it was certainly the case when we came to screen that first episode. As you can imagine, the technology was extremely basic back then in comparison with the way in which the *Street* is produced today, but at the same time television was also very cutting edge, because it was such a new thing.

When it was decided to go ahead with the idea of *Coronation Street*, it wasn't just a case of Tony writing his scripts or the actors being assembled to play the characters he'd created; it was also about managing a whole new operation for the people who worked at Granada. That's what made it so exciting, and I think we all had a sense of that when we arrived that first week to start preparing for the show, which was going to go out on the Friday.

I'd done the pilot, so that meant I'd already met one or two other members of the cast apart from Jack, but not everyone I'd met before was there, because having done the two pilots some of the actors involved in them had not gone on to be part of the first programme. It was all very friendly as we were introduced, and I remember how respectful the younger members of the cast were towards their elders. As well as Jack Howarth there were people like Doris Speed, who was to play Annie Walker, the Rovers Return landlady; Arthur Leslie, who was going to be her husband, Jack; my *Street* parents, Frank Pemberton and Noel Dyson, who had been cast as Frank and Ida; Margot Bryant, who became such a favourite as Minnie Caldwell; and Lynne Carol, who had been given the part of Martha Longhurst; but perhaps the person who seemed to command the most respect straight away was Violet Carson, who went on to have such an impact on the programme playing the redoubtable Ena Sharples. Someone else who was younger but was to have a huge impact was Pat Phoenix, who brought the character of Elsie Tanner to life. The other people in that picture I mentioned and who were there for the first week of rehearsals were: Ivan Beavis, cast as Harry Hewitt; Anne Cunningham, who played Elsie's daughter, Linda; and she was married in the programme to Ivan Cheveski, played by Ernst Walder. He was supposed to be Polish in the *Street*, but in fact was an Austrian actor. Betty Alberge was also in the picture and appeared right at the start of the first episode as Florrie Lindley, who had just taken over the running of the corner shop. The previous owner, Elsie Lappin, played by Maudie Edwards, was not in the picture for some reason, but did appear in the first episode, as did Patricia Shakesby, playing Ken's girlfriend, Susan Cunningham. There were also two other people who played main characters: Philip Lowrie, who was Elsie's son, Dennis; and Alan Rothwell, Ken's brother, David. Bill Croasdale and Penny Davies also appear in the picture; both of them had parts as police officers in the second episode, but were there during that first week because the programme was going to be recorded after we'd gone out live with the first.

It was a good atmosphere and the only really uncomfortable moment for me came when we had to sit there and watch everyone read through their scenes. I found that quite frightening and it never really became comfortable for me, but at the same time it was something that had to be done and we all got on with it. I'm sure there were others who felt the same as I did, but you make the most of it and start to get used to the routines and structure of the programme. Although it was an experienced cast not too many had done a lot of television, not even Vi Carson, who was probably the best-known actor there. She had been hugely successful appearing with Wilfred Pickles in his very popular radio show *Have A Go*, and was also well known as Auntie Vi from another radio show, *Children's Hour*. She could play the piano beautifully and had a lovely voice, but she didn't really have any television experience. In fact, none of us were recognisable to the general public. Our faces may have popped up briefly in a film or on television, but that was about it. Little did we know then how things would change almost overnight for all of us involved in those early episodes of the show.

The first week was a pretty pleasant experience really, because although it was new and quite exciting the pace wasn't particularly hurried, and I think we all knew our lines on the day we arrived at the studios because we'd had the script for quite a while, so learning wasn't a problem and it was reinforced by the way we went about all the rehearsals. Everything built towards getting those first two episodes done on the Friday and, of course, making sure it all went well for the live broadcast.

On the day, we just went through everything we had to, including the dress rehearsal in the afternoon, and then when it was time we just went for the live screening. I'm sure we all had butterflies in our stomachs as the clock ticked down and we knew we were about to go on air, but at the same time we were all professional actors and that part of you quickly kicks in. You get into the part and hopefully do exactly what you have been hired for, and that is to portray your character as truthfully as you can and bring him to life on the screen for the viewers. It's something I tried to do during my first-ever scene on *Coronation Street* and I try to do it to this day, 50 years later. With acting, there never comes a time where you feel you can just relax because you know it all. The fact is, you are learning all the time, and in many ways that's exactly what makes it so interesting: there are always things to be brought out of a character and the lines you are given.

The great thing about that first show was the way in which it very quickly established the Street as a believable place and introduced the people who were to become its main characters. The strength of the programme has always been the fact that it is character based, which was something that came across strongly the very first time it was screened. The viewers were slowly introduced to the programme, with the outdoor set of the Street being shown at the beginning as two girls played outside the corner shop at the end of the road. The episode then took you inside the Street as one by one certain characters were introduced. Florrie Lindley, the new woman running the shop, is told by former owner Mrs Lappin about some of the people she might want to be wary about giving credit to, and she names the 'Tanners at number 11'. The viewer is then taken into the Tanners' house for a scene involving Elsie and her son, Dennis, in which they bicker, with her accusing him of taking two shillings from her purse, and during the course of the dialogue we also discover that Dennis is not long out of prison. Elsie says during the course of their row that she wishes Dennis could be more like Ken Barlow at number three, and then the action switches to their house.

In my very first scene on *Coronation Street* Ken's mum, Ida, enters the room carrying a pot of tea. Ken is sitting at a table with his father, Frank, eating a meal and is asked by his mother if he would like some sauce with his food.

'No, no thank you,' says Ken.

They were my first-ever lines on the show. Just four words, but at the same time the context in which they were said helped establish something about the character of Ken early on, and also the sort of relationship he had with his father and mother. Ida goes on to tell Ken that she 'got it special, you always liked it when you were little'. It's obvious that brown sauce is something Ken has clearly grown out of as he's matured, and when he then sees his father pouring sauce onto his plate, it's quite clear he doesn't approve.

'What's up?' asks his dad.

'Nothing,' replies Ken unconvincingly.

'What's that snooty expression for then?' Frank adds. He then proceeds to smother the rest of his food with the stuff and this is clearly a step too far for Ken.

'Oh no,' Ken says instinctively, and at the same time he obviously regrets blurting the words out. Frank sees this as the opportunity to give vent to his feelings about a son he believes has become a bit of a snob during his time at college.

'Don't they do this at college then?' Frank says angrily. 'I bet they don't eat in their shirtsleeves either!'

It's all good character-defining stuff, and by the end of that scene it was pretty obvious that there was conflict between Ken and his dad, and that Ken was looking for something better than what Coronation Street had to offer. In the same scene he further antagonised his father by saying that he was going to meet a girl at the Imperial Hotel instead of letting her anywhere near the Street. In fact, the girlfriend, Susan, turns up at the Barlows' and is more than happy to chat to the family as Ken's brother, David, mends his bike in front of the fire.

That episode also introduced Annie Walker to the public, and once again her character, which Doris Speed was to develop to such good effect in the years that followed, came shining through, making the viewers aware of the sort of person she was.

As I've mentioned, television was a very different thing back then. There wasn't the technology that's available today and there certainly wasn't the choice, with only a couple of channels on offer, something today's youngsters would find unimaginable. I also think the style of the *Street* was very different in those first two episodes compared with today's programme. Back then I think the dialogue tended to go on for longer, and as a consequence, so did the scenes. There was a greater emphasis on having just two or three people in those scenes, and a lot of them in those first two episodes were quite dramatic. What Tony Warren also managed to do very early on was to conjure up some good storylines that would naturally flow from the first show into the second, and could be taken on from there in different directions if he wanted them to.

In that very first episode there was the young, educated Ken at odds with his father and clearly feeling he wanted something better from life than being stuck in Coronation Street, but at the same time he was portrayed as a nice young guy who was happy to help out if he could, as in the way he paid for a packet of cigarettes for Dennis Tanner in the Rovers when Elsie's son didn't have any money. There was also Elsie's daughter, Linda, who had returned to her mother's house, having left her husband, Ivan, and there was Florrie Lindley getting to grips with running the corner shop. Places like the shop and the pub were very important tools in those days, because they allowed different characters to meet, which meant the stories didn't have to be confined to the various sets of individual houses, and it also meant that other possible storylines could be brought into the show. All of those storylines were developed further in the second episode and so too were the characters. Tony was very clever in the way he did that, and it didn't take long for people like Ken, Elsie, Annie Walker and Ena Sharples to become established as part of the fabric of *Coronation Street*.

Having got that first episode out of the way, none of us really had time to sit and ponder on how it had gone and what the reaction would be, because we had to get on with recording the second one, which was going to be transmitted five days later. Once we had done those first two episodes, I think there was a feeling of relief that we'd got the week out of the way and settled into some sort of a routine, but I think there was a very matter-of-fact atmosphere as we dispersed for the weekend. Looking back now, I believe we all felt we had done our jobs well and that the programme was up and running.

I'm sure we all felt we were working on something that was extremely good and very much cutting edge for its time. We were portraying a slice of working-class northern life, and I'm sure that was what struck a chord with the public. It was new, it was different, but at no time during the course of that week did any of us realise exactly what we had set in motion.

5

SIGNING ON

I think we were all a bit taken aback by the reaction of the public to the show after those first two episodes, and at the same time it quickly became clear that the programme had something about it that the viewers obviously liked.

During the first month seven episodes were broadcast, and as well as establishing those characters from the first two shows, others gradually began to be introduced. That first episode featured the Barlows, Elsie Tanner and her children, Albert Tatlock, Annie Walker, Ena Sharples and Florrie Lindley. The second introduced Jack Walker, Martha Longhurst, Harry Hewitt, Christine Hardman and Esther Hayes, who was played by Daphne Oxenford, an actress who had originally auditioned for the role of Annie Walker. The episode also saw the appearance of Margot Bryant, playing the meek and mild character of Minnie Caldwell. Margot had a non-speaking role in that show, but in the next programme, which was another live broadcast, she had a few lines, and it was also the episode that saw Arthur Lowe make his debut playing Leonard Swindley, something he did beautifully for some time to come. Later on in that first month, young Jennifer Moss appeared as Harry Hewitt's daughter, Lucille, and Doreen Keogh also joined the cast playing barmaid Concepta Riley, who went on to marry Harry at a later stage. So in the first month before the year ended, an awful lot happened in seven episodes, and the fact that it was shown twice a week meant the programme got a lot of exposure, and I think it came across as something that was new, fresh and bright on the television screens of Britain. I can't be sure of exactly what it was that made the show popular so quickly, but as I've already mentioned, I think the early characters created by Tony Warren had a lot to do with it. They were strong and left an impression with the public. It didn't take long before viewers knew exactly what to expect from Ken and his family, and from the likes of Ena, Elsie and Annie Walker. At the same time the characters were being developed and with them came different storylines that sustained the interest of viewers. There was little doubt as the year came to an end that within just a few weeks *Coronation Street* had established itself with the public and become a very popular programme.

The almost overnight success of the show came as a bit of a shock to some of the cast. We were suddenly getting recognised when we went out in Manchester, and I don't think that had really happened to any of us before. In my own mind, I wasn't looking any further than the episodes I'd been contracted to do. Each week at the end of doing the two episodes I would hop on a train and head back to London, and then make my way back up to Manchester on the Sunday or Monday to start all over again. Sometimes I would share a car with Frank Pemberton, because he too lived in London, and although we would talk about the programme, I don't think either of us was thinking too far ahead after that first month, but pretty soon into the new year things started to change rapidly, and it became obvious to Granada and the rest of us that we were involved in something that was a bit special.

I have already said that all of the actors were aware from an early stage of the quality of writing and production that was involved in *Coronation Street*, but because there hadn't really been anything like it before we had no way of measuring it in terms of appeal and popularity. However, early on in 1961 the organisation that measured audience figures reported a huge increase in the people watching the programme, which was obviously great news for everyone at Granada and also for the ITV network.

At the beginning of March the *Street* became a networked show, which meant that it was seen in every region, and instead of going out on Fridays and Wednesdays the programme was switched to Mondays and Wednesdays. In the autumn of that year another survey revealed that we were being watched by a staggering 15 million viewers every time an episode was shown, which proved just how popular *Coronation Street* had become less than a year after it was first shown. Having thought no further ahead than those initial 13 episodes it soon became clear that the programme had a lot more to offer, and as an actor it was very exciting to be involved in something that was not only good, but also very successful. From a practical point of view it also meant that there was more work, which is something an actor can never take for granted. Usually you are working from one job to another, whether it's a film, a play or some television work, and you never look further ahead than that. If you want job security, then acting is probably not the best profession in the world for you to turn to. That is the case now and it most certainly was the case back then, so when we were first given six-month contracts at the turn of the year and then in June 1961 several of us were asked if we wanted to sign a long-term contract guaranteeing work for a year it was quite amazing, because for an actor that was pretty much unheard of. It was incredible security, because until then, like most other actors, I had been leading a hand-to-mouth existence, never thinking further ahead than a few days, weeks or months. Suddenly that all changed, and with it came the realisation that I was part of something that had really taken off and hit the pulse of the viewing nation in a very big way.

I remember walking down the corridor at Granada Studios during those early days and coming the other way was one of the producers, Stuart 'Harry' Latham. We both realised we were working on something that was a bit special, but neither of us could quite put our finger on exactly what it was.

'What have we got here, Bill?' he asked me, almost pleadingly. 'What have we got?'

I think he was simply voicing what most of us were feeling; we were all being swept along by a unique programme, and it was lovely to be a part of it. When we first went on air and began to be recognised locally I don't think any of us thought too much about it, but quite literally within weeks of the first broadcast we had all been catapulted into a very different world. I suppose these days we're more used to it, and the word 'celebrity' is bandied about on a regular basis, but in those days there weren't really television celebrities. There were film stars and the whole Mersey thing with the Beatles began to happen a couple of years after we started, but as far as national television was concerned there had never been anything like *Coronation Street* and the twice-weekly viewing figures the programme attracted. I think it was lovely for people like Jack Howarth, Doris Speed, Arthur Leslie and Margot Bryant. They had all worked long and hard in the theatre all of their lives, and then suddenly this enormously popular and successful television work had come along and they were able to enjoy it, basking in the sunshine in the later years of their careers. Once we settled into a routine, the work was really quite gentle. We stopped doing the live broadcast, and instead both episodes were recorded on a Friday, so the pace wasn't particularly hectic and they could enjoy the whole experience. For the younger members of the cast it was thrilling and exciting to be given such a platform, and from a personal point of view I was getting great job satisfaction. I felt comfortable playing Ken, even though I was actually seven years older than him, it was enjoyable and I liked all the spin-offs that came with the job. In short, I was very happy with my role and with my job.

There were some people during those early days who were seeking to make their characters in the programme more powerful, fighting to make sure they carried strong storylines and were always involved. Pat Phoenix was probably the leader when it came to doing that; she seemed to be in there fighting for her character, always trying to push the role of Elsie. She also loved doing things like personal appearances and lapped up the adulation she got from the public. Pat was very much in the mould of the classic movie star of the 1940s and 1950s; in fact, I'm sure she would have loved to have been one, and I'm also sure she would have been very good at it. She loved the glamour and recognition, which was in stark contrast to someone like Doris Speed, who was never really interested in any of the extramural activities that appearing on a show like *Coronation Street* offered.

She was just interested in playing Annie Walker, and Arthur Leslie was such a great foil for her in the show, with his familiar 'Eee, Annie' phrase he used whenever he felt she was going too far or had said something out of place. Both had come from theatrical backgrounds: Jack's parents were actors, and Doris was born when her mother and father were on tour as a music-hall double act. Like Jack Howarth, Arthur had a lot of experience in rep and ran his own company, and before *Coronation Street* came along virtually all of his acting life had been spent in the theatre, while Doris gained her experience in rep, musical comedy and radio, where she once worked on a *Children's Hour* play with Tony Warren, who at the time was a child actor. She'd never really had any television experience, but had had a small part in *Skyport*.

Arthur was a lovely, gentle man, and I think the character of Jack that he played in the show suited him. There was a lot of Arthur in the way he played that role, and as a consequence I think the personality of Jack Walker benefited. Arthur was very unassuming and clearly loved being in the *Street*; the chance to be in the programme had come along when he was about 60, and I think that, having spent all of those years in the theatre, he was really able to enjoy television and brought all of his experience and considerable acting skills to the part. We didn't realise when the *Street* started, but Doris was actually 61 when it began, and once again I think she really enjoyed and appreciated being part of something that was new, successful and, at the same time, very enjoyable. She wasn't at all interested in the trappings of fame and lived very modestly with her mother in a semi just outside of Manchester.

Doris played everything beautifully out front, with those wonderful eyes of hers, and she made the character of Annie very much her own. Off-screen she was a lovely person, and she used to make me laugh in the way that she loved being conspiratorial over the most trivial of things. I might be in the rehearsal room one morning and she'd call across to me.

'Bill, I wonder if I could have a word?'

You'd go over to her and she would beckon you to a quiet part of the room and then whisper to you in hushed tones.

'Have you heard they're moving the time that the tea trolley comes around each morning?'

It was so funny the way she would make something so innocuous into a major piece of gossip. She loved to smoke as well and was a voracious reader of books. I heard that one day, many years later when she had retired from the *Street* and lived in a home in Bury, she stubbed out her cigarette, put down the book she had been reading and then just laid back and died peacefully. During her time on the *Street* she was always marvellous to work with, and although her Annie Walker could be quite sharp with some of the locals, she always seemed to have a soft spot for Ken. Annie was always trying to make sure the Rovers was a cut above the rest, and she certainly had grand ideas for both herself and the pub on occasions. Jack Walker indulged her to a certain extent, but was always there to keep her feet on the ground if she started to get too carried away. I think Annie liked Ken because she saw him as a bit of an intellectual, and someone who had done well for himself by getting a degree. It was something she would have loved to have done, and always seemed impressed by the sort of education he had got.

As you might imagine, those early days of the *Street* were very different to the way things are today. The number of actors employed on the show was very small compared with today, and everything about the show was much more basic. These days we have a purpose-built Street exterior set and we also have a building that houses all of our dressing-rooms. Back then it was a very different story: we didn't have our own individual dressing-rooms; all we had was a big rehearsal room with the floor taped out for the various sets, and then there were chairs all around the edge of the room, which were each allocated to a member of the cast. So if, for instance, there was a scene involving Frank Pemberton and me, we would have to get up and move to the part of the room that had been put aside for the Barlows' set and then rehearse our scene and lines in front of everyone else.

Something else that seemed to play a big part in the day, particularly with Arthur Leslie, Vi Carson and Doris Speed, was the *Daily Telegraph* crossword puzzle. They would each sit there doing it, and the first one to complete it would get up from their chair with a slightly self-satisfied look on their face, as if to say, 'I've done it. I'm finished.'

There was a great unity amongst us, and a feeling that we were very much in it together, because the cast was so small. Routines were developed very quickly, like having your own little area where you sat, and we would all look forward to the arrival of the tea lady and her trolley, which was well stocked with cakes. We got to know each other well and Granada itself had a very homely feel to it. We were only a tiny little bit of the ITV network when the show began, and the Bernsteins, Cecil and Sidney, who ran Granada, would sometimes turn up to see us, adding to the family feel of the place. Other characters were gradually introduced during 1961, including Emily Nugent, played by Eileen Derbyshire; Len Fairclough, played by Peter Adamson; Alf Roberts, played by Bryan Mosley; and Billy Walker, played by Kenneth Farrington. All of them went on to have major roles in the programme and, of course, Eileen is still in the show today.

In fact, she's now the second longest-serving on the programme and made an immediate impact when she turned up on-screen playing a very shy helper at the Mission Hall. I believe she was actually asked about joining the *Street* in December 1960, but already had a commitment in the theatre. She was then asked whether she wanted to wait until a new family was introduced into the *Street* or take a small part playing the role of Emily. Sometimes things are just meant to be, and Eileen immediately brought something to the part and made it her own. She's a very fine actor, able to handle heavy scenes and lightness with great skill, and off-screen she is a wonderful person. She very quickly began to have some wonderful scenes with Arthur Lowe, and the public loved the interplay between them as the show developed. They went on to work together after Emily moved on to have a baby-linen shop and then merged with Swindley's haberdashery, where he became her boss. Arthur Lowe was a master when it came to being able to deliver lines that were funny and offered light relief within the show. It was something he went on to do with great effect when he played Captain Mainwaring in *Dad's*

Army. I used to love watching Arthur work, because he was such a neat and tidy actor, and his delivery was superb. Quite often he would have a piece of dialogue and use just one word during the course of it to speak in a very broad Lancashire accent: the effect was wonderful, and he also had a very expressive face, which helped the viewers know exactly what he was thinking.

As other characters like Valerie Tatlock, played by Anne Reid, Doreen Lostock, played by Angela Crow, and Jed Stone, who was played by Kenneth Cope, were added during 1961, the show seemed to go from strength to strength, with the public clearly liking what they saw. One of the most memorable events of that year for all of us was the day the whole cast went off to Blackpool because Violet Carson had been asked to switch on the famous illuminations. She lived in the town and she was very much part of the area. We got an absolutely wonderful reception from the public, and they literally lined the streets and cheered as we did a procession in an open-top bus.

We had quite a grand reception with the mayor, and when we looked out of the window at the town hall, all we could see were people waiting to catch a glimpse of all of us. Vi Carson then went on to switch on the famous lights, and as she stood on a podium with the mayor, ready to flick the switch, a big board behind her was lit up with pictures of all the cast displayed on it. That got a big cheer, but nothing like the one Violet got from the crowd a few seconds later. She had arrived for the night looking terrific in a glimmering outfit with her hair looking immaculate, but just as the crowd's attention was taken by our pictures being lit up, she took out a hairnet and old raincoat, so that by the time the crowd focused on her again, she had quickly managed to transform herself into Ena Sharples! Violet was a wonderful woman who had a dignity and natural authority about her. She had this marvellous face, and I used to say that it looked as though you could break rocks on it, and it made her character of Ena look even more formidable. She was very much the strong personality in the cast and would sort out any problems with the management. In many ways she became a sort of spokesperson for us, and you certainly didn't cross her.

Noel Dyson was there with all of us that night, but in fact, by the time we travelled to Blackpool, she had already left the show. Noel, who played Ken's mum, Ida, had decided that she wanted to leave the programme, just as Anne Cunningham had. In Anne's case, it was decided that her character of Linda Cheveski should emigrate to Canada with husband, Ivan, but for Noel they made sure the departure was more permanent and dramatic when she was run over by a bus. She had already done the episode by the time we went to Blackpool, but they decided to put out a filler episode that same night instead, and Noel was able to celebrate with the rest of the cast. Asking to be written out can have repercussions for other members of the cast. Once your character goes the departure can have a knock-on effect, and the producer and writers have to decide what they want to do with other characters who were closely associated with them. In Noel's case, she had become established as the wife of Frank as well as the mother of Ken and David. That meant it could potentially have had an effect on Frank Pemberton, Alan Rothwell and me. Noel was also concerned because she realised this fact, and I know she was relieved to find out from Harry Kershaw that nothing bad would be happening to the three of us as a consequence. It's a situation that has occurred from time to time over the years since then. Sometimes it comes about because the actor wants to leave, and the other situation is when the writers and producer decide it is time to kill off a character. On this particular occasion, I think it was felt that the show was still relatively young and something like a death was a natural part of what would be happening in *Coronation Street*. The Barlows were one of the *Street*'s established families, and it also gave the writers scope to write different storylines for Frank and myself.

The episode I played in when Ida died offered me the chance to get stuck into some very good, meaty acting, and I think the way in which the storylines were then developed helped give a better insight into the character of Ken Barlow and the relationship he had with his father. Ida's death was a tragedy for both men, and although their relationship could often be stormy, with Ken's views and attitude rubbing Frank up the wrong way on a number of issues, the fact was that they had been thrown together by her death and they had to get used to living with each other without the buffer that Ida had often provided.

I think there was quite a significant moment in the programme when it came to the emotional scene that showed a hearse driving off, with Eric Spear's *Coronation Street* theme music in the background. It made me realise just what a flexible piece it was, because it could be played at a moment like that and sound just right for the occasion, adding even more emotion to the scene, and when the rest of the cast watched that scene played back I don't think there was a dry eye in the house. It wasn't just the fact that the programme and her death were very emotional, it was also because we were saying goodbye to Noel Dyson. She had been there with us for almost a year, and because we were very much a team, I think we all felt it and missed having her with us. She was also a sort of 'mother' figure to everyone and would fuss around the rest of the cast if there was anything wrong with us, like a cold or sore throat, giving us different medicines and generally trying to make sure we were all right and looked after. She was a lovely person, but I think that she really hadn't thought of being in the show for longer than those initial few weeks, and because her husband was in London it probably became more difficult to keep commuting. She wanted to do other things and asked to go.

When Noel went, she came into the Green Room one day and presented the rest of us with a little vine as a parting gift, saying, 'When this vine dies, the *Street* will end.' Right from the start there was always someone to look after it and make sure it was watered and cared for, but there have been a few panics along the way, the most notable of which came when we were given our own purpose-built studio, Studio One, in 1990. The new complex had dressing-rooms, a make-up room and a new Green Room that were just for the cast of *Coronation Street*. We were all very happy with our new home, which meant that the programme had its own self-contained environment, but then one day soon after the move somebody asked where the vine was. Nobody could recall exactly what had happened to it and suddenly we were all searching for this plant. Actors can be pretty superstitious, and we certainly didn't want the vine to go missing, having seen it flourish for almost 30 years. People looked everywhere, and it was eventually discovered in an old skip, along with a lot of stuff that was due to be thrown out – panic over. The vine was saved and a cutting was taken from it, which is still going strong to this day!

In the same month that Ida was killed off and we all went to Blackpool, *Coronation Street* found itself at the top of the ratings, and we remained there for the rest of the year. A couple of months later the programme had to deal with a strike that was called by the actors' union, Equity, protesting against pay and conditions. It meant that the ITV network was badly hit, with some shows having to come off air to be replaced by the showing of old films. In contrast, because of the long-term contracts signed by the core of the cast on *Coronation Street*, the show was able to carry on, and as there was no real opposition and we were being shown twice a week, we also claimed the top two spots in the ratings. The producers had also apparently heard about the possibility of a strike and quickly added Peter Adamson to the list of actors the show had on long-term contract, because Len Fairclough had become such a successful and well-liked character, with his no-nonsense macho-man image. The terms of those contracts meant that we were able to work right through the strike. Had that not been the case then *Coronation Street* might well have disappeared from the screens for good, despite its popularity, because the other thing the programme clearly needed was continuity.

So the good news was that we were able to carry on when other shows were being hit hard and quite literally disappearing; the bad news was that nobody else except the 14 actors who had been offered and signed contracts were allowed to work on the show. The 14 were Pat Phoenix, Doreen Keogh, Betty Alberge, Doris Speed, Arthur Leslie, Ivan Beavis, Peter Adamson, Jack Howarth, Lynne Carol, Frank Pemberton, Philip Lowrie, Margot Bryant, Violet Carson and me. We had no way of knowing how long the strike would last for and consequently the scripts had to be tailored for the situation, making sure that only the 14 of us carried the storylines.

It meant that the Rovers started to look very bare on occasions, because we weren't allowed to have any extras in the background in the way we usually did. Most scenes in the pub would have people coming and going or playing darts as some of the regulars chatted at the bar, but all that had to stop.

It also meant that some of the people who had been quite prominent in the *Street*, like Anne Reid, Eileen Derbyshire and Arthur Lowe, could not act on the show. The strike went on for about six months in the end, which was much longer than most people had expected, but apart from the restrictions it put on everyone, there was also scope for some very good stories to be played out, some of them quite heavy and dramatic, while others had a much lighter, comedic feel to them.

During the course of the dispute, in February 1962, I was involved in a very good episode that I really enjoyed doing. It revolved around an article Ken had written for a left-wing magazine called *Survival*, in which he wrote a piece criticising the residents of Coronation Street. Ken's father thought it was a bit harsh, but was comforted by the fact that it had been printed in a magazine that his son assured him would never be read by anyone in Coronation Street. Unfortunately the article was then picked up by the local paper, which printed some of the most damning phrases, and when Len Fairclough read it he was furious. He confronted Frank Barlow outside the Rovers and the two men had a stand-up row. When Ken came home to find his clearly shaken father sitting in a chair in the Barlows', he decided he would go to the pub and confront his critics. Ken refused to back down from what he had written in the article, even though the atmosphere in the pub was becoming distinctly edgy, with Len getting very worked up. Eventually he threw a punch at Ken, who hit him back, but was then floored by Fairclough as the end music played and the titles rolled.

That fight sequence had to be shot straight through, which basically means that there is no stopping to get things right or do it again; you just begin the scene and carry on until the end of it. We obviously wanted it to look as realistic as possible, and I knew I was quite an athletic sort of guy, so I told Peter that the thing to do was for him to come at me and actually try to throw a punch and hit me. I was confident that at the last second I would be able to dodge the blow and no harm would be done. I think Peter had played some sport during his life, but he wasn't particularly quick and I thought that my agility would help make the scene look authentic. So when it came to shooting the scene Peter did exactly what I had suggested, and I literally felt his punch whistle past as I dodged the blow, but ended up in a heap on the floor as I was supposed to. The result looked so good that the first thing I heard when we'd finished was the floor manager anxiously asking if I was OK. Something like that wouldn't happen in today's *Coronation Street*, because for a number of years now we have been using stuntmen, who either do the scene themselves or choreograph it for us, letting the actors know exactly what they should do and how they should do it.

I really enjoyed playing those scenes as well as all the drama with Len; I also had some very good, meaty scenes with Frank for that episode. It was very much what the *Street* was about at the time, and although there were restrictions on who could be acting, the fact that the show was very much character based meant that we could get away with just a few people carrying the whole storyline. In that particular episode I think there were only eleven actors used, and the main story centred around five of the characters – Len, Harry Hewitt, Albert, Frank Barlow and me – but it certainly worked, and worked well. I also doubt that the viewing public would have noticed that so few people were in it, partly because we didn't have a huge cast then anyway, even before the strike, and there were certainly nothing like the numbers there are in today's programme.

That episode was written by Robert Holles, and although Tony Warren had done all the original scripts and laid down the foundation for all the major characters, other writers began to produce some terrific scripts as well, people like John Finch and Jack Rosenthal. Jack went on to display a really deft touch for drama with a lovely light comedy running through it and wrote some tremendous television plays that have become classics, including the enormously popular and critically acclaimed *Bar*

Mitzvah Boy and *The Knowledge*, and the comedy programmes *The Dustbin Men* and *The Lovers*. He was also the man behind *London's Burning*, which he wrote as a one-off drama, and he co-wrote the film *Yentl* with Barbra Streisand. Jack also had a brief stint as the show's producer during 1967.

In another of the episodes broadcast during the strike, he wrote a script that essentially centred on Dennis Tanner putting on a concert at the Mission Hall. After entering the *Street* in that first-ever episode as a rather surly, dark figure just out of prison, Dennis Tanner's character had been opened up by the scriptwriters, and Philip Lowrie, who in my opinion was a very fine actor, also displayed a great ability to play comedy – not in the belly-laugh sense, but in being able to bring laughter to a drama serial in a very subtle way. He was a natural and was able to play the lines beautifully.

The concert that Dennis put on was a great success, at least in terms of the number of tickets he sold. In fact, he sold about three times the number he should and it all started to go terribly wrong. He'd also arranged for three exotic dancers, which, because of the strike, could never be seen, and there were some sea lions as well. The ploy of using animals in the show to help supplement things during the strike came about because a storyline had been created for Dennis where he got a job with a theatrical agent, handling all manner of things, both human and animal. In this particular episode, with Dennis staging the show, there was an awful lot of activity backstage at the Mission Hall, but despite the sound effects suggesting there was a large and vocal audience out front, nobody was ever shown, because of the strike, so you would get various actors from the *Street* talking to the camera as if they were shouting to a crowd in front of them and somehow it worked.

I think the thing that made that happen was some great acting and a marvellous script. As part of the ending, Dennis manages to smuggle two sea lions and the three exotic dancers into the Rovers while Annie and Jack are out for the night, only for them to return home and discover the sea lions in their bath and the dancers in their bed! The comic timing of Doris Speed in the final scene is wonderful. In fact, having a rich vein of comedy and people who were able to play it also became a feature of the show from the very beginning.

When the strike ended it allowed the show to bring back the actors who had been missing, and at the same time some significant new characters were introduced, such as Jerry Booth, played by Graham Haberfield, who joined the show as an apprentice to Len Fairclough in his builder's yard. The Jed Stone character had enjoyed popularity when he made his *Street* bow the previous year as the cheeky Liverpool spiv who was always trying to get some sort of dodgy deal going, and he went on to lodge with dear, sweet little Minnie Caldwell. They were wonderful together as Minnie used to fuss over him, and despite his obvious shortcomings she tried to always see Jed in a good light. Her other great love was Bobby the cat.

Minnie and Martha had become part of the fabric of the *Street* in those early days as two of a trio led by Ena, and the three of them would often inhabit the 'snug' bar of the Rovers Return, providing some very nice comedic moments that ran alongside the other, more dramatic storylines. They would sit there talking and gossiping, with Ena very much the one in charge and the person who set the agenda. Martha tended to be her second in command, with Minnie coming across as a lovely, sweet old lady who wouldn't say boo to a goose, but in real life she was a very different character.

It was quite amazing, really, because if you were out with Margot Bryant she might still have looked like Minnie, but she certainly didn't act like her. She could be horrendous, swearing and having a go at the waiters. I think she seemed to like the idea that she could shock people because her behaviour was so unlike anything that came across on the television screen. Of course, it would be wrong to expect all of the actors on *Coronation Street* to be just like the characters they play on-screen, but Margot was just so much the opposite of Minnie that it actually became a bit shocking. I think someone once asked her what she would have liked to have been had she not been involved in acting and she said, 'A pirate!'

She was frightening, and could be quite vitriolic; her whole demeanour was quite disarming, although I'm sure I often saw a little twinkle in her eye when she was clearly surprising some unsuspecting soul with the way she was behaving. She was a trained dancer and had done chorus work, even dancing in a West End show with Fred Astaire. Margot was great fun, but certainly nobody wanted to get on the wrong side of her, although there was one member of the cast who took his life in his own hands one day by playing a joke on her.

Graham Haberfield was a lovely guy and one of life's born jokers; he could never resist a practical joke and was always larking around. I liked him a lot and we got on well, often playing jokes on each other. He was so happy to have been given the chance to join the cast of *Coronation Street*, having just left Bristol Old Vic Drama School. He was an extremely good actor, and the viewers immediately took to his character and the way Graham played Jerry.

During those early years of the *Street*, you would often have this thing where a guy would come around to the studios selling various things cheaply. It could be all sorts of things, from perfume to clothes; it was all legitimate and certainly none of it had 'fallen off the back of a lorry', as the saying goes, so when he turned up one day with real fur coats the girls showed an immediate interest. Things were very different back then and there was no guilt about wearing fur coats or any real awareness about the plight of the animals they had come from. They were just seen as the sort of luxury item that most women would buy if they could afford them. The coats were so good and so cheap that I think pretty well every female member of the cast bought one, and each day at rehearsal you would see this clothes rack at the far end of the room with a line of identical fur coats hanging from it. The only difference was in their size, and probably the smallest coat there belonged to Margot. She was a tiny woman, and whenever she put her coat on and wandered off she had this oval shape to her. Graham had obviously seen this and one day got a piece of paper and scribbled down 'I am a shit beetle' before sticking it on the back of Margot's black fur coat, and from the back she did rather have the shape of a beetle. So when it was time for us all to go home, she went to the rack and put her coat on without seeing this piece of paper stuck on the back. She walked out of the room, and nobody who saw what Graham had scribbled dared say anything. Margot then proceeded to walk through reception at Granada and out onto the street as she made her way home. We never found out when she discovered the piece of paper and, of course, none of us was going to ask about it. One thing's for certain, I wouldn't have liked to have been there when she did find it. She never said anything about the piece of paper the next day and we weren't going to mention it. Luckily for Graham, she never found out who did it!

The relationship Minnie had with Jed during the course of the show was tremendous, but in later years Margot's memory started to deteriorate and she would get a little muddled. There was one episode where Jed had to go to Liverpool, and everybody knew that using 'Liverpool' was another way of saying he was going off to jail. At the end of the scene, he got into an unmarked police car just as Ena appeared, asking where he was going. Minnie was supposed to say Liverpool, and after a knowing look from Ena the episode was then due to come to an end.

That was all fine, but when it came to actually filming the scene Margot said Birmingham instead of Liverpool. Everyone laughed at the time, but it was an indication that perhaps things were getting a little difficult for her. She eventually left the show in the mid-1970s and in later life had to go into a home. Eileen Derbyshire used to visit her regularly, and I went along on a couple of occasions, but sadly she didn't really recognise me and she died about nine years after she left the programme.

Lynne Carol was the other member of that famous snug trio, and her very gossipy character fitted in perfectly, allowing some very good stories to be written for them. Lynne apparently helped create the way Martha looked on-screen, buying the coat, hat and glasses that were to become part of her regular on-screen dress. Despite the fact that her character was very popular, she was killed off in 1964 by a young producer who thought the show needed a bit of a shake-up. It wasn't one of the nicest of times for any of us, because he seemed to want to make changes for change's sake. At the time I think quite a few of the cast thought they might not survive, and one of them was me.

6

BEING KEN

I had been in *Coronation Street* for more than three years and the character of Ken Barlow had become well established, having been involved in more than 200 episodes since we first began, but in the spring of 1964 the show was hit by the news that there were going to be changes. A young guy in his late twenties called Tim Aspinall had been appointed as the new producer of the programme, and he clearly intended to shake things up. It's not unusual for a new producer to want to make changes, and having fresh ideas or tweaking things here and there can help a programme like *Coronation Street* to improve and evolve. The trouble was that Tim Aspinall seemed more intent on carrying out a culling exercise and it ended up not only having an impact on those actors who lost their roles in the show, but also on those who were left, because the great team spirit and feeling of unity that we had was attacked.

He basically decided who he wanted out and then sent Margaret Morris, who was head of casting, into the Green Room one day to announce his intention to drop some characters from the show almost with immediate effect, while others, including myself, were sort of put on warning that we were likely to be given the chop at a later date. He had a kind of hit list of characters and there was no privacy involved in the way the people were told. I think everyone felt stunned at the news and at the way we had heard about it. Lynne Carol's character, Martha Longhurst, was going to be killed off, Frank Pemberton was also going to go, so too were the whole Hewitt family, Betty Alberge was also on the list, as were Anne Reid and I, along with Jack Howarth, while both Graham Haberfield as Jerry Booth and Susan Jameson, who played his wife, Myra, had already expressed a wish to leave the show and pursue some other acting opportunities. The news of the big shake-up also got out into the press, which made the atmosphere even worse. Violet Carson was very upset at Lynne's departure; so too was Peter Adamson. I think Vi went to see the management and may even have threatened to leave the show herself, but the death of Martha went ahead in an episode that saw Frank Barlow holding a celebration party at the Rovers after he had sold his DIY shop to a supermarket chain for £6,000. Having already had a £5,000 Premium Bonds win a few weeks earlier, he was then due to move away from the Street. Just as everyone was gathered around a piano that Ena was playing, Martha slowly wandered off to the snug, sat in her chair, took off her coat and hat, and died. Violet's protests had fallen on deaf ears, and in the end she could do nothing to prevent the departure of Lynne.

I think everyone in the cast felt it was a huge mistake to kill her off, and to this day I still believe it was. The trio of Ena, Martha and Minnie offered the opportunity for some lovely lines of dialogue during the time the three of them were together, and although both Ena and Minnie continued to visit the snug, I think that not having that extra voice and character was a real loss to the show. Over the years *Coronation Street* has proved time and again that the programme is bigger than any one actor, and that is the way it should be. I have no problem with that, and if decisions are made for the right reasons and they ultimately benefit the show, that has to be a good thing, but I certainly didn't feel that was the case with some of the decisions Tim Aspinall made.

In the end he wasn't in charge for very long, and it was decided to bring Harry Kershaw back as producer. By the time this had happened Martha had gone, along with Frank Barlow, and so too had Harry and Concepta Hewitt. Their daughter, Lucille, was spared, apparently at the intervention of Cecil Bernstein, who told Aspinall that not having any children in the *Street* was ridiculous. There was a possible storyline of Valerie, who had married Ken in 1962, going to Australia with him, but thankfully that never happened when Harry Kershaw returned to the show.

Although there had been a trickle of people coming and going since the programme made its debut, I think that period of change and uncertainty in 1964 was something that was both unsettling and quite sad. Seeing someone like Betty Alberge leave was a great shame. She'd been in that very first scene when she took over at the corner shop, and she was a good actress who was popular amongst the rest of the cast. We had all lived through her trials and tribulations while she tried to pass her driving test during her time on the show. She took it so many times I think we all lost count, but did eventually pass, although I think we were all a bit concerned for the rest of the motorists on the road at the time.

I'd had an excellent working relationship with Frank and we'd played some very good scenes with each other. He had a great way of running through his lines with me whenever we had a scene to do, and quite often there would be a lot of dialogue involved, so the last thing you wanted was to forget a line or stumble over words. Frank had this thing where we would sometimes do the lines at great speed, other times we would do them in different accents, and it really did have the effect of helping you to remember, so that when the time came to speak them for an episode, you were word perfect. He also had this thing where he would sometimes write a particular word out if he thought it might be something that could cause a problem when he came to do it. He would write it on a piece of paper and look at it during a scene, or maybe put it on a beer mat if he was in the Rovers. One day he even wrote a word on the shell of an egg in a scene we were doing while sitting at a table in the Barlows', but the trouble was that he got so carried away with the scene that he whacked his spoon into the egg and in doing so smashed the shell to pieces and with it the word he had marked on it. Fortunately it didn't matter and Frank got through it without having to refer to the dialogue safety net he had created for himself. I believe Frank found it very difficult to get work after he left, and in later years he suffered a stroke, which made things worse for him. He did come back to the *Street* briefly in the early 1970s, but really Tim Aspinall's decision to axe him in 1964 spelled the end of his time in *Coronation Street*. I think it's different when a character goes because the actor wants to leave the show, but when it is a management decision to get rid of someone and that actor doesn't necessarily want to go, it's a very different proposition, especially if you have been playing a part that you like. That would certainly have been the case for me if I had been killed off, because I was enjoying playing Ken and genuinely felt his character was starting to evolve and grow. There had been some good storylines for me right from the start, with the relationship between Ken and his father, the different girlfriends, the death of his mother and then the marriage to Val. I thought there was plenty of mileage left in Ken and, happily, so too did Harry Kershaw. I suppose the fact that I'm still here more than 50 years later hopefully proves that he was right. Harry was like the father of the show in those days. He cared about *Coronation Street* and had a very clear idea about its identity and the sort of characters and stories the show should have in it. You felt safe in his hands, because not only was he a very warm and friendly man, he was also a very strong personality.

Although it hadn't been pleasant to be told that I was on the shortlist for the chop, it wasn't so much the decision that I found upsetting, but rather the way in which it had been made and then delivered to the people concerned. To have effectively been given your cards without any prior warning and with such a lack of subtlety and concern was appalling. From my own point of view I knew that I was at least going to be employed for another six months, and I also realised that very few actors were ever lucky enough to have the sort of continuous work I'd had for more than three years. I'd be lying if I said that I wasn't sad at the thought of leaving, simply because I had enjoyed myself so much and also because I thought Ken had more to give as a character, but I comforted myself with the thought that I would be able to pursue other acting roles in the theatre, on film and in television. However, I have to admit that when they decided to bring Harry back it was lovely to get a call one night from him to let me know there had been a change of heart.

'Forget all that business about you going, Bill,' he told me. 'We want you to stay.'

One of the good things Tim Aspinall did do during his short time as producer of the show was to introduce the Ogden family into the *Street*, and they became wonderful characters in the years that followed, with some very rich storylines. The public loved Stan, Hilda and their daughter Irma, who married Ken's brother, David. They also had a rather wayward son called Trevor, but he never really featured heavily in the show, and in terms of longevity it was Stan and Hilda that the public took to. They were beautifully played by Bernard Youens, who was always known as 'Bunny', and Jean Alexander. Despite being cast as this very northern working-class man, Bernard was in fact from the south coast and had previously been working at Granada as a continuity announcer. He'd had breaks in his career but had also got a lot of experience from his time in rep, and it's Bernard I later had to thank for introducing me to the game of golf. Jean was another person with great experience from touring with various theatre companies and she was superb as Hilda, able to play the interfering gossip one moment, some very touching scenes at other times and then getting marvellous comedic moments from her relationship with Stan. They became a very welcome addition to the cast, and off-screen both of them helped add to some of the communal pastimes we indulged in during the week. I've already mentioned the passion some of the cast had for doing the *Telegraph* crossword each day, and when Jean and Bernard joined they loved to play Scrabble. The game really took off and sometimes they would go on for a long time before they were settled.

Having survived the great purge by Tim Aspinall, I was delighted to be able to carry on being Ken. I had enjoyed the role from the moment I played him and felt his character was growing along with the show. When you are working on something like *Coronation Street*, you become aware that there is this sort of parallel world that you inhabit. Obviously you are living your own life, but at the same time there is a regular ongoing fictional life that has been created by the writers of the programme. It's not like a play in the theatre that stays the same throughout its run on the stage, and it's not a television drama that will only be seen once. A drama serial has running stories that are topical and keep moving. The show is a year-round operation and the episodes have to reflect that. Although we were only transmitting two episodes each week, which is nothing like the busy schedule we have these days, it was still a constant production for the studios, and because of its popularity the producer and writers were always aware of making sure that the show maintained its strength and moved with the times, keeping the audience entertained and happy with what they saw each week.

One of the other things that happened following Harry Kershaw taking over was the return of Graham Haberfield. He had started in the programme as an apprentice with Len Fairclough, and his character, Jerry Booth, returned to work with Len once more, which meant we could renew our own friendship off-screen. For some reason or other the two of us got on well as soon as he joined the cast, and I think Graham's sense of humour always appealed to me. I have already mentioned his antics with regard to Margot Bryant, and certainly no member of the cast was immune as far as he was concerned. One of his favourite and most disconcerting jokes was setting light to your newspaper just as you were sitting back in the rehearsal room preparing to read it. I think in many ways the reason we got on so well was the fact that we both loved this kind of schoolboy humour, probably because neither of us had grown up!

He knew I'd been in the army and always used to call me 'The Commander'; we'd often have rather silly mock sword fights in the corridor and play jokes on each other. On one occasion I saw him hide around a corner, and I knew he'd seen me and was going to try to surprise me. So I ran up the corridor as quietly as I could and thought I'd get to him first. I swung my foot around the corner, hoping to give him a kick on the shin, but instead of catching his leg my foot hit something far softer and then I heard Graham cry out. Instead of standing upright he'd decided to go down on all fours in order to surprise me, and my foot had hit the top of his eye and there was blood everywhere. I had to get a taxi and go off to hospital with him to have some stitches put in the wound before we both raced back to go through our technical run-through. I think that while we'd been away the old rumour mill had started and people were saying that we'd had a fight, but of course nothing could have been further from the truth. You couldn't relax when you were around Graham, but I always found him to be great fun.

Like any other television show, *Coronation Street* would get feedback from the audience in the form of letters that were sent in. One day a letter was received saying that the beer that was served in the Rovers never looked very authentic. The guy who was in charge of the props took this to heart and decided to do something about it. The sets were very different in those days, and they were all tucked together in very close proximity to each other. It meant that if you had to play a scene in one set and then had to dash off to play another scene shortly after in another set, it could be done pretty quickly and without too much fuss. We were about to shoot some scenes for a particular episode and one of them involved Graham's character, Jerry Booth, having to go into the Rovers for a drink, and then once he'd done that he had to dash around the back of the set and be in position for another scene where he was due to be kissing his girlfriend. He did the whole thing during dress rehearsal and it went well, but he didn't actually have a drink during the course of it. When the time came for him to do the scene for the cameras Graham did exactly as he had in rehearsal, but of course this time he had to drink his pint of beer before dashing off for the love scene with his girlfriend. By the time he reached the back of the set poor Graham had thrown up all over the floor, but still managed to carry on and complete his kissing scene. We found out later that in order to make the beer look more authentic the prop man had come up with the idea of adding gravy browning and soda water; the effect was absolutely disgusting when you drank it and that was why Graham had been sick.

It was typical that something like that should have happened to him, and once he'd got over it I think Graham was able to see the funny side of it all. He was an adopted child and always wanted to find out who his real father was, but I don't think he ever did. He was always very keen to learn and was always asking me questions about this and that. His acting was superb, but he did have an alcohol problem. Things happened around Graham, and he seemed to either be creating problems or, when he was sober, apologising for them, but he was such a likeable guy.

On another occasion he was out on the town with a few people from the *Street* and one of them was a stuntman. Graham had a bit of a bee in his bonnet about the police for some reason or other on this particular night – I think they may have stopped him for speeding or something like that, but whatever it was had upset him – and as they walked past a police station he spotted this glass window and was going to throw a brick through it. The stuntman guy who was with him saw what Graham was going to do and decided to take the quickest action he could in order to prevent this happening, so he punched him. Apparently poor Graham reeled backwards and then fell down into the gutter, hitting his head on the kerb. Some of the others who were there panicked.

'You've killed him,' they said.

'Well, if he is dead, it's his fault!' said the stuntman.

Happily Graham was fine once he'd slept off the effects of the punch and the booze that all of them had consumed that night, and despite scrapes like that you just couldn't help liking him. Everyone loved having him around, and it was a huge shock to us when he died at the age of just 34, in 1975. We turned up one morning for rehearsals and there was a message for us to say that the producer, Susie Hush, was coming down to have a word with us all. When she told us that Graham had died that morning, I don't think any of us could quite believe it. From what we heard, there were no signs that he was ill: Graham had been in bed and his wife, Valerie, had gone to see if he wanted a cup of tea; when she brought it to him he'd gone, just like that, and had died of a heart attack at such a young age. It was a real tragedy, and I'm just glad that I have such lovely memories of him and his mischievous sense of humour.

After the business with Tim Aspinall had been sorted out and Harry had returned to the *Street* there was a much more settled feel to what we were doing, and I'm sure that this in turn helped the cast and the show itself. I could actually feel Ken's character developing, and I'm sure that was the case for a lot of the other actors. I suppose we were all keen to push our own characters as much as we could in those early years, and none more so than Pat Phoenix. As I've said, she loved the fame that the show brought her and the rest of us, and lapped up the adulation of the public. The Elsie Tanner character almost became a brand for her, so much so that later on in the show when she married an American soldier in 1967, she insisted that his name was Tanner as well so that she wouldn't have to change. I got on well with Pat and liked her larger-than-life personality; she was also a very good actress and did a great job playing Elsie, making her one of the best-known and most popular characters in the *Street*, which made it quite upsetting for me when we had a row that resulted in her not speaking to me for two years.

The whole thing came about because of a particular scene some time after Ken and Val had been married. There was some storyline where effectively Elsie and Ena Sharples had taken it upon themselves to sort of gang up on Val because she had done something they didn't like. I think they were supposed to be making certain accusations when Ken came along and stood up for his wife, telling the pair that if they didn't stop he would take action. This was supposed to stun them into silence as Ken stormed off, and it would end there, with Ken having put the pair of them in their place.

As always the writing seemed to be perfect and hit the spot. I was happy with the script and the way the scene would pan out, but when it came to rehearsing it Pat decided to have a word with the director. She basically told him that she didn't think Elsie would take that sort of thing from Ken. I pointed out that it was the way the scene had been written, but she insisted that at the end of what I said, Elsie would utter a few words dismissing Ken completely. When something happens like that it's really up to the director to decide. They can either be strong and insist on the thing going ahead as it was written, or they can be much more flexible, and it became clear that this particular director was not going to stand up to Pat. Her suggestion that she should be so dismissive of Ken really annoyed me. It wasn't an ego thing; it was simply that if we went down that route the scene would lose any dramatic impact it was supposed to have. The writer had clearly realised this, and it was obvious that the scene worked really well.

We rehearsed the scene, and when it came to the end Pat just said something like, 'Oh, get off!' I was very upset about this and extremely annoyed. I have never been the sort of actor who shouts and screams if I'm not happy about something; I prefer to talk the whole thing through and come up with a solution, but on this particular occasion there seemed little chance of Pat doing anything other than altering the scene to suit her and her character. To add insult to injury, just before we were due to do another run-through she came over and said that at the end of the scene, after she had told me to 'get off', she then wanted me to pause so that she could pick up an ashtray and threaten to throw it at me.

I was absolutely furious at this point and told her that there was no way I was going to do what she had suggested. We then had a huge row in front of the whole set, and in the end the scene was not one thing or the other, with any dramatic impact it was supposed to have being lost. Pat's request for me to pause at the end, and the row we had after it, turned out to be the last words we spoke to each other off-screen for the next two years. I have to admit that I didn't like that; it was horrible to have it hanging there for such a long period of time, and I found the whole situation very upsetting. I don't like conflict or animosity; I just see it as a very negative thing. I also didn't like the fact that one of my colleagues wasn't talking to me, because, as I've said, we all got on so well as a group, but the fact was that she'd altered that scene and the director had gone along with it. I thought it did a disservice to the show and it was damaging to my character. I actually liked Pat; she was a very outgoing sort of person. She was also a very powerful personality and I wasn't, and it was she who chose to stop talking to me, not the other way round. As strange as it may seem, we just kind of avoided each other for those two years, unless we had to play a scene together.

The end came one day when she had invited everyone to her house for a party; all the cast had been invited except me, but on the day of the party we were due to shoot a scene where I was required to go into the Rovers with her. Just as we were about to make our entrance, she said to me, 'You can come tonight if you want.'

It was completely unexpected, but I immediately accepted the invitation, and from that moment on there wasn't a problem. We spoke quite a bit at the party and I got on very well with her for many years to come. We never spoke about the incident again. It had been very unfortunate, and it was nice when the whole thing was resolved and we could get back to normal.

I think in many ways the problem arose out of the fact that we both felt quite passionately about the characters we were playing. We'd been Ken and Elsie since the programme started, and you obviously take a real interest in what is written for them and the situations they find themselves in with regard to the storylines. Acting is about getting to the core of what you are asked to play and then letting the words and the actions ride out truthfully. When it came to playing Ken, my thoughts then were the same as they are now. It's my job to really understand the character and then take him through whatever adventures have been written for him. I have always felt that I'm the guardian of Ken and I'm always watching out for him. It's my job to portray truthfully what this guy would say and do. I'm not Ken, but I am his caretaker. I'm responsible for him and I care about him. That was as true back then as it is to this day.

All of the characters were beautifully drawn right from the very start of the programme and that continued to be the case, both for the original cast who remained during the course of the 1960s and the new characters who were introduced, like the Ogdens, Jerry Booth and Jed Stone. John Betjeman once described the *Street* as Dickensian because Dickens created very strong characters in the stories he wrote and, of course, much of his output was produced in instalments for people to read and enjoy, just as *Coronation Street* produced a weekly stream of stories for the viewing public. From the very first time I played Ken I knew that Tony Warren had given the character a very solid foundation, but it was only as the years began to go by during the 1960s that I started to realise I was changing and getting older, but, of course, so was Ken, and it was a very natural process. In those very early episodes and for some time after them, my accent had a distinct Lancashire tone to it, but as time went on that accent began to change and I started to sound pretty much the same way I do today in the show. I'm not really sure how or why that happened, only that it did and it seemed a perfectly normal sort of thing. Nobody really noticed, and I think because it happened in a gradual and natural way, it was just part of the process that saw the character developing. In many ways it's a joint process, because as an actor you get hold of the character and play it in a certain way, and the writers will probably see that and then develop Ken, or whoever, according to what they see on the screen. It's a living organism, and that's why it works so well. I've always felt that the writing in *Coronation Street* is so good that as an actor you feel the dialogue has been tailor-made for your character, it all fits so well. Ken, in concept, might have been a lot different in Tony Warren's eyes to the way he is now, for instance, but over the years he has developed in just the same way that anyone would in real life. That process started back then and will never stop, and I'm glad to say that the character of Ken Barlow has continued to develop and evolve over the years.

Looking back now I realise that being Ken in the 1960s wasn't just about playing the character, it was also about getting used to what he meant to the public and the effect it had on me as a person. It was inevitable that as the popularity of the programme grew, so too would the fame it brought to each of us. I would be lying if I said that it wasn't exciting, and I think each of us dealt with it in our different ways. One of the things that I think we all noticed was the way in which we became part of what was happening during the 1960s. We were of the times, and those times were certainly changing. Television was growing as a medium and that meant that anyone who appeared on it was guaranteed a certain amount of recognition, so it was inevitable that as a group of people who appeared regularly on British screens twice a week, we would attract a certain degree of fame. You have to remember that these were the days of pop stars like the Beatles and the whole swinging '60s thing was happening, and although *Coronation Street* was a drama serial, it soon became part of the fabric of what was going on in the country at that time; it was part of the popular culture.

During the mid and late 1960s Granada was a busy place to be, with lots of shows and dramas being made there. You never really knew who you might bump into as you walked down a corridor or stepped into the make-up room and wardrobe departments. I recall seeing a very young and slender Tom Jones making a phone call in the corridor one day, and also going into make-up one morning and sitting there as John Gielgud and Ralph Richardson sat beside me having this wonderful conversation. They were doing a play at the studios and I overheard Gielgud say, 'I'm as nervous as a kitten, Ralphie, nervous as a kitten!' It was wonderful hearing that such great actors got nervous as well, and as the conversation went on it didn't really matter what they were talking about, their voices just sounded wonderful. To hear them chatting about mundane things was lovely and also rather amusing.

Getting a taste of fame in those years was very nice. You were pushed into it, and I sort of went along with everything without thinking about it too much. Before any of us knew it we were what are now called 'celebrities', but in those days you were just famous. I don't think that side of things went to my head; after all, it wasn't as though I'd had a deprived childhood. I was very middle class, my father was a doctor, I'd been to public school and served in the army as a captain. So in that sense, by the time I joined *Coronation Street* I'd already done things. My parents were pretty down-to-earth people and I was always very close to them. I don't think I went into orbit too much when fame came along, but I did succumb to some of the temptations that were on offer.

I was in a job that I liked, I was being pretty well paid and it was a very exciting time in the country as a whole. I was also married to Anna Cropper, an actress I'd met when we were in rep at Nottingham and then later on in Oldham. She was a very good actor and taught me a lot about the profession and the craft itself. Anna actually appeared in the *Street* during 1962, when she played the part of Joan Akers, a woman who had taken Concepta Hewitt's baby son, Christopher. Anna and I married in 1961, not long after I had started appearing in *Coronation Street*, and set up home in north London. As I have mentioned, quite a few of the cast in those early days used to travel down to London at weekends, and I did the same before buying a little place in the north. Anna and I had two children, Vanya and Linus, so we kept our house in London and really that became a base for them, while for five days during the week when I was working on the programme, I would live in the house I'd bought nearer to the studios in Manchester.

It is probably not the best way to maintain a marriage, but at the same time I am not looking to make excuses for some of my behaviour during the 1960s. When fame comes along the first phase of it can be very nice. You get recognised, getting things like a table in a restaurant is easy and generally you feel that everything is lovely, but then the realisation hits you that there is no going back from it. You can't undo the fact that you have become well known and then it is a case of having to deal with it. In many ways something like fame forces you to face your own weaknesses, and they very soon become exposed. Temptation is lurking around the corner, because so much is on offer to you. In my own case I succumbed to my weaknesses and because of this indulged in things like affairs, which I am certainly not proud of. It was nobody else's fault, no one forced me to do what I did, and I still regret the way I behaved and ultimately what it did to my marriage. I wasn't strong enough to resist the opportunities. The 1960s were a very infectious time, and I was part of it.

7

TIME TO QUIT

On the face of it I had a lovely life and should have been extremely happy. I'd been in *Coronation Street* for about ten years and the show was a big success. But at the same time, as a new decade approached, I found myself feeling physically and mentally depleted. I couldn't put my finger on exactly what was wrong, only that I certainly didn't feel happy. It was probably a combination of things going on in my life at that time that made me feel the way I did. As I have mentioned, I am not proud of some of the things I did during the 1960s, and having indulged in things like drinking too much and misbehaving with the affairs, I had come to a point in my life where I'd never felt worse. I didn't feel good; it was as if there was something wrong and something missing, but I wasn't sure what it was. I felt very low and wasn't sure what I should do about it. One day I confided in a friend, telling her how rotten I felt, and she suggested that I should go to see someone she knew in south London.

'Look, if you're feeling bad I know someone who is a homoeopathic doctor, but I think he's more than that,' she told me.

I knew I had to do something about the way I was feeling, and so the next time I was in London I made my way to the address she had given me in Dulwich where this doctor lived. His house was on a nice tree-lined road, and after I rang the doorbell I was shown into quite a large room that had long benches in it. It was obviously his waiting room, but it looked much bigger than any waiting room I had seen at a doctor's before. After a while, the woman who had opened the door to me came in and said that the doctor would see me. I was told to go up some stairs and that he would be in his study and the door would be open. I did this, and when I walked in I was confronted with one of the most untidy rooms imaginable, with piles of books and papers everywhere, and in one corner I spotted a curtained-off area. There was a huge desk with a roll-top that seemed to dominate the room, and seated behind it was an amazing-looking man. He was very small and thin, with a bald head and a long grey beard. He also had the darkest-brown eyes you could imagine, and although he was obviously old there was no way you could really put an age to him. He could have been anything from 60 to 100. He had very penetrating eyes and I got the feeling that he was able to see exactly what was going on in my head and in my soul, but at the same time I didn't feel uncomfortable.

His name was Dr Thomas Maugham, and he asked me why I had come to see him. I explained I was feeling really low, both in a physical and a mental sense. I felt depleted and wasn't very happy with my life. He stared at me for some time, but although it should have been a little unnerving, I felt perfectly at ease and relaxed in his presence. After a while he went behind the curtained area and came out with a bottle that contained some pills. He tapped one into my hand and said that I should dissolve it under my tongue, and then went on to tap some other pills into a brown envelope for me to take away. He told me when I should take them, and then said that he held a meeting in his waiting room every other Thursday and asked whether I would like to come along to the next one. I had no hesitation in accepting the offer, and the next Thursday I turned up at the house once again.

However, this time the waiting room looked very different: instead of it being deserted, it was absolutely packed with people. Dr Maugham came in and everyone in the room fell silent. Then he began to speak, and a most wonderful thing began to happen for me. Whatever he said seemed to be just the sort of things I had been waiting to hear all my life; I just knew that he was speaking the truth, and I felt an immediate connection with what was going on. It all had real meaning to me, and the evening turned out to be a wonderful experience. There was also some meditation involved, and when I left I knew that I had managed to find something that I could really relate to. It's difficult to say exactly what it was, only that I'd managed to find something I'd been looking for.

I had another appointment booked to see Dr Maugham in his capacity as a homoeopath, and the night before I was due to see him I had a very vivid dream, the sort that stays with you and that you're very much aware of the moment you wake up. The dream involved me going to see this guy in his untidy study, and as I entered the room he leaned forward and spoke to me.

'Bill, why don't you come and join us?' he said.

When I arrived at Dr Maugham's surgery I went upstairs to his study, and the first thing he said to me was, 'Did you get my message?' A tingle went down my spine, and I knew that this man was a very special person. He had an understanding and a state of being that was way ahead of anyone I had ever met before. He was a Master, and meeting him quite literally changed my life. I was suddenly able to begin my spiritual development, something I had probably been trying to do all of my life but had never quite managed to find the right way in which to begin my journey. I know all this might sound strange to many people – and that's fine, I can understand that – but put simply, I began a process of self-development and a search for the truth. For the next four or five years I would regularly visit Dr Maugham, driving down to London on Sundays and then driving back the same day.

After feeling so awful within myself, I began to gradually feel much better. There was a relief, and much of that was due to the fact that I slowly started to get a better understanding of all sorts of things, and I was also able to banish the fears of death and infinity that I'd had all of my life. They had been very real fears for me, but in the end I came to realise they were great gifts as well, because they had spurred me on to find out whether there was life after death, what happens and what the truth is. I wasn't interested in joining any particular group or religion, because I felt so many religions had gone wrong in the way they interpreted the spiritual message.

When I met Dr Maugham, it was as if I had been searching for somebody like that all of my life. He suddenly had answers for me, and I began to realise that the whole point of life is to search for the truth. It's not easy, and the first thing anyone has to do is to overcome their own feelings and beliefs. It was the beginning of a journey for me, and it is a journey that I am still on. In fact it never ends, and when I started it back in the early 1970s I began to feel that I had a better understanding of what life was about and its purpose. I knew I wanted to become a better person and to serve and contribute to society. I had felt guilty about myself and some of the things I had done, and I also felt I wasn't a particularly pleasant person. As the 1970s began I think I was a pretty degraded person in many ways, but I came to understand that I wasn't a hopeless case.

I realised that we're all imperfect, but at the same time I wanted to improve myself as a person and move in the right direction. Once you take that decision, it makes a huge difference and it begins a process of self-evolvement. One problem I did have was coming to terms with the profession I was in. I started to understand how destructive the ego can be and how you have to try to surrender it if you are going to improve as a person, but, of course, I was probably in the most ego-driven profession there is, so I wondered what I should do and whether giving up acting was the answer. I asked Dr Maugham what he thought, and he basically said it was in my own hands and I should do what I wanted to do. Having been so strongly drawn to acting in the way I had been, I knew I wanted to continue doing what I felt I was good at and enjoyed so much. When I told him this he simply said that I should carry on, and looking back on it now I realise that there was good reason for me to carry on. There is no doubt in my mind that my acting career has given me a certain platform and enabled me to do many other things, including helping charities, which I have always enjoyed. I think it was all part of a process I was going through, but it was a genuine dilemma for me at the time, and because of it I actually did wonder whether I should quit *Coronation Street* and stop acting altogether. I'm extremely pleased I decided to carry on, and in the years that have followed since I have been fortunate to be involved in a programme that has not only provided me with regular work, but has also given me the enjoyment and variety from a job that not many people are lucky enough to experience.

For the most part the 1960s were a very happy time for me, and it was only towards the end of them that I began to feel things weren't right. Up to that point life just carried on as normal, and I enjoyed being part of a very successful programme. My dissatisfaction was never with the *Street*, it was all about the way I felt as a person, and the programme during the 1960s was as exciting as ever, with some very good storylines written for Ken.

There were things like the time I had to talk down Christine Hardman from the roof of the factory, and the two of us actually had to be harnessed to the top of an old school building that was directly opposite Granada Studios. It was hardly sophisticated stuff compared with the way outside filming is done these days, but it was still pretty good for its time. The storyline for the episode involved poor Christine, whose mother had died in early December 1960, becoming so depressed and disillusioned with her life that she decides to end it all by throwing herself off the roof. The police try to talk her down, but to no avail, and in the end, with people gathered in the road below watching what is going to happen next and fearing the worst, Ken walks into the scene chatting to Elsie. When he sees who it is and what she is attempting, he climbs onto the roof and begins to try to talk Christine down. The filming went on for quite a while, and at one stage I think we might even have been left up there while some of the crew went off for refreshments, because the building we filmed in also doubled as a sort of canteen, with drinks served on the ground floor. Eventually Ken manages to make her see sense and she backs off from her threat to jump. I remember seeing the episode and feeling a bit disappointed, because although it was actually filmed on a roof, you didn't get any real sense of perspective in terms of how high up we were, although right at the end the camera did pan down from the roof to ground level as the gawping crowd dispersed.

I seem to recall Granada having to take out some sort of insurance on us, just in case anything went wrong. We were both assured that it wouldn't, but I doubt that they could have got away with shooting the whole thing like that now, even if they wanted to. Of course, this was in the days when there was no such thing as health and safety; we simply got on and did it ourselves, because there were no stunt doubles at the time, and it usually came down to someone coming up with an idea just to make sure the scene worked with the minimum of fuss being made. Nevertheless, the scene and the drama of that episode showed exactly what the *Street* was all about. It was able to deal in things that were relatively frivolous, like gossip, and then introduce a serious and dramatic story to run alongside it. The formula worked very well, and it can still be seen today in *Coronation Street*. The strength of the scriptwriting has meant that such storylines can be interwoven and intermingled in episodes to give the viewer both drama and the more light-hearted stuff all in one programme, with neither of them seeming out of place.

One of the other major things to happen to Ken in that first decade of the programme was his marriage to Val and the birth of his twins. As the character was developed by the writers it was probably inevitable that he should go on to be married, although in many ways it went a little against the grain to begin with, because Ken was this young, educated guy who the ladies seemed to like, and he was also likely to want to move away from the Street. After all, with his degree and the fact that he clearly wanted something more than a life in Coronation Street, Ken was the sort of young character who might have drifted away and not come back. Instead what happened was that the writers clearly saw potential in having someone like him in and around the Street. He was very different to the average resident in many ways, and yet he was very much the same, whether he liked it or not. Getting married and having kids at a relatively young age was typical of the sort of things most of the others had done in their lives. Ken was just part of a new generation and he happened to have had a better education than the rest of them. His character very quickly became established, and I have to say that I liked him from the start and have never had a problem playing him, even though as Bill Roache I am very different to him and have different views on things like politics.

Ken has always been very earnest and honourable in his views, and he's tried to do the right thing. The trouble is that like any other human being he is flawed: we all are. When it came to the sort of job he would do, it was clear that teaching fitted perfectly with him as a person. Not only did it help satisfy him intellectually, it also allowed him to help others and at the same time give him a degree of control, which he probably always wanted. I always thought of him during that first decade as a young man who was basically well intentioned, but who also had a very stubborn streak in him when it came to his principles and what he thought was right. Sometimes this got him into trouble, as it did in 1967, when he took part in an anti-Vietnam War meeting. The story was that the meeting was banned from taking place, but Ken, sticking stubbornly to his beliefs, took part in it anyway and in the end faced the prospect of a fine or going to jail for a week. In typical Ken fashion he refused to pay the fine and so ended up in Strangeways Prison, leaving a distraught Val to cope on her own with the twins, while he rather selfishly stuck to his principles even though they had an unhappy impact on his family. In many ways it summed up what Ken was like and the sort of character the writers had created.

However, despite having principles and trying to do the right thing most of the time, Ken also emerged as someone who liked the ladies. Nothing wrong with that, of course; after all, he was a young man and it was a pretty natural thing to do. However, it didn't stop when he met Val, and in the mid-1960s both Anne Reid and I enjoyed some very good dramatic moments when Ken went off and had an affair with a newspaper reporter named Jackie Marsh, who was played by Pamela Craig. He clearly felt guilty about this, but at the same time carried on seeing this other woman behind Val's back and even planned a weekend away with her under the pretence of attending a teachers' conference. Eventually the guilt did get the better of him and he decided not to go, feeling relieved that he'd kept the matter from Val, only to later find out that she'd known all about what he'd been up to. There were some very good scenes written for us when this happened and Anne played them beautifully. She was a very accomplished actress, and having those scenes and that sort of marital conflict was, of course, a taste of things to come for Ken when he went on to marry Deirdre and had some tempestuous moments with her. I always enjoyed acting with Anne and I think she felt the same with me. Certainly those scenes were also good for the development of Ken, because a different dimension was introduced. He was a married man with kids, and, while full of good intentions, he was also liable to stray and clearly had trouble resisting the temptation of another woman. Once that sort of character seed has been sown, it allows the writers to use it at a later date if they want to. Mind you, by that time Val hadn't exactly been a model of propriety, as in 1964 when she packed her bags and tried to move in with a teaching colleague of Ken's called Dave Robbins. He'd lodged with the Barlows for a time and Val had become attracted to him, mainly because of the lack of interest Ken had shown towards her, who seemed to see her very much as the housewife whose main priority should be to look after the home. The whole thing sadly backfired on poor Val, because when she turned up at Dave's he made it pretty clear that he wasn't going to take her in, and she had to go back to Ken.

I was lucky to have some other dramatic moments with Anne during those days. One involved the time that Ken went to the Rovers when he was supposed to look after the twins and there was a fire in the Barlows' house. Val came home to find the place full of smoke, with no sign of Ken. The fire was put out when Ken returned and he was horrified that the twins could have been killed, but the fallout his absence caused gave rise to some more very dramatic and tense scenes, which Anne and I enjoyed playing. There was also a story from 1968 when the Barlows had moved home from their terraced house into one of the new maisonettes that had been built across the street. Ken was out one evening, directing a play at the technical college he was teaching at, and Val was taken hostage by an escaped prisoner called Frank Riley. It was very dramatic stuff and we did it over two episodes, with a bit of a cliffhanger in the first as the police arrived. In the next programme they burst in and rescued Val, who then discovered that Riley was a convicted rapist. Ken suspected that something had gone on during her ordeal, and despite Val claiming that Riley had not touched her, Ken clearly doubted this and the storyline created some very tense and interesting moments. It was a big subject for the *Street* to tackle, and through the years the programme has done similar things with other issues and dealt with them in a very clever way.

The programme was also popular in Australia, and in 1966 there was even a visit by some people from the *Street*, including Pat Phoenix, Doris Speed and Arthur Leslie, to places like Melbourne, Sydney and Adelaide. In the same year the cast were invited to Downing Street by Prime Minister Harold Wilson, and it was obvious the show had very much arrived.

As the decade came to an end it was very clear that *Coronation Street* had not only gone from strength to strength, but also that it had earned a particular place in the hearts of the British viewing public, and some of the big stories that were written in those first ten years drew enormous audience figures. One of them was the marriage of Elsie Tanner to American soldier Steve Tanner, in 1967, which was watched by almost 9.5 million people. There was even a special-edition magazine brought out to commemorate the occasion and it was one of those classic *Street* moments that really seemed to hit the pulse of the nation.

There was another big change towards the end of the 1960s when the *Street* made its debut in colour. It happened in December 1969 and was obviously going to herald a new era in many ways. Until then it had been in black and white, and although all the other programmes had been shot in the same way, there was no doubt that colour was the future of television, even though not that many people had colour sets in their homes at the time. I remember that there was a bit of a debate about whether the *Street* would actually benefit from being shot in colour, because it was seen by many as a very gritty, northern working-class drama. Like so many film dramas in the 1960s, *Coronation Street* seemed to be suited to black and white, so there was a certain degree of reluctance to move forward, but of course it was inevitable that colour should happen and I don't think we lost anything by being seen in colour. It also meant that we were able to actually start wearing white shirts on the show, because until then all we could ever wear were these slightly grey or green shirts, because the cameras couldn't cope with the brightness of white, although colour, when it did come, brought its own problems as well. Things like the products displayed in the corner shop had to have their colour toned down, and I think that in general they had some teething troubles with balancing the colours early on. We also began to work differently, because the *Street* was taped instead of the show being on film. It allowed the editing process to become more sophisticated and easier to manage.

It was originally planned that the first colour episode would be filmed on location in the Lake District, with a Street outing. The story was going to centre around us all going off on a coach trip with stops along the way, and the drama would be created by the fact that the coach had mechanical problems and was dangerous to drive. Eventually the inevitable happened and there was a crash just as the episode ended. With the wonderful countryside that part of the world provided, it was thought that it would be a great way to introduce colour to the show, but unfortunately the cameras couldn't cope with it and eventually the episode had to be filmed in black and white. So the first colour programme was actually the one that followed, when many of the Street's residents involved in the outing were seen being treated for their injuries at hospital.

From my own point of view I have another lasting memory from the episode that was filmed on location. We did one scene at about nine in the morning, and it involved some of us sitting around a table outside a pub having a drink and something to eat. I think I actually did have a real lager and then a sandwich before we all clambered back on the coach to shoot another scene. The trouble was certain lines had to be delivered at a certain spot as the coach travelled along a small stretch of road, but because the scene was not shot in one take it meant that a small circular route was devised for the coach to travel on, so that the scene could be shot in the same place for the sake of continuity. It would have looked extremely odd to have a very different change of scenery outside the coach windows during the course of me delivering some lines. So around and around we went on this tight little circuit as the interior coach scene was shot. The trouble was that the movement of the coach, combined with what I'd eaten and drunk, started to make me feel decidedly uncomfortable. In fact, it made me feel extremely sick, and after trying to soldier on for a while I had to give in and ask them to stop, before scrabbling off the coach to be sick at the side of the road.

After feeling so low at the start of the 1970s, my meeting with Dr Maugham and the journey I began with regard to my spiritual beliefs slowly began to help me feel better about myself and life in general. Once I had resolved the dilemma I had about carrying on with acting and with my career in *Coronation Street*, I really began to settle into the job with as much enthusiasm and enjoyment as I'd ever had. I'm sure none of my colleagues noticed any real difference in me when I turned up for work, but at the same time I doubt that I had exhibited any symptoms in previous months that showed just how unhappy I felt about myself. I don't know if it had a knock-on effect with regard to my work, but I do know that once I began to feel happier within myself, everything connected must have started to improve and get better – not in a blinding flash or an immediate change, but in a gradual way that has carried on ever since.

I certainly felt happy in my work as a second decade began, but in the *Street*, just as in life, you never really know what is in store for you. Ken ended the 1960s as a married man with a couple of kids, and as such looked pretty settled, but as the 1970s began it didn't take long for his life to take a new twist and at the same time give me as an actor one of my most enjoyable and satisfying moments in *Coronation Street*.

8

SHEDDING A TEAR

In any drama serial there have to be twists and turns that not only keep the programme fresh and interesting, but also act as a way of moving the show on. Throughout the '60s *Coronation Street* thrived because that's exactly what happened on a regular basis. The characters had been established, when new ones came in they were quickly integrated into the fabric of the show, the scripts were strong, the production and direction superb, and technically the programme had embraced changes like colour and new editing methods. From my own point of view I was happy with my decision to carry on, and on a personal level my life outside of the *Street* was beginning to have more meaning and depth than it had for quite some time.

For Ken, there was personal tragedy in the Barlow family in 1970 when his brother, David, died in a car crash in Australia with his son, and there was also a trip to America for Ken, although unfortunately they didn't seem to think it was actually worth me going out there to film any scenes. There was also another very big story in the *Street* that year when, after the breakdown of her marriage to Steve Tanner and his subsequent death, Elsie Tanner married Alan Howard, played by Alan Browning, who had arrived in the programme as a businessman friend of Len Fairclough. Two years later, fact mirrored fiction when Pat Phoenix and Alan actually did tie the knot in real life, which I'm sure must have really blurred things for some of the viewers.

The biggest shock for the cast that year was the sudden death of Arthur Leslie. The news stunned everyone, and it was very difficult to take in. He died while on holiday in Wales, and apart from the natural feeling of grief that hit everyone on the show there was also the very practical problem for the writers of having to suddenly work poor Arthur's death into the programme. As Jack Walker he had become a very big part of the show, and his partnership with Doris Speed was absolutely wonderful. I think Arthur poured an awful lot of himself into the role of Jack, who always came across as a very kind man and someone you could depend on. In the programme his character's death came about a month after Arthur's, and it was decided that Annie would remain in charge of the Rovers, with her son, Billy, coming back in to help her run the pub.

In Arthur's case the producer and writers had to react quickly to a situation they hadn't created. I'm sure they would have liked Jack Walker in the Rovers for many more years to come, but unfortunately Arthur's sudden death changed everything. Towards the end of the year the writers were faced with another unexpected departure from the programme, and this time I knew it might have consequences for me.

Anne Reid made it known to the producer, June Howson, that she wanted to leave the show. Once an actor has made the decision not to carry on in the *Street*, you can always go upstairs at Granada to where the producer has their office and tell them you want to leave. It has always been very good like that, and as long as they know with sufficient time in advance, they can then carry on and begin to plan your departure. From Anne's point of view, she made it clear that she didn't want to come back at some later stage, which effectively meant that they had to kill her off. I had really enjoyed playing opposite Anne: she had gone to Penrhos, which was the sister school of Rydal, where I had gone as a boy, and it was always a pleasure working with her. The viewers had taken to the way she had played Val, making her very likeable and popular, which was why nobody wanted her to go. However, Anne had made the decision and was determined she wanted to move on to other things, so all that was left was to decide how she would depart and what to do with Ken. I remember she came to me and actually said, 'Bill, I'm very sorry, but I want to leave.' I think she thought that if she left, the likelihood was that I would have to go too.

The Barlows were very much a couple; they might have had a few problems in their marriage, but basically it was seen as being a good one, and if Val went where would that leave Ken? I think they thought about possibly having him emigrate with the twins but then decided that he should stay and survive her as the widowed father of young children. The producer called me in and said they'd decided that although Anne wanted to leave they were not going to kill off Ken as well, but instead were going to keep him, which was a relief for me because I was enjoying playing him.

In the end they really made sure Val wasn't coming back, because she was both electrocuted and then burned in early 1971. Once again it was all very dramatic, with Ken and Val due to celebrate a new chapter in their lives. He had been offered a teaching job in Jamaica, and the family was due to jet off and start a new life in the sun. They were having a farewell party at the Rovers, and as Ken arrived at the pub Val was still at home getting ready. He made a phone call to ask her where she was, and Val told him she would be there soon, but that was the last conversation they ever had on the programme, because after talking to Ken she went on to try to dry her hair. She picked up a hairdryer and tried to fix a loose plug, then jabbed an adapter into the wall. She got a shock that killed her, but then as she fell she hit an electric fire, which went into a packing case and set the place on fire. There was supposed to be a scene at the end of it all with Val on the floor with the flames lapping all around her, but in the end there were some problems with doing that because of the studio time we had, and instead the credits rolled as the flames were shown engulfing one of the children's teddy bears.

What happened in the aftermath of all of this produced a scene that I referred to earlier as giving me a lot of satisfaction and enjoyment. All actors love getting their teeth into something that is substantial, and quite often that means that you are playing a scene that has a lot of emotion attached to it. That was certainly the case when I had to walk through the charred ruins of the

Barlows' flat after Val's body had been removed, and with the encouragement of the director, Carol Wilks, I was able to produce one of my best moments on the show. She simply told me that the whole ending was going to be on me, with the camera following me as I walked through the debris. So I was just allowed to do exactly what I wanted to do, which was wonderful. I walked through the room and then found Val's powder compact, which I picked up. I then walked on with it in my hand before sitting on the stairs, and with the camera still rolling I began to cry. It's a strange thing, but some actors can cry and some can't. I've always found it easy to do, and for that particular scene I really did cry. I think it was a really nice ending, and the director was pleased with what I'd done. Strange as it might sound to some people, when you do an emotional scene and you end it by crying, it can feel very satisfying, and I was very happy with the way it turned out. I think it also showed people like the producer and writers that I could do a scene of that kind, and when they know you can do the crying bit it's very useful for them to store that away for future use.

I was sorry to see Anne go, not only because I got on well with her and had enjoyed acting alongside her for ten years, but also because she had brought the character of Val to life and made her very much part of the *Street* for the viewers. When she left she bought me a lovely little silver goblet, and inscribed on it were the words, 'We must do this again some time.' It was a really nice thing for her to do and, of course, she went on to have a lot of success in the years that followed, including some wonderful work with Victoria Wood. As ever with *Coronation Street*, the programme carries on and evolves as characters come and go. In the same year that saw Anne leave, two other characters were introduced who would go on to have long careers in the programme, when Mavis Riley, played by Thelma Barlow, and Ivy Tilsley, played by Lynne Perrie, arrived.

By this time the show was being seen in more than ten countries around the world, from places like Holland and Nigeria to Australia, New Zealand, Hong Kong and Singapore. The programme clearly had appeal not only to people in Britain, and I have no doubt that a lot of other countries started to think about trying to recreate the same sort of winning formula themselves. Certainly in the United States, some years earlier, they had decided not to take the *Street*, but were inspired by the concept and created their own show, set not in a small working-class community but in a rather more middle-class environment. They came up with *Peyton Place*, which was a huge success over there and was also popular in this country. The *Street*'s popularity in Australia also later prompted a response from media magnate Kerry Packer, who owned a television station that decided they would create their own kind of *Coronation Street*, an idea that was to lead to the birth of *Neighbours*. I think a lot of people saw just how well the *Street* had done, and by the start of the 1970s it was clear that the programme wasn't a flash in the pan. We had established ourselves as a show that was both popular and entertaining, moving into a new television era where the medium was a real part of family life in Britain. Ironically, despite the success of the programme in the early and mid-'60s, the Bernsteins had been urged by others in the industry to take it off the air. It sounds incredible now, but that was very much the norm in those days. Quite often a drama serial was started by the BBC, and even though it was doing well, they would take it off. I suppose the thinking was that nothing like that was going to go on for any great length of time and so they might as well take it off the screens with the public still thinking highly of it as a successful programme. Happily the Bernsteins resisted the temptation to follow suit and instead kept the show going, but I doubt that even they would have thought that something that they put on the air all those years ago would still be going strong more than 50 years later.

In 1972 I met two people who would go on to have a lasting effect on my life. One was a strikingly beautiful woman called Sara Mottram; the other was a young actress straight out of rep who joined the cast of *Coronation Street*, and she was called Anne Kirkbride. Both became my wife: one off-screen, the other on it.

When the programme first started one of our floor managers was a guy called Dick Everett, and he later went on to become a producer of the show. Away from the *Street*, both Dick and his wife were heavily involved in a local amateur dramatics society in Wilmslow called the Green Room. One day Dick asked me if I could help out with a charity evening they were having, which was going to be based on the television show *Going for a Song*, where antiques were brought on and you had to try and guess what they were. I basically told Dick that I'd help out if he couldn't find anyone else, which of course he couldn't. So I turned up on the night, and the job of bringing the antiques on was given to a tall, blue-eyed, dark-haired woman who was extremely beautiful.

During the interval I went to find the toilet, asked the woman where it was and then walked past her. Of course that beautiful woman was Sara, and she later told me that during that brief moment a thought flashed through her head, which told her she was going to marry me. We chatted at the party after the show, and then began to see each other. My marriage was over by then and I certainly had no thoughts of getting married again, but I came to realise in the years that followed that Sara had a very strong intuition, and her thought that night later turned out to be absolutely true.

I have to admit that I can't really remember Anne Kirkbride joining the *Street*. She was just 18 when she came into the programme from Oldham Rep, where she'd started off as an assistant stage manager and then got the chance to act, and I had actually seen her there. Anne had already done a bit of work for Granada in a television play and then got the chance to have a bit part in the *Street* where her character, Deirdre Hunt, was seen chatting to Alan Howard in a pub. I'm sure Anne had no idea that Deirdre would become such a popular part of the show, but I think it says an awful lot for her as an actor that she is still going strong some more than 38 years later, and from a personal point of view she has been an absolute joy to work with on-screen and a wonderful friend off it.

Of course, Ken's marriage to Deirdre some years later produced some spectacular storylines for both of us, not least of which was the scene I have already mentioned at the start of this book. Ken and Deirdre's relationship only really started in the late 1970s and they didn't actually marry until 1981, but before that, following the death of Val, and after a suitable period of time, the writers decided it was time to marry him off again. Having been a married man with children in what was supposed to be a pretty settled relationship, the writers were faced with the problem of exactly what to do with Ken after Anne Reid's departure. Did he soldier on as the single-parent dad looking after his twins, or did they devise a different lifestyle for him? In the end they decided that Ken would allow the twins to move north of the border to live with their grandparents in Scotland, leaving Ken to pursue what was essentially a single lifestyle. It was at that point that the twins pretty much disappeared from the *Street*, but not before another member of the Roache family made an appearance in the programme. The writers needed to include the twins in the show for some different storylines. They had a little girl called Wendy Jane Walker who played the role of Susan, and of course needed someone who looked the same age to be her twin brother, Peter. I think my own son Linus was a little older than he was supposed to be for the purpose of the story, but it didn't seem to matter too much, and so at the age of nine he appeared in *Coronation Street* as Ken's son, Peter.

During the two years following Val's death, and with the twins up in Scotland, the writers allowed Ken to get involved with several women, but underlying a lot of this was the fact that he also seemed to be on the lookout for another wife. Despite his education and the fact that he was supposed to be the Street's intellectual, Ken was very much a northern working-class man at heart. He was the sort who wanted to have a wife who would stay at home, look after the kids and make sure the house was run smoothly, while he went off to work to pursue a career. It was very old-fashioned in many ways, but he could never see it that way and it was often left to the women he had relationships with to remind him of that trait in his character. In 1973 Ken was married off again, this time to Janet Reid, a character who had been around in the Street and whose reputation was not exactly spotless. She had jilted Len and been involved in trying to break up the marriage of Elsie and Alan Howard, so in many viewers' eyes she was seen as a bit of a baddie.

The writing should have been on the wall for Ken, but it didn't stop them getting married, and in doing so, it opened up a whole new set of possibilities of storylines for the show. Janet clearly saw Ken as someone who might provide the sort of lifestyle she wanted if he was pushed and manoeuvred in the right direction. She had plans for them to move away from the Street and into a bigger house, and went along with the idea Ken had of getting the twins back to live with them, while all along having no intention of sharing a home with his kids. It soon became clear that the marriage was not going to be a happy one, and that Janet was no Val. Judith Barker, who played Janet, did so really well. So well, in fact, that she suffered a bit from some viewers who clearly did not like her character and what she was trying to do in *Coronation Street*. It is something we all have to get used to as actors in the programme, because the public's perception of you can often become blurred and some people have trouble separating the real person from the character you are playing. After all of the years I have been in the show, I've got used to people sometimes calling me Ken instead of Bill. I can perfectly well understand it, and even my own father once called me Ken by mistake. I thought it was quite amusing, and at the same time I realised that it was also a compliment to the way I was portraying the character. If my own father saw Ken as a believable character then I couldn't have been doing too badly in the way in which I played him.

Ken's marriage to Janet was hardly a happy one, and less than a year into it I was given another one of those scenes that I loved and which I still remember vividly today. Ken was teaching at Bessie Street School and it had been decided that it might be a good idea to get the twins back so that they could live with him and Janet. Of course Janet had no real intention of letting this happen, and although the children could have places at Bessie Street, she had already investigated the possibility of them going to a boarding school, which Ken was absolutely against.

One evening Ken came home to what appeared to be a very cosy meal for two. Janet had bought a bottle of red wine and poured Ken a glass as he searched for a folder in a drawer. As he did so, he came across a brochure for a boarding school and asked why it was there. He began to look increasingly angry and shouted at Janet, even calling her a 'bitch'. To many people it must have appeared most unlike Ken, and for that reason I think the dramatic effect was intensified. Janet had not only gone behind his back, she was proposing to send the twins to a boarding school, which went against all of his principles, and at the same time she clearly had no intention of sharing a home with his children. I was really able to let rip when it came to doing the scene and threw myself into what was happening. I then picked up the bottle of wine and smashed it down on the table, but at the same time it hit one of the glasses that had been placed there, shattering it to pieces, and it even made a dent in the table. It took poor Judith totally by surprise and genuinely made her scream and jump back with the shock of what had happened. It all added to the drama of the scene, with the tension and violence of it coming across beautifully. I later heard that it had been used as an exercise in drama schools, which I think was a nice compliment to everyone involved in creating the moment. When something like that happens in the programme and you know it has really hit the spot, it's not just down to the way you have acted. Working on a programme like *Coronation Street* is a team effort, and that is certainly the case when it comes to creating a memorable scene. It involves writers, the producer, director and all the technical people as well as the actors, and I think it's very satisfying for everyone concerned when it turns out so well.

Later that same year Janet walked out on Ken, with the marriage clearly over, and despite bumping into each other some time later, both of them realised that there wasn't going to be any reconciliation. The two didn't meet again until 1977, when a distraught Janet turned up, having split from her boyfriend, Vince Denton. Ken thought that Janet wanted a divorce, but instead she practically begged Ken to take her back. He refused, but did allow her to stay the night, which produced another dramatic moment, because when he went up to her room to wake her in the morning he discovered her unconscious from an overdose of sleeping pills. She was pronounced dead on arrival after she had been rushed to hospital. Again it was another dramatic scene for Ken, and of course for Judith, who played Janet.

Although the whole suicide thing was shown early in 1977,

Judith had been approached at the end of the previous year about coming back to play the storyline, and was in the middle of a theatre run at the time. When Judith came to do the scene in the bed where she was going to be discovered unconscious, she actually fell asleep because she was so exhausted with all the work she was doing with the play. When it came to having the camera shooting her supposedly unconscious from the overdose, she was snoring away happily.

While Janet departed from the *Street* there were some very notable additions during the 1970s. As well as Deirdre, other characters like Rita Littlewood, Vera Duckworth, Gail Potter and Eddie Yeats were created, while Bet Lynch, who had been in the show as a factory girl for a few weeks in the mid-1960s, came back at the start of the 1970s and established herself playing a barmaid in the Rovers. And in 1976 a character was created who was to have a big impact on Ken in the years that followed, when Mike Baldwin first made his bow in the *Street*. Another actor who came to prominence during the '70s was Stephen Hancock, who played Ernest Bishop. He went on to marry Emily, who had worked for him in his photographer's shop, but when he went bankrupt he took a job at Mike Baldwin's factory. Towards the end of the decade Stephen asked to leave and therefore had to be killed off. It was decided he should meet a violent end, and he was shot when there was a raid on the factory. Naturally there were the usual funeral scenes with Street residents in attendance, and I'm afraid that occasions like that are often a recipe for disaster for me: because it's supposed to be such a dramatic scene I have quite often been known to get a fit of the giggles, or 'corpse', as it is known in the trade. I remember doing it when we rehearsed a funeral-parlour scene for that story, and there have been other occasions during my time on the show when it has happened.

Back in the days when we did the show live you tended not to giggle when the programme was being broadcast, simply because you were terrified, but when it came to rehearsals that could sometimes be a different matter. Frank Pemberton had one of those big, open faces, and he once had a line that for some reason made me start to giggle. The director asked me whether I was all right, and I assured him that I was, but once again when we came to do the line, I just couldn't stop giggling. The silly thing is that if you actually recounted the line to someone else they wouldn't find it at all funny, but for whatever reason, if something sets you off – that's it!

If you're going to do a really tearful sort of scene you can only really do that once with all the emotion involved in it, so when you do the rehearsal you're going through the motions to a large extent, and that's when the giggles can strike. I once had a director come down to the floor and tell us that we were being unprofessional when this happened, but he didn't really understand. We were getting rid of the giggles, and there was no way the same thing would have happened when we actually came to do the scene for real. The trouble was when he came down and said that it only made us want to giggle even more. It's relatively rare, but it can sometimes happen in a performance, and when that happens it's frightening, because it's like a nervous reaction and you just can't stop.

There was another occasion in the *Street* when I had to walk into the corner shop and play a scene with Gail, played by Helen Worth. As I walked in there was a bit of chewing-gum on the floor and I simply stubbed my toe on it. Nothing funny in that, I'm sure you're thinking, but for whatever reason I couldn't stop giggling. So out I went to start the scene over again, and as soon as I stepped inside the shop I began to giggle again. Eventually I managed to get through this without giggling, and then Helen started! Eileen Derbyshire is another of the *Street*'s big gigglers, and I also had a scene with Pat Phoenix once where there were a couple of lines in the script that simply lent themselves to a bit of innuendo. I think I had to try to open a door with a key and I had to say something like, 'I can't get it in,' and 'It won't fit.' Silly schoolboy humour, I know, but it was enough to set the both of us off.

Perhaps the worst example of the giggles that I ever experienced came away from the *Street*, during a theatre production. I had formed William Roache Productions with Sara, and we were going to put on a comedy play called *The Little Hut* at the Guild Hall in Preston. The play revolved around the story of a shipwreck, with me, Sara and Bryan Mosley playing the lead roles; we also had another actor called Lawrence Mullin, who was in the *Street* at the time playing Mike Baldwin's sidekick, Steve Fisher. When we did the first week of rehearsals we couldn't seem to get to grips with it at all, but by the second week it was all beginning to fall into place, so I began to relax a little, and I think that was a fatal mistake. Bryan could always seem to make me laugh. Like Frank Pemberton, he had this big, open, childlike face and large eyes. During the course of the play there was a line where Bryan had to say, 'He's running amok.' That was all it was, but when he looked at me and said it, I was gone and just couldn't stop giggling. The director, Diana Harker, was sitting in the stalls watching all of this and said that we should go back and do it all again, but the same thing happened. I just couldn't stop giggling. We did it over and over again, but the result was the same each time. We had a break and the three of us tried to run the scene, but it was hopeless; it ended up with us rolling around on the floor laughing. The problem was that bad. On the night we opened, when we got to the line that had caused so much trouble for all of us, we just sort of slightly turned away from each other and muttered our way through it. I don't quite know what the audience thought of us, and I honestly thought I might have to give up acting because of what had happened. There I was, a professional actor, and I was unable to deliver a line because I was giggling too much. I seriously began to wonder whether it was something that was going to plague me, but I think that particular episode was an extreme case. Bryan knew he could usually set me off whenever he wanted to just by looking at me in a certain way, and I used to have to tell him to stop it sometimes, because I had no defence to it. I tried to get my own back on him once, but instead of setting him off, I ended up giggling instead.

I have already mentioned the shock death of Graham Haberfield, a lovely colleague to work with and a fine actor whose character, Jerry Booth, was much loved by the public. Apart from our practical-jokes antics, Graham and I used to play golf together, a game I took up because of Bunny Youens. Bunny suggested one day that I should play the game and then promptly booked me a lesson at Prestwich Golf Club. That was it. I was hooked. Graham, Bunny and I used to play, along with Eddy Shah, who I knew from his days as a floor manager at Granada, long before he went on to make his fortune in the newspaper world with *Today* in the 1980s. The four of us would also occasionally be joined by Alan Browning, and I loved it. We used to get Thursday mornings off in those days, and our game of golf became quite a regular thing. Bunny and Graham often used to slink off a bit early to get the drinks started in the bar, but I really got enthusiastic about the game, and thanks to Bunny and Graham I went on to have many happy moments on the golf course, playing in some great pro-celebrity tournaments and meeting wonderful people along the way.

As the decade came to a close I was certainly feeling more settled in my private life, having married Sara in 1978. We did it with the minimum of fuss and kept the whole thing very low-key. I just asked producer Bill Podmore for a day off, and we got married in a local registry office, with Alan Rothwell as my best man. Sara had become a very important part of my life, and along with the fact that I had begun my own spiritual journey at the start of the 1970s, I think her love and support certainly helped to make me a much happier and more contented human being.

As for *Coronation Street*, the programme was in very good shape. I think there had been a bit of an audience blip in 1973, but that was soon corrected, and the storylines and new characters that had been introduced gave the show a richness and vitality that continued to make it very popular across all strands of life in Britain. In 1979, the Variety Club held a dinner in honour of the show at which Sir John Betjeman presented Doris Speed with a lifetime-achievement award. He also made those comments likening the *Street* to the works of Dickens, and it was clear that the programme was highly thought of by many people who were very good judges of quality work.

Another person who made his admiration of the *Street* known was Sir Laurence Olivier, and he actually agreed to be in an episode. He was going to play a tramp outside a department store as Hilda Ogden tried to be the first in the queue to buy a cheap colour television, but he then had to do some re-shoots for the film *Marathon Man* and wasn't able to appear. Having met Olivier all those years ago when I was desperate to break into the acting profession, I came across him once again quite by chance during the 1970s at Granada. I was in one of the corridors at the studios one day making a telephone call, and just as I'd finished I heard a man's voice behind me.

'I'd just like to say how much I enjoy your performances in *Coronation Street*,' he said.

I turned around to discover it was Laurence Olivier, who apparently was there to do *Cat on a Hot Tin Roof* with Robert Wagner and Natalie Wood, and also *King Lear*. I thanked him for his kind words and then said I was delighted to see him, because I had a story I thought he would be interested in. I went on to remind him of the time he had invited me to have a chat with him, and thanked him for being so kind on that occasion and for taking the trouble to try to help me. He thought it was a wonderful story, and I told him that he had given me the will and enthusiasm to carry on trying to make a career in acting. I also said that he was probably responsible for me actually being in the *Street*. It was so nice after all of those years to be able to say thank you to a wonderful actor and a great man who was so helpful to me, and I hope it was nice for him to see where his words of encouragement had led.

As for Ken, the end of the decade saw the possibility of a new woman in his life. Deirdre's character had grown considerably since entering the *Street* and had become popular with the viewers. She had married Ray Langton and had a baby daughter, but Neville Buswell, who played Ray, wanted to leave the *Street* and so a plot was devised that saw him move to Holland. Their marriage wasn't going well, with Ray having had an affair with a waitress called Janice Stubbs. Initially Deirdre and their daughter Tracy were due to move to Holland with Ray, but then she decided to stay. It meant that Neville could leave the programme as he wanted to, while Deirdre could carry on, and it also meant she was a single mum. In 1979, one of the most dramatic storylines involved a lorry crash outside the Rovers. Deirdre has left Tracy outside in her pram and is convinced she has been killed, because the lorry has shed its load right through the front of the Rovers, and as they sort through the wreckage there is no sign of her daughter. She is eventually found, and it transpires that she had been taken by a former friend of Deirdre's moments before the crash. Mother and daughter are reunited, and Ken is there not only to try to help people get clear of the rubble, but also to act as something of a shoulder for Deirdre to cry on. The two begin to see each other, and even when old flame Billy Walker arrives back on the scene and invites Deirdre to Jersey with him, where he wants to open a wine bar, she decides to stay put. However, when a letter arrives from Ray saying that he is going to cite Ken in a divorce proceeding, he is beside himself. It's very typical of Ken, because as well-meaning and good-natured as he can be, there is a selfish streak in him too, which Deirdre sees for the first time, but as the years will show it will certainly not be the last time this character trait causes problems for their relationship. As the year goes on they manage to resolve their problems, with Ray finally agreeing that Deirdre can divorce him, and she and Ken end the '70s seeing the New Year in together.

So by the end of the nineteenth year of the show Ken had seen his parents, brother and two wives die, while becoming the father of twins who, conveniently, lived in Scotland. I say conveniently because I doubt very much whether he could have enjoyed the company of so many women had he been a full-time single father. If there was one thing Ken wasn't short of during those first two decades it was women, and it is a theme that has continued throughout my fifty years on the *Street*.

I suspect it was good for people like Tony Warren initially and then other writers who subsequently took over the duty of producing scripts to have someone like Ken around. Certainly in the early days he was the young guy with an education and because of that a possible bright future ahead of him. He was quite eligible in that sense, and after the relationship with fellow student Susan he was then catapulted into a relationship with an older woman, in the shape of Marian Lund, a university librarian who was supposed to be 11 years older than him, played by Patricia Heneghan. Ken eventually gave her up over a pint and a chat, when her boyfriend came to see him in the Rovers and said that they were engaged. It was all very civilised and allowed Ken to move on and meet someone else, who turned out to be Val.

It was at this stage that Ken began to look much more like a settled young man, especially when he and Val announced their plans to marry, even though he was still pretty young and I thought the writers might want to keep him single. Once the decision had been made to marry him off it looked as though he would then start to settle down to quiet domesticity, and in a way that's exactly what he wanted, but the writers were very clever. On the one hand they had created this caring, principled, stubborn individual who was bright and intelligent, but on the other they also saw that he had a definite weakness when it came to women, and out of that came the affair he had with Jackie Marsh, even though he knew he was risking his marriage as a consequence. In fact, although I tend to think of Ken as this well-meaning guy who always tries to do the right thing, I think that when it came to women, particularly in the first 20 years of the show, he wasn't very nice at all. In many ways he was pretty ruthless. I think he's mellowed over the years, thank goodness, although as recently as 2009 he still managed to have a bit of a fling with actress Martha Fraser, played beautifully by the wonderful Stephanie Beacham.

Certainly in the 1970s he was very much out for himself, hence the affair with Jackie Marsh, but despite his roaming eye the thing he always seemed to be looking for was the normality of married life. He was a sensitive, thinking chauvinist who liked the idea of having a wife who was always there for him, but at the same time he found nothing wrong with flirting or going off with another woman. The death of Val hit him hard, and in the episodes that followed the scene I've already described with me finding her compact, Ken briefly came into contact with a woman called Yvonne Chappell, who was a receptionist at a hotel he booked into. The storyline was that Ken was due to go to Glasgow for Val's funeral, but couldn't face it. Instead he checked into the hotel, but Yvonne made him realise that life had to go on and he eventually travelled to Scotland. The writers then decided it would be good to have the two of them get together at a later stage, which is exactly what happened. They got on well and Ken became very enthusiastic about Yvonne, to the point of actually proposing, but she turned him down, saying that all he was basically looking for was a replacement for Val. I had some quite long scenes on location with Alex Marshall, who played Yvonne, like when we were supposed to be having a romantic day on a boat and Ken went to the trouble of borrowing a sports car for the occasion. But, despite his best intentions, she wasn't interested in marrying him, and it was left to me to look hurt, baffled and a little angry as she left Ken in the car after turning down his proposal.

Yvonne may have been able to resist Ken's charms, but there was one young, impressionable girl in the *Street* who couldn't. Her character was called Norma Ford, and she was portrayed by Diana Davies. I had a lovely relationship with Diana off-screen as well as on it, and when we weren't in front of the camera she was always joking around and pretending to look after me. She had a great personality and she played the part of Norma really well, who came into the programme as an assistant to Maggie Clegg in the corner shop. She was in the show for about two years and brought the character to life. Diana was able to play the light comedic moments, but at the same time she had a rather sad quality to her, in the way she was clearly desperate for Ken to take more than a passing interest in her. He was pretty awful to her really at one stage, simply using her for some convenient female company just to restore his own self-esteem, but before that happened there was a very funny moment that had consequences beyond the *Street*.

There was a story written for the two of us that saw Ken give

Norma English lessons for the grand old sum of 50p an hour. It was clear that Norma really fancied Ken, but those feelings weren't reciprocated. In an effort to let her know exactly how he felt, Ken decided he would recite a poem to her. It was beautifully written by Harry Kershaw, and I think he was rightly proud of the finished product. At the end of one episode Ken duly begins to recite this poem to Norma, and it is very romantic indeed. So much so that a member of the public actually got in touch with Granada and asked if he could have a copy of it to send to his girlfriend. The trouble was that the guy hadn't realised there was another part to the poem, which was going to be read by Ken in the next episode, a few days later, and it basically ended with him saying to Norma that there was no way their relationship could carry on. Heaven only knows what happened between the guy and his girlfriend after she'd read the full version of Harry's work!

Norma still hoped there was a chance of her and Ken getting together. I think she just felt he needed time, but he had other things on his mind in 1973, when he fell hook, line and sinker for Elaine Perkins – and who could blame him, because she was played by Joanna Lumley. Ken had got himself a job as head of English at Bessie Street School and was at a drinks party held at the house of his headmaster, Mr Perkins. In the scene Ken is obviously keen to get away and seems to be finding the whole thing rather boring and stuffy, but then he is introduced by the headmaster to his daughter and his attitude changes instantly. Rather than wanting to get away, Ken is more than happy to stay and chat to the beautiful Elaine, who is both sexy and intelligent, with the kind of background and group of friends that Ken himself had probably always hankered after in many ways. I don't think Ken was ever a real leftie when it came to politics, and although he expressed socialist views from time to time, I always felt that he was much more a sort of liberal, fair-minded guy who was always looking to right the wrongs of society. He was happy to carry the banner if it came along, but he wouldn't really instigate things, and whether he liked it or not, he seemed to quite enjoy the comfy middle-class background that Elaine clearly came from, and in many ways embraced it.

The two begin to see each other and Ken totally falls for Elaine.

She likes him, but sees Ken as just another man in her life. She's fiercely independent and has her own life to lead. Elaine is quite happy for Ken to become part of her life but not to the exclusion of her friends or what she might want to do. He becomes increasingly frustrated with her independence and the fact that she is not prepared to take him as seriously as he is taking her. The simple truth is that he is in love, but although she likes him a lot, it is no more than that for her.

I loved playing opposite Joanna. She was, and still is, ravishingly beautiful, incredibly intelligent and incredibly nice. It's unfair really, and she hasn't changed a bit over the years. She went on to do great things after appearing in the *Street*, including *The New Avengers*, but I felt she was always destined to do well. She has a lovely personality. She's open and childlike in her enthusiasm, and she has a great love of life. She also has a wonderful sense of humour and has that great ability not to take herself seriously, although she's made sure a few politicians have had to do just that in recent years with her tireless work for the Gurkhas. She was an absolute delight to work with, and I was always sorry that she wasn't reintroduced into the show at some later stage. I think there was some talk of that happening in 2009, but nothing ever materialised. Ironically, although Ken never did quite manage to persuade Elaine to make their relationship more permanent, in real life Joanna Lumley is a Barlow, having married the conductor Stephen Barlow.

When Ken realises there is no chance of him being able to persuade Elaine to take their relationship more seriously he storms out of the house, leaving Wensley Pithey, who played headmaster Wilfred Perkins, to ask his daughter what had happened.

'Ken is a man who needs his pride; you didn't dent it, did you?' he asks her.

'I rather think I did,' she replies.

Despite the crushing disappointment of being rejected by Elaine Perkins, Ken then shows his resilience when it comes to matters of the heart, because as soon as he gets back to Coronation Street he makes his way to the corner shop and promptly asks Norma if she wants to go out with him that night. Against her better judgement she says yes, but then Ken shows just how self-centred he was in those days by having a drink with Rita in the Rovers and then agreeing to see her that night instead of poor Norma. I remember the scene in the Rovers with Rita. She is upset because Len has gone off to the Continent and not taken her with him, so they decide to console each other and spend the night together. I remember that during the Rovers scene Ken confides in her that Elaine was 'out of my league', as he puts it.

'There were other fellers more glamorous, more successful, more wealthy and more interesting than me,' he tells Rita.

That line kind of summed up his perception of Elaine and her world, but it also gave an insight into the world of Ken Barlow, because even if he didn't really like to admit it to himself, he was very much of Coronation Street, for better or for worse, and often that fact was a source of frustration for him.

There were other women in Ken's life during the '70s, including Wendy Nightingale, who was married, but Ken still persuaded her to move in with him, which she did for a time while he was separated from Janet. Needless to say it didn't work out, and although there were a few other girls who briefly came and went throughout that period, Ken stayed well clear of any long-term commitment. I think it's been very clever of the writers throughout my time on the show to have this theme running through Ken's character. I think that in the 1980s, when he was given the tag of 'boring Ken', nobody really stopped to look at the fact that when it came to his relationships with women, his life was anything but boring. In those first two decades of the show he was certainly very active when it came to different women, and although the number of girlfriends slowed down slightly in the next twenty years, the storylines tended to be bigger and more involved, as when he had affairs with Wendy Crozier, Alma Sedgewick, Maggie Redman and Denise Osbourne, producing some great drama along the way. The stories and episodes involving Ken's relationships with these women really seemed to hit the spot as far as the viewers were concerned, and the response they got was tremendous. I have to say that Ken's treatment of women through much of his life has often shown him in a pretty poor light, but as an actor it has provided me with great opportunities to be involved in some very strong storylines over a long period of time, and none of them has been stronger or more enduring than Ken's relationship with Deirdre.

As we saw the new decade in together on the show back in 1979, neither Anne Kirkbride nor I could have believed that we would still be working together as a couple some 32 years later, but that's exactly what has happened, and of all the women in Ken's life there is no doubt at all that Deirdre has been the most enduring.

10

DEIRDRE

As an actor on *Coronation Street* you have no real say in the destiny of your character: that's down to the producer and the writers. Your job is to portray as honestly and truthfully as you can the stories they come up with and to make them as believable as you possibly can. One of the great strengths of the programme has been the quality of its writers and the storylines and plots that have been devised over the years. It is not easy to keep a show fresh and vital, so to have done that for more than 50 years is quite remarkable, in my opinion. I often marvel at the fact that characters are given stories that I would never have thought of, or which may not seem quite right to begin with but then turn out to be perfect for the show.

When it was decided back in the late 1970s that there should possibly be some kind of romantic storyline linking Ken and Deirdre, it might have seemed a little strange to some people. After all, he was quite a bit older than her, and although she'd been part of the show for eight years their paths had never really crossed before. Ken may have had an eye for the ladies, but Deirdre had not been one of them, and for her part it had been Ray Langton who had provided the main romantic interest in her life. However, when Neville Buswell decided he wanted to leave the *Street*, in 1978, his departure had a real knock-on effect for both Anne Kirkbride and me. Neither of us was aware of it at the time, and I don't suppose the writers had thought that far ahead, but the fact was that having Ray Langton go off to Holland set in motion the possibilities for a whole new storyline involving Ken and Deirdre.

This sort of thing can often happen when a character leaves the *Street*, either by asking to go, in which case the writers get more notice of their departure, or when there is the sudden and unexpected death of one of the actors. Just as in life, someone dying will have an effect on those around them, and that is exactly the same in the *Street*. A departure from the programme has a ripple effect, and it just depends who those ripples touch. Having Deirdre as a single mum in the programme opened up the possibilities of her meeting someone else. She was young and attractive with her life ahead of her, so there was every reason for the writers to use this and try to link her with a man.

Once she'd turned down the chance to go to Jersey with Billy Walker, another romantic avenue needed to open up for Deirdre, and the writers decided it would be Ken, although as the programme entered the 1980s it looked as though their relationship might be short-lived, because he backed away from any sort of long-term commitment. Having already been married twice, Ken wasn't keen on the thought of a third wedding, and during most of 1980 there was no real hint of what was to come, but that began to change during the following year. Ken clearly liked Deirdre, and they began to see each other once more, but the writers decided to add a different dimension to the relationship, one which I'm sure was only meant to be temporary at the time, but which laid the ground for some spectacular storylines in the future. They introduced Mike Baldwin as another male admirer for Deirdre.

The thing between Ken and Deirdre that year started pretty slowly. In fact, before the two of them went out he had stood back while she had a date with someone called Dirk Van Der Stek, who was supposed to be a colleague of Ray's from Holland. Ken clearly didn't feel happy about this and pretty soon began seeing Deirdre, but on one occasion when they were supposed to go out Ken's car broke down, leaving Deirdre hanging around waiting for him, and Mike Baldwin quickly stepped in to take her out for a meal. Mike and Deirdre then started to see each other, leaving

Ken feeling jealous, but despite his growing feelings towards her he managed to accept the situation, and it looked as though it was all over between Ken and Deirdre.

Looking back now, it is interesting for me to see just how important those few episodes broadcast in 1981 were for me and for the character of Ken. I don't think Anne, Johnny Briggs or I had any idea of how intertwined our three characters would become in the years to come, but the Ken, Mike and Deirdre stories went on to form a huge part of the show and provide some of my happiest moments as an actor on *Coronation Street*.

Ken and Deirdre were brought together again when they found themselves washing up after Mike Baldwin's flat-warming party. In typical Baldwin fashion, he took the rest of the partygoers off to the Pandas nightclub, including Sonia Price, who had been Ken's date for the night. Ken then began to see Deirdre again and their relationship blossomed, despite Uncle Albert feeling less than enthusiastic about what was going on.

Throughout my time on the show there have been a series of relationships that Ken has formed, some fleeting, others more lasting, and not all of them of the romantic kind. One of the relationships that worked so well on-screen, and was a great pleasure for me on a personal level, was acting opposite Jack Howarth. Having known Jack all of those years ago as a schoolboy it was wonderful to act with him professionally, and I was so pleased that we were able to do so for such a long time. After the death of Val the writers had Ken renting number three Coronation Street, but then it was sold to Ernest Bishop as he prepared for his wedding to Emily Nugent. It meant that Ken moved into number one with Albert and began a two-way relationship with him that was often a little bumpy and uncomfortable, but underlying all of that was an affection the two had for each other. Albert was one of these wonderful older characters that the *Street* has had over the years, and they simply don't care what they say and when they say it. The Ken and Albert relationship worked really well, and it was always good to be in a scene with Jack. When it was clear Ken and Deirdre's relationship was back on again, and the two planned to marry, Albert became very concerned. He knew she wanted a bigger house away from Coronation Street, and even Albert's own daughter, Beattie Pearson, was not prepared to take her father in, so it looked as though he would be left on his own. There were some very good scenes written around that time that really examined the nature of Ken's relationship with Uncle Albert. Ken was told by the doctor that Albert was too old to live alone, after he had collapsed on the street, and so Deirdre agreed to live at number one and a new strand of the Ken and Albert relationship was woven into the show.

The wedding itself was a huge event, with the press very excited about the prospect of Ken and Deirdre marrying, and just to add to the occasion, it took place only a couple of days before Prince Charles married Diana. Both Anne and I were delighted that the writers had decided to marry us off, because in the time we had been working closely together on-screen it was clear that we worked well together. It's a funny thing and not easy to define, but when you are acting closely with someone in something like *Coronation Street*, being able to get on and feel comfortable with them both on- and off-screen is really important. Annie was lovely from the start, and I think that we both felt very comfortable with each other on-screen and also got on well as colleagues. It's something that has never changed and, in fact, it's probably got better as the years have gone by.

If you look at our relationship in *Coronation Street* today, I think we look and sound just right. We have been together on and off for more than 30 years, which is incredible really, and so much of what we do in front of the cameras is instinctive now. Anne, as Deirdre, will say or do something, and I, as Ken, will react in a certain way that has become so familiar to her over the years. We really are a bit like an old married couple who have had their ups and downs, lived through them and come out the other side. The writers know they can use our history as a couple and also as individuals to come up with storylines, and I think it was very much like that right from the start of the marriage. The wedding on 27 July 1981 attracted a staggering 21 million viewers, and with a figure like that it was clear that the marriage had captured the imagination of the public. Curiously, the ceremony was performed

A shot of the original cast in 1960. It's a picture I still have hanging
outside my dressing-room at Granada.
(© ITV Picture Archive)

My first screen wife, Val,
beautifully played by
Anne Reid.
(© Getty Images)

The wonderful Joanna Lumley was a romantic interest for Ken when she played Elaine Perkins in the 1970s. (© ITV Picture Archive)

A shot of the cast from 1969. The numbers have grown considerably since then. (© Getty Images)

A publicity shot taken during the famous 1983 scene involving Mike Baldwin, Deirdre and Ken, but the real drama took place in the Barlows' hall. (© ITV Picture Archive)

Anne Kirkbride, Johnny Briggs and I won an award for the iconic Ken, Deirdre and Mike Baldwin scene in 1983. (© PA)

Smiles outside the High Court with some of my *Street* colleagues during my libel case, but there wasn't much to be happy about in the end, even though I won. (© PA)

I got the chance to show Prime Minister Margaret Thatcher around the new Studio One complex in 1990. (© PA)

A happy moment, posing with my MBE after receiving
it at Buckingham Palace in 2000. (© PA)

A night out with Verity, Sara, Will and a friend.
(© Champions (UK) plc)

The end for Mike Baldwin, as he dies of a heart attack in the arms of his long-term enemy, Ken. (© ITV Picture Archive)

With my recording partner, Peter Kay. It was fun being part of a hit record. (© Champions (UK) plc)

One of many great scenes with Maggie Jones, who played Blanche so brilliantly. Here I am as Ken in 2008, trying to tell her that I am not a homosexual! (© ITV Picture Archive)

With my beautiful wife, Sara, in 2008. (© Getty Images)

by a guy called Frank Topping, who was actually a Methodist minister and combined this with a show business career. The age difference of nearly sixteen years between the older Ken and his young bride didn't seem to worry anyone, and it looked as though the two of them might settle into a fairly conventional marriage, but little did we know that the writers had something very different in mind some eighteen months later, and I have to say that I will always be grateful for the invention they showed.

From a personal point of view, the early 1980s were not particularly happy for me as an actor, because I didn't really feel pleased with the way they were writing for Ken. As I have mentioned, I think he was beginning to look very ordinary and quite nerdy, and that in turn had a knock-on effect for me, because I started to lose confidence as an actor. Once that happens things can fall apart pretty rapidly, and I went through a time where I was really scared of 'drying', which is not being able to remember your lines, and if that happens it's not only extremely inconvenient for your colleagues and everyone else involved in the production of a scene, it also drains you mentally. You start to wonder about your own ability to remember lines and act in the way you had, which can be very damaging. The feeling that Ken as a character was just drifting along and not really getting involved in any particularly good storylines also added to my unease, and the combination of all of this was what led to me going 'upstairs' to see the producer. Whether that led to them developing the storyline they came up with or whether they already had it in mind to create something quite dramatic I don't really know, but the fact was that things did start to change for Ken. Apparently at a story conference in the summer of 1982 the idea that Deirdre should have an affair was hatched, and when the other man turned out to be Mike Baldwin the show suddenly had a love-triangle saga that would prove hugely popular with the audience and at the same time split the nation.

The storyline hit the public pulse and it seemed the country was equally divided as to who Deirdre should end up with: Ken or Mike. I remember that Ken got a lot of sympathy in some quarters, while other people believed Deirdre should go off with

Mike, who was seen as the more exciting prospect. People would take it really seriously, and when the affair between Mike and Deirdre started to happen and poor old Ken knew nothing about it, I would get letters addressed to me at the studios that said, 'Dear Ken, I think you should know that Mike Baldwin is seeing your wife!' The blurring of me and Ken was obviously a bit too much for some people, but I can understand how that happens. In fact, sometimes we, as actors, get a bit confused ourselves, and I have been known, during the middle of a Ken and Deirdre scene, to suddenly refer to Deirdre as Annie.

I think one of the main reasons for the affair taking such a grip on the nation was the way it was played out, because the public were allowed to see it slowly developing in front of their eyes. It didn't really matter whether they agreed or disagreed with a certain character and their actions, the main thing was that the programme allowed it all to unfold, and as a consequence the drama built episode by episode, until you knew there was going to be some sort of explosion.

It all started innocently, with Deirdre and Mike having a chat in the Rovers, and when Mike's pregnant girlfriend, Maggie Dunlop, left him, it was Deirdre who consoled him over a drink in the pub. The whole relationship really began over the Christmas period of 1982, with Deirdre having a dance with Mike, while virtually being ignored by Ken on the night. Her increasing frustration at what she perceived as a lack of attention from Ken was compounded one evening when she thought the two of them were going to see a film, only for him to announce that he wanted to stay at home and watch a documentary on Channel 4. Deirdre went to the cinema on her own, leaving Ken at home with Uncle Albert, and on the way back she stopped off at Mike's flat. Things began to take a new turn after that, and with Ken reserving his enthusiasm for the possibility of a new job as deputy director of Social Services, rather than for his wife, Deirdre eventually started the affair with Mike after the two of them went out for a meal together. I think a lot of women may have sympathised with Deirdre during the course of this period, because Ken was cast as the sort of husband who took her very much for granted, while Mike was giving her the sort of attention she would have loved in her own marriage. When Ken applies for the job he is clearly excited and enthusiastic, emotions that were lacking in their relationship at that time, and when Deirdre questions him about it, Ken delivers a line that is like a dagger to her heart.

'You've got to have something interesting to get excited about,' he explains when she comments on his high spirits. Unfortunately for Deirdre, although the thought of a new job excites him, she clearly believes that his marriage to her does not. The writers did a great job with the way they kept the storyline vibrant and fresh. By this time the viewers knew what was going on, but Ken still didn't, so he carried on as normal, picking up none of the signs of despondency that Deirdre was displaying. That was when I got the sort of mail I described earlier, warning Ken about the affair, a sure sign that it was having a gripping effect on the audience, which is exactly what you want. There were some very dramatic moments for Anne, because not only was Deirdre seeing Mike behind her husband's back, she was also feeling guilty but couldn't seem to help herself. The whole affair took another direction when it was decided that Emily would find out about what was happening and confront Deirdre.

The writers have always been very good at giving a character just one or two lines that really hit the spot and sum up all that is going on, and in a heated scene with Emily, as she tries to get Deirdre to end the affair, there was a wonderful line that painted the picture perfectly and conveyed all the frustration she felt.

'Being married to Ken these last few months has been about as exciting as being hitched to a block of wood,' Deirdre tells Emily.

The term 'boring Ken' first really started to appear around the time of the affair, and it was used thereafter by several newspapers whenever they wanted to describe the character. I always felt it was a little unfair, particularly when you think about the number of women who have played a part in Ken's life, but perhaps it was a line from one of the episodes at this time that started the whole thing off. Needless to say, Ken's high hopes of a new job all came to nothing, and as he sat in a chair feeling sorry for himself,

Deirdre hit him with a few home truths, telling him that there was nothing wrong with his life that a little enthusiasm wouldn't put right. She had discovered the reason for Ken not getting the job, and the main one was that they didn't feel he had enough 'go' in him. Ken became angry at hearing some home truths from her, finally spitting out the words, 'I'm boring,' as he sank deeper into his own self-pity. When Deirdre finally confessed that she had been having an affair with Mike, it led on to the famous scene with me slamming the door and Annie crying her way through it, while delivering a tremendous performance at the same time. It was a mark of not only her acting ability, but also her professionalism that she was able to continue that scene in such a dramatic fashion.

Annie was, and still is, a joy to work with. I think she's a lovely person and she's like a mother at times, not just to me but to anyone on the *Street*. She's always caring and fussing around us. If I have a cold or don't feel too well, you can bet that Anne will delve into her bag and bring out a potion or some pills to help me feel better. She's very sensitive, but also very strong, and when it comes to her lines she is word perfect. We've had some wonderful times together on the *Street*, and it's very important that you have a way of being sympathetic to someone you are working with over a long period of time. Anne and I know each other as actors so well that we can speed up or slow down a scene instinctively and the other person will react accordingly. We've had romantic storylines and others where we've been shouting and screaming at each other, but, as odd as it might sound, when we've had those sorts of scenes we've come out of the studio and almost inevitably one of us will say to the other, 'I really enjoyed that.' It's because as an actor you always want to have something to play that is very positive, and a conflict scene is exactly that. Anne and I can play scenes with confidence and with ease because we work so well together, and I feel extremely comfortable playing opposite her. I've been very fortunate to have her as a friend and colleague for so many years, and long may it continue.

The force of my performance during that famous scene clearly surprised her, but once it was over there was that wonderful feeling of knowing that we'd both been involved in a piece of acting and television drama that was special. Certainly the whole Ken, Mike and Deirdre saga was special for all three of us, and it pleased me to have such strong storylines that I could get stuck into. What was so good about it was that it involved three principal characters and there was a lot of energy poured into it by all three of us.

My confidence began to return during that period, and I certainly think it gave the writers and producer something more to think about in the years that followed. The love triangle gave them scope for various twists and turns, and there was a new dynamic created: not only was there the affair to refer to and mull over at different times, there was also the fallout from it. While Ken and Deirdre patched up their marriage and gave it another try at that point, the storyline had also created another of the classic *Street* double acts – Ken and Mike.

11

TROUBLE WITH MIKE

Ken's dislike of Mike started long before the love triangle with Deirdre. The truth was that Ken never liked him, but having his wife go off and have an affair with Mike turned dislike into hatred, which was wonderful for the programme. Just the mention of Baldwin's name was enough to get Ken twitching with barely contained anger, and for Johnny Briggs and me it was absolutely wonderful. At best the two characters sometimes tolerated each other in an uneasy truce, but at worst the two of them not only threw insults at each other, but punches too. It was a relationship that ran for many years, and although towards the end of Mike Baldwin's time on the show you might say there was a little mellowing going on, it was never a relationship that was going to be anything other than uneasy.

Quite naturally, as actors we loved every minute of it, and although by nature I am not the sort of person who shouts and screams or in any way resorts to physical violence, it was still great fun to be able to do it through Ken. I have always said that the writers write and come up with the storylines, and it is my job to portray what they have written. As Bill Roache I don't have to agree or disagree with what is written, I just have to believe that what I see in a script is what Ken would do, and once the dislike of Mike Baldwin had been created it was quite easy to see that here was a man who would always be able to get under his skin. It didn't matter how much Ken tried to control himself; it was simply like a red rag to a bull and he had to react. The great thing was that once this obvious dislike and hatred had been established, it allowed the writers to dip into it on numerous occasions, knowing that an explosive and dramatic situation was guaranteed. The other wonderful thing was that their dislike for each other had an effect on other characters, and so they were dragged into this whole swirl of acrimony that epitomised Ken and Mike's relationship.

I have touched on the fact that there is always a blurring of the characters and actors for many people when they watch the show. I know that when the Ken and Mike thing was at its height during the 1980s there were lots of people who thought we actually didn't like each other, and the other question that seemed to interest the audience was how Johnny and I really got on together. We both liked playing golf, and I remember we were at one of these pro-celebrity functions where I did a bit of a question-and-answer session. One of the questions I was asked was how I actually got on with Johnny.

'I hate him,' I replied in a deadpan fashion.

For a second or two I think the questioner may have believed I meant it, but then I smiled and everyone laughed. I also used to sometimes plant a kiss on his cheek at these days, and people would love to take pictures of the two of us. We used to joke about the perception some people had of our relationship, because they obviously weren't sure of how we got on together. The truth was that we got on perfectly well and just did our jobs as professional actors; we were never bosom buddies or close friends, but we got on well enough and were really good colleagues. I also think we were very grateful to be playing characters who would have these moments of conflict on a regular basis, while also going about their everyday lives as part of the *Street*. Professionally we had some great stuff going on together, and even after some of the most dramatic or violent scenes we played we would both go off and have a coffee together, knowing that we'd just enjoyed what had gone on and had great fun doing it.

Having managed to make sure that Deirdre stayed with him and didn't go off with Mike Baldwin, Ken then had to face another trauma a few years later when the writers came up with a plot that involved another woman who was close to his heart. They decided that it would be a good idea for Ken's daughter, Susan, to fall in love with Mike, with all the emotional shockwaves such a storyline would create. Once again it was a great idea, and once again it allowed me to really get my teeth into some very meaty scripts.

A lot of parents wouldn't be too happy about a 20-year-old daughter being involved with someone who was old enough to be their father, but when that person happened to be Mike Baldwin, you could almost see the steam coming out of Ken's ears. It was another wonderful story, and it gave me a lot of scope on different levels. First there was my obvious dislike of Baldwin, second there was the emotional side of my father-and-daughter relationship with Susan and third there was a sort of inner turmoil that underpinned the whole thing, where Ken had to battle with his own stubbornness. He loved his daughter and, having been absent for much of her life, he carried a lot of guilt as well, but at the same time he could not tolerate the prospect of her being married to the man he disliked most in the world. When it became clear that Susan and Mike's relationship was a serious one he was beside himself and desperately tried to get her to stop seeing him. The subplot to all of this at the time was that Susan had no idea why her father had such hatred for Mike, because although the viewers knew the history of what had gone on before with Deirdre, she was unaware of it. Having that kind of story running through it made the whole saga much more dramatic, and the audience knew that as Ken became more desperate he would have to let his daughter know the truth.

I remember it being a very dramatic and emotional scene, because not only did I reveal the fact that my wife had had an affair with Baldwin, I did so knowing how much it would also upset Deirdre, and once again Anne turned in an excellent performance, conveying the despair and embarrassment she must have felt at such an intimate part of her life being laid bare to her stepdaughter. Before Ken tells Susan, who was played by Wendy Jane Walker, he has one last stab at trying to get her to see sense, and when that doesn't work he hits her with the emotional bombshell that he hopes will finally put an end to her relationship with Baldwin.

'He tried to take my wife; he didn't manage it, so now he wants my daughter,' he tells her.

The line summed up all the anger and frustration he felt about the situation, and in many ways showed how ruthless and self-centred Ken could be when the figure of Mike Baldwin entered his life. In an instant he had upset two of the people he loved most, his wife and his daughter, but that didn't really seem to matter to him as much as making sure Baldwin did not get what he wanted. He clearly began to see Mike as someone who was on a one-man crusade to wreck the life of Ken Barlow, and he was never able to fully control his emotions or actions when it came to dealing with him. Having that level of anger and drama to deal with is great for any actor, and it was lovely for me, because I was able to really throw myself into the scenes and enjoyed some marvellous moments in the process.

Those kinds of moments were very satisfying, but as part of the ongoing conflict with Baldwin over his relationship with Susan, I also had to play in a scene that, although dramatic, was not nearly as satisfying from a personal point of view. Over the years in the *Street*, Ken has got involved in one or two conflicts that have seen him resort to violence. Playing those scenes can be great fun, and when you feel that they have been done as authentically as possible there is a great deal of satisfaction to be had from the moment. When I had the fight scene with Len in the Rovers and told Peter Adamson to actually try to hit me, I think the whole thing worked really well and came over on-screen just as I had hoped. I liked actually acting the whole thing out and really going for it in front of the cameras, but when I had a fight scene with Johnny as part of the storyline involving Mike Baldwin and Susan, I just didn't feel the same way about it.

The script called for me to walk into Mike's factory, go straight over to him, speak a line of dialogue and, without giving him the chance to do or say anything in reply, hit him, knocking Baldwin to the floor. When it came to the take I walked in looking angry and determined and marched up to Johnny, who was busy with some of the factory workers.

'I've had enough of your poison in my family, more than enough,' I snarled at him.

And with that I threw a punch with my left hand that knocked him to the floor, and I turned on my heel, mission accomplished, and walked out of the factory as a stunned workforce watched their boss reeling on the floor. The trouble was that when I actually did the scene there was no follow through, as there had been with the Len Fairclough fight; instead, I had to walk up, utter the lines and then throw the punch. The scene would then be cut, and the next shot was of Johnny propelling himself backwards onto the floor. They were then going to piece it together to make it look as though the whole thing had been done in one take. I had serious doubts that it would work on-screen when it came to be shown, but I think it did in the end, and I think the reason they did it like that was to try to capture the high drama of the moment, but it certainly wasn't as much fun to do as that previous scene with Peter Adamson.

When Ken failed in his attempt to stop Susan from going ahead with her marriage to Mike, he displayed a side to him that was not particularly appealing: when he refused to walk down the aisle with her, to give his only daughter away. It was a mixture of stubbornness and petulance at not getting his own way, and it looked as though Ken would be prepared to miss his own daughter's wedding as a result, but the writers came up with some wonderful scenes that eventually led to the storyline taking a twist as the viewers waited to see what would happen. Ken was still adamant that he was not going to attend the wedding, and even when Susan pleaded with him to walk her down the aisle, he wouldn't change his mind, but he was then confronted by his son, Peter, who told him a few home truths. The character of 21-year-old Peter was played by David Lonsdale at the time, and he did a great job in hitting just the right note as he calmly, but with an understated sense of emotion, spelled out the way he felt about his father. Peter told Ken that he packed his children off to Scotland to live with their grandparents, and was never really there when they needed him. Ken clearly didn't see it like that and was somewhat in denial over the whole issue. I have always believed that at the core of Ken's character there is a very decent and honourable man who will always try to do the right thing. He is subject to the same weaknesses, faults and emotions we all are, and sometimes he doesn't deal with that part of his character in the way that he would like to. He will often erect a barrier or construct some strange kind of logic that he sees as justification for his actions, even though in his heart of hearts he knows it is wrong.

In the scene with Peter some of the things he heard from his own son were clearly hard to take, and the fact that they were said in such a heartfelt way only helped emphasise their truth. The conversation had an effect on Ken, and after wrestling with his emotions, he turned up at the church for the wedding, with his presence causing a stir among the assembled guests, who clearly thought he wasn't going to attend his own daughter's wedding. At the reception Mike even thanks Ken for coming, but it is made very obvious to Baldwin that the only reason he came was because of Susan.

That mini truce apart, it was clear their relationship was never really going to improve. Ken detested Mike, and he was locked in a kind of hatred that in many ways was a far stronger emotion than the love he had for those closest to him. Mention the name Baldwin and Ken's whole demeanour changed, which was always a delicious prospect for me. I remember in one programme Ken tried to sum up what he thought of Mike.

'He's everything I detest: unprincipled, superficial, materialistic, flashy and a manipulator.' Ken said this as he sat there trying to logically list the character traits in Baldwin that he despised so much.

It was a marvellous list, and you could almost see Ken's nostrils twitching as he spat out every word with just the sort of venom you would expect from someone so clearly consumed with hate for another human being. Of course, those sorts of feelings were exactly the kind of emotions I, as Bill Roache, would not want to entertain. I accept that human beings are fallible, but one of the main things I began to learn after embarking on my spiritual journey was that hate is such a negative thing. It does no good at all and is not a positive thing in the way that love is. I know for a fact that loving other humans and the world we live in is not only a good thing for those around us, it also helps you on a personal level. Put simply, I have always believed that trying to be nice is so much better than being nasty, and if you do that there is usually a positive response from people. Of course, there was no chance of that happening between Ken and Mike, which was why the whole relationship was so satisfying to play as an actor. Giving your mannerisms and expressions to a character is one thing, but acting is about playing someone else. I care about the character of Ken and on the whole I think he's a pretty decent person, but his views and emotions are not necessarily mine. It's my job to portray Ken as honestly and truthfully as I can: if a script calls for him to be angry or to hate another character, it's not for me to pass judgement; all I have to do is believe that given a certain set of circumstances he would react in a particular way, and then it's up to me to portray that for the screen.

A few years down the line saw Susan's marriage to Mike hit the rails. He wanted to have children, and when she became pregnant but then told him she'd had an abortion, it was too much for him to take, and he told Susan that she had not only killed his baby, she had also killed their marriage.

The ongoing feud between Ken and Mike had been established ever since the days of the love triangle with Deirdre, and often it was used as a kind of volcano by the writers, because although it was there you never really knew when it was likely to erupt and how strong that eruption would be. As the 1980s came to a close, a storyline was hatched concerning the Barlow marriage that was every bit as powerful as the one that had heralded the early years of the decade – only this time it wasn't Deirdre who strayed, it was Ken, and just to add a little spice to it all, there was a significant cameo role played in the whole affair by Mike Baldwin.

By 1989 Deirdre was working as a councillor, having won an election, and Ken was happy as the editor of the *Weatherfield Recorder*, having first owned a third share of the newspaper before eventually getting the opportunity to buy it outright. He clearly enjoyed being a local press baron, and the paper provided a perfect platform for various campaigns and crusades. One such series of articles concerned the leaking of a story about a hostel for homeless youths being opened in a community centre and Deirdre's bosses thinking that the leak had come from her, given the close connection she had with the *Recorder*'s owner and editor. In fact, Ken had got the information from the chief executive's secretary, a woman called Wendy Crozier, who was very well played in the programme by Roberta Kerr. Deirdre then tells her bosses who the mole is and Wendy gets her marching orders, prompting Ken to give her a job. The two of them work closely together, and with Deirdre so involved in her job Ken begins to feel a little neglected. Not only that, he also has the attractive Wendy working in close proximity to him, and I'm afraid it all gets a little too much. He succumbs to temptation, but just as an added little twist, Ken and Wendy are spotted at the airport by Mike Baldwin, and it doesn't take much for him to put two and two together. Mike is more than happy to share his suspicions with Deirdre, and although Ken bluffs his way out of it, claiming he is not having an affair when she confronts him with the allegation, he is decidedly uncomfortable, knowing that he is living a lie. Despite the fact that Ken is feeling guilty about his affair with Wendy, it doesn't stop him from warning Baldwin to stay away from Deirdre and to stop spreading rumours. I thought it was great that the writers were able to create a scenario where the boot was very much on the other foot as far as Ken and Deirdre were concerned. A few years earlier it had been her who had gone off behind Ken's back; now it was the other way around. I have to say that at the time I was a little worried about having Ken go off with another woman. It had happened when he was married to Val and started seeing Jackie Marsh, but having patched things up with Deirdre I wasn't sure that seeing him going off with Wendy seemed right. Of course, I need not have worried, because the writers did their usual great job with the scripts, letting the plot fall nicely into place as the episodes went on and the drama built.

A lot of the affair was conducted at Wendy's house, and that meant us having to go on location to do the filming. When something like that is called for, people will have certain ideas about what would be suitable for shooting the sort of scenes the script requires. All of this was done at a time of great change for *Coronation Street*, because in October 1989 the programme went from being broadcast twice a week, on Monday and Wednesday nights, to adding a third night, when it was shown on Fridays as well. This obviously meant a change in the way the show was made and also in the way we worked through the week. As a consequence of the change we began location shooting on Sundays, and the first one of these was taken up with the scenes Roberta and I had to do. I think we had about six of them in all that day, and we used a house owned by a couple who we later learned were quite religious. Unfortunately some of the scenes we did that day weren't exactly what they might have been expecting when they agreed to have their house used for the shoot, because much of what went on involved us having to use their bedroom. For one of the scenes I was told by wardrobe that the director, Brian Mills, had instructed it should be a 'knickers-only' scene. Stripping down to my pants didn't bother me, but what I was concerned about was looking a bit overweight on-screen. Brian assured me it would be fine and even said that I could look at the playback afterwards. As always he was right, and just as he had done with all of those scenes involving Anne, Johnny and me six years earlier, everything turned out really well.

It wasn't long before Deirdre's suspicions surfaced again and she once more confronted Ken. This time, weighed down with the guilt and the pretence surrounding the affair, Ken admitted to it. The scene was highly charged and dramatic, and once again it involved just Anne and me. I was slumped in a chair as she looked down at me and tearfully asked me where I had been and who with. She already knew, of course, and it was a very tense atmosphere. I looked up at her with tears welling in my eyes, and when she walked out of the room I broke down and began to cry. They were very dramatic moments for both of us, and although we were acting, it is certainly true that because you are so closely associated with your character and we had essentially been a married couple for all of those years, there is an extra dimension added to a scene like that. You can empathise with the characters and feel what they must be going through. It's slightly strange in that sense, because as actors in the *Street* we live in a kind of parallel world, dipping in and out of their lives. It may be fiction, and as a professional that is something you are aware of, but at the same time your work requires you to play that fictional character as honestly as you possibly can. When Deirdre had the affair, Ken felt angry and hurt; when it was his turn to be the unfaithful one, I had to express another mixture of emotions.

First and foremost he had made the decision to embark on the affair, and he was feeling guilty, but in the way that human beings often do when they know they have done something wrong, he was trying to justify it in his own mind and, in a strange way, to Deirdre as well. Of course she was having none of it, and instead of Ken deciding to either end the affair or leave Deirdre, he actually tried to ask her for time to decide what to do. Once again the story caught the nation's imagination and provoked all sorts of comments and opinions in the press and media. The Christmas episode that followed Ken's confession attracted huge audience figures, and the general consensus was that Ken was very much in the wrong and Deirdre should kick him out. We had a marriage-guidance counsellor speaking out and congratulating the programme for the amount of research we'd done into a marriage breakdown, saying that the emotional side of the affair had been portrayed just right. There was also a lecturer in developmental psychology who was asked by one newspaper to give an opinion on the effect it would have on a twelve year old like Tracy.

I think, for most people, Ken was seen as a nice, well-meaning guy, and there had been a lot of sympathy for him after what Mike Baldwin and Deirdre got up to, but that attitude changed among a lot of the viewers after Ken's affair, and as Bill Roache I experienced at first hand just how deeply some people felt about what had gone on. I recall dropping my children off at school one day and a woman dragged her daughter away, saying, 'Don't go near that man!' It was another example of how the actor and his character sometimes blur in the minds of the public, but a few years later the same woman came up to me and apologised for her actions that day. She then went on to explain that at the time her husband had just done the same thing, and she told me how painful it had been for her to watch those episodes on-screen, but she also said that watching them had, in the end, proved to be a help to her.

Deirdre eventually kicked Ken out and he went to stay with Wendy. It didn't take Mike Baldwin long to offer a consoling shoulder for Deirdre to cry on if she wanted it, but although he had no time for Ken and the way he'd treated her, he was not about to try to worm his way into her affections again. As for Ken, he had to sell the *Recorder* in order to give the house to Deirdre, and the relationship with Wendy began to deteriorate. At one point his car broke down and he couldn't even afford to have it repaired, choosing instead to sell it to Curly Watts, who became a hugely popular character in the *Street* after joining the programme in 1983 and was played so well by Kevin Kennedy. Ken, however, hadn't told Curly about the car's condition and afterwards refused to give him any money for repairs, so he was clearly not a popular figure when he later walked into the Rovers. Ken looked emotionally battered and just about the last thing he needed was the gloating figure of Mike Baldwin goading him. It was all too much for Ken and he completely lost it, flying at Baldwin but coming off second best, and was left on the floor before finally being bundled out of the pub.

Soon after that incident, Ken told Wendy that he had made a mistake leaving Deirdre, but by then it was all too late. He had lost his wife, his job, his home and his mistress. As a new decade dawned, things looked very different for him and Mike Baldwin: the only sure thing was that having established them as arch-enemies during the turbulent years of the 1980s, the writers were certainly not going to pass up the opportunity to continue their feud for many years to come. The Ken and Mike enmity had become a well-established part of *Coronation Street*.

She had gone into Edwina's room and found her lying at the top of her cot, completely motionless. I ran up the stairs and tried to rouse Edwina, but there was no response. I tried everything I could think of, including the kiss of life, in order to try to get her to move and show some signs of life. It was a horrible experience and a mixture of fear, disbelief and utter panic gripped the both of us as we battled with this nightmare situation. It was terrible. The paramedics were called and went clambering up the stairs of our house, which was now full of the sound of people crying. There was me and Sara, together with Sid and Kay, while poor little Verity, who was only three years old, wasn't sure what was going on. It must have been awful for her, and the house was in complete turmoil. Everything was happening so fast, and it was hard to try to get to grips with exactly what we were all experiencing. It soon became apparent that there was nothing that could be done to revive little Edwina. Our darling little daughter was gone.

When the realisation of her passing hit us, I don't think either Sara or I could quite comprehend what had happened, it was such a shock. I'd never known grief to be a physical pain before, but it really hurt. I think we were both numb to begin with, but then there was the realisation that we were experiencing every parent's nightmare. Your children are not supposed to die before you, but that was exactly what had happened to us that night, and it wasn't something that was easy to come to terms with. After it happened, I just couldn't talk. If I tried to speak to anyone I simply burst into tears. In the days that followed I didn't want to see anyone, I didn't want to leave the house, and if the phone rang I couldn't say anything before starting to cry once more. It was a very tough time for Sara and me, and it was a test of our own relationship as well. We helped each other and were at least able to talk, but for about three days neither of us could eat and we quite literally survived by drinking hot chocolate.

I had to ring the office and tell them, which was a very difficult thing to do, and they were very good about everything and told me to take my time before coming back to work, but even as I spoke to them and they were being so sympathetic, I burst into tears once more as I was talking. The post-mortem later revealed that one of the tiny tubes to Edwina's lungs had become blocked with catarrh, cutting off the air supply, and the doctor told us that very little can be done when that happens.

I honestly didn't know how I was going to cope with the funeral, when I was supposed to carry little Edwina's coffin; it all seemed too much and I was hurting so much with the pain of her going, but on the morning of the funeral I had a psychic experience that gave me strength and helped me cope not only with the day, but also with coming to terms with what had happened to Edwina. I woke up that morning and began to think of how terrible the day ahead would be, but as I lay there I suddenly saw this wonderful golden light and in the middle of it was the face of little Edwina, looking down and reassuring me that she was well and happy, and telling me not to worry. The pain and grief of her going did not suddenly disappear with what I saw, but it gave me a new strength. I told Sara what had happened, and although she hadn't seen what I had, she too said she felt stronger. That got us through it, and I carried the coffin on the day of the funeral with a greater inner strength than I could have imagined. The days that followed were very difficult – there was still a lot of grief and that was coupled with a sense of guilt – but at the same time my spiritual beliefs certainly helped me get through the period. It had been something like 14 years since that first meeting with Dr Maugham, and I understood that there was a reason for everything, and I also knew that Edwina would be in a loving place and that we would meet again. Everything I'd learned up to that point concerning my spiritual beliefs and about what happens when we pass was verified and endorsed. The knowledge that life goes on and can never be extinguished was a huge help and comfort to both of us.

I gradually began to do the more normal things in life, like going out and driving the car. It was difficult for me to talk about Edwina in those early, raw days without crying. Gradually, you have to move on, and both Sara and I were then able to start thinking about how much we had enjoyed having Edwina with us, and you are thankful for that precious time, knowing just how special it was.

I was away from work for about two weeks in all, and I have

to admit that going back to life on *Coronation Street* was pretty tough. I knew that a lot of people simply didn't know what to do, which means you spend a lot of time trying to put people at their ease. Some people just touch your arm and don't say anything, but it shows they care. I was dreading the first day back because of all of that, but once that first day was over, and everyone was so very lovely and caring, it made things easier. What had happened didn't affect my work, but when I did go into Granada I knew what I didn't want was to have to play some sort of frivolous part, but that never happened and gradually I got back to something like normality. I had to get on with my job, just as any other parent who goes through that terrible experience has to, and I was very fortunate in having the sort of job and colleagues that I did, with a wonderful support network that has always been there ever since I first started working on the show.

There was an amazing response from the public when they found out what had happened, and I had a huge amount of letters expressing sympathy and showing real love and affection towards Sara, Verity and me as a family. It was lovely to have that wave of warmth from complete strangers, and it certainly helped to give us strength. I also got letters from people who had experienced similar losses to our own, with mothers writing about losing daughters and sons. It's a truly terrible feeling, and there is no way anyone can properly understand the hurt and despair it brings unless it has happened to them, but at the same time the love we received as a result of our loss was truly overwhelming.

The public were wonderful, and I have to say that the press were extremely good as well. As you might expect, there were quite a few reporters who were sent to our house when news about what had happened to Edwina became public, and I understood that someone in my profession and in the job I did on television was always going to be of interest to the newspapers. They had a job to do, and I understood that. One of the reporters came to the front door and asked what I would like them to do. I asked him to please leave us alone, and that was exactly what they did. They didn't try to pester us or intrude on what was a very difficult and upsetting time.

Having the *Street* to go back to was a great help to me. It occupied my thoughts when I was at the studio, and I had something to focus on as I gradually came to terms with our loss. I knew that whatever had happened, it was my job to continue to be Ken Barlow on *Coronation Street*; there was a kind of public face that I had to portray, and in many ways that probably helped. Sara and I did a lot of talking in the days, weeks and months that followed, and she showed a great deal of strength in the way she coped with everything. I also think it demonstrated the strength of our own relationship, because there is no doubt that we really leaned heavily on each other during that period. It was a very important time for little Verity, too; she was young, and it had been an upsetting and bewildering experience for her. We were very much aware that she needed the comfort, love and strength of her parents as she came to terms with all that had happened. There was an enormous hurt within the family, and I wasn't at all sure whether we would have another child, but a little over a year after the death of Edwina, Sara gave birth to our son, William, and it was wonderful to be able to find such joy with his arrival. Both he and Verity, along with Linus and Vanya, continue to give me that joy to this day. They are all wonderful children, and I feel extremely fortunate to have them.

The loss of Edwina was not the only one I suffered that year. In April, the wonderful Jack Howarth sadly died. Not only had our association gone back to my schooldays at Rydal, I had also forged a very close working relationship with him on the *Street*. As Uncle Albert, he and I often had scenes together, some of them heated, some comic, but always enjoyable to play. He often put Ken in his place and had the ability to be the grumpy old man one moment and then produce a delightful comedic moment the next without breaking his stride. He was very much part of the old school of acting, hence his advice to me to not shout on-set and never put my hands in my pockets.

The idea that the writers had of keeping him and Ken together after the death of Val worked brilliantly, and when Deirdre came along, having Albert there in the middle of all that went on in their marriage was another move by the producer and writers that I think clearly worked. The public seemed to take to Albert as a character in his own right from the very first time he appeared on-screen, and it is a tribute to his ability as an actor that Jack became such an integral part of *Coronation Street*, appearing in more than 1,300 episodes during his time on the show. In the year before he died, he was awarded the MBE.

The programme also lost another of its iconic characters when Bernard 'Bunny' Youens died in the summer of that year. He'd had strokes and a heart attack, and it was very sad when he died. I'd had some very pleasant times playing golf with him, and the character he created had become part of *Coronation Street* folklore. His on-screen marriage to Hilda was a joy to watch, with both he and Jean Alexander combining to produce one of the *Street*'s classic couples. They were funny and sad, you always knew they were never quite going to achieve what they set out to do, and they were often the butt of the jokes. Despite their rows and problems over the years, and the fact that Stan Ogden was basically bone idle, they still had each other, and often it seemed like it was them against the world. After Bunny died the writers then had to decide how Stan would leave the *Street*, and they eventually did it with him dying in hospital after becoming bedridden during the course of the show. The scene following his death when Hilda unwraps Stan's belongings, sitting at a table in front of the famous 'muriel' and flying ducks on the wall, is beautifully played by Jean. She eventually comes across his glasses case and glasses, and tearfully holds them as the realisation sinks in that after all of those years, she is now alone and without the man who, despite all of his failings, she very clearly loved. The two of them worked so well on-screen and got on well off-screen, and it must have been very sad for Jean, because, like the rest of us, she had great affection for Bunny as a person and the character he created as an actor. Jean stayed on the show for another three years, but then decided to leave. It certainly shocked fans of the *Street*, and there were even campaigns started in the papers to 'Save Hilda'. Her popularity was reflected by the viewing figure for her last performance, when it was shown on Christmas Day in 1987, attracting a staggering 26.6 million people.

Another original member of the cast had died the year before

Bunny passed away: dear Vi Carson. She hadn't been well for some time and had, in fact, made her last appearance in *Coronation Street* during 1980. Her characterisation of Ena Sharples had become one of the most recognisable in the *Street*'s history, with her trademark hairnet. She stood no nonsense from anyone, and over the years had some marvellous scenes. As queen of the snug in those early days with Minnie and Martha, she would hold court on any given subject and spout forth her opinions and stories. As well as the fierce and acerbic lines she often delivered, there were also some wonderfully funny ones. On the subject of dying, she once said that she would like to go just as her mother had.

'She just sat up, broke wind and died,' she told an approving Minnie and Martha.

It was wonderful stuff, and Violet was a lovely person. She was very kind and caring, and I think she was also a little overwhelmed by the success of Ena and the effect her character had on the nation. Although she was really the only well-known one amongst us when we did that first episode, I don't think she was prepared for the fact that the character of Ena would be so popular, and with it so too would she. Violet wasn't the kind of person who sought publicity – she liked her work and just wanted to get on with it – but having made her name through radio, perhaps the instant recognition she got because of appearing in such a popular television programme was something she just didn't expect. It was lovely to have worked with her, and there was great affection for her amongst the cast and everyone on the programme, as well as the British public, who clearly took Ena and Violet to their hearts.

Vi had not been in the best of health for some time, and in May 1982 she was too poorly to attend the opening of the new permanent exterior of *Coronation Street*. It was a lovely occasion, with all the cast dressed in character as the Queen and Prince Philip toured the set and chatted to us all. Until then we had been using an exterior set that had been constructed about fourteen years earlier; the difference with the new one was that it was solid and permanent, made from real bricks and roof slates to give the Street an authentic look. It really was a proper street with proper terraced houses, but the realism only stretched as far as the front of the properties: behind them there were no rooms, but there was a walkway at the top of the houses so that if a character had to look out of a window, this could be done. There was also a slight change to the design of the Street, because they put a little alleyway between the Rovers and number one, putting an end to the speculation from some eagle-eyed viewers as to why the pub's toilets seemed to run straight into poor old Albert's house, because there had been no gap between the two in any of the old sets.

I wasn't really aware of it at the time, but there was a big change in terms of the original cast during those early years of the 1980s. In 1983, Doris Speed was another of the originals who left the programme, due to illness. In the same year, Peter Adamson, who wasn't part of the original cast but who had become such a big figure in the story of the *Street* and joined very early on in the programme's history, also left. In his case, the management were eventually left with no option but to sack him. Peter had been involved in a court case where certain charges were brought against him, but he was acquitted. Lots of people thought it was the court case that led to him leaving the *Street*, but that was not the case. It was in our contracts that we should get permission from Granada if we wanted to talk to the media. Peter talked to the press without getting permission and was warned about it. He did it a second time and received another warning, before doing it a third time and receiving a suspension. While he was on suspension he did it again, and the company really had no other option but to cancel his contract. It was sad, but at the same time he had been warned, and I don't feel that Granada was at all heavy handed in its approach. He knew the rules and chose to completely ignore them. It was sad that he should leave in those circumstances, because he had been such a big part of the programme since his character first hit the screens. Peter was a very good actor and an intelligent man, and he made Len into one of the programme's big characters for more than 20 years. When he was written out of the show they killed him off in a car crash, leaving Rita as his grieving widow, but she finds out at his funeral that in true Len fashion he'd been seeing another woman.

If Len had been a big character, then so too had the woman

who was always part of his life in one way or another during the time he was in the show, with their sometimes on, sometimes off romance. In 1983 Pat Phoenix announced that she was going to be leaving the show, and at the beginning of the next year the episode in which she made her last appearance was shown. After the run-in I'd had with her in those early days when we hadn't spoken for two years, I got on well with Pat. She was very childlike in many ways, and I mean that in the nicest sense: she loved life and she enjoyed being who she was. She also became quite interested in spiritual matters for a time, and she would come to see me and have little chats and discussions, which I very much enjoyed.

After those two years we got on fine, and I think everyone knew that her decision to go would be a big loss. Pat brought a lot to her role as Elsie, and her character had a huge impact, particularly in those very early days. Her decision to leave surprised the public, but she wanted to pursue other work away from the *Street*, and the storyline created for her exit involved Elsie going off to live with old flame Bill Gregory at his wine bar in Portugal. I think everyone was shocked and saddened three years later to learn Pat had been diagnosed with lung cancer, and when she died, in 1986, there was a huge turnout at Manchester Cathedral, which included her husband, Tony Booth, together with his daughter Cherie and her husband, Tony Blair.

By the time 1984 came around, I found myself the only surviving member of that group of actors who first appeared on the programme in 1960. I didn't really think much of it at the time, but now it's strange to think that all of those characters disappeared from the screens. Equally, it emphasised the strength of the show, because the actors who came in to play new characters did such a good job, allowing the programme to evolve and change, but at the same time retain all the essential qualities that had made it popular in the first place.

One of the things that seemed to be a pretty regular occurrence for everyone on the show around that time was the appearance of one of the cast as the subject of *This is Your Life*; in fact, we got to know the presenter of the show, Eamonn Andrews, quite well because of it! I can't quite remember which one of us was the first to appear on the programme, but they pretty much started going through the cast one by one. I remember dear old Jack Howarth saying that he didn't want to be the subject, because I think he was worried about how tearful he would become as people trooped on to say nice things about him. It was actually very funny when they did get him, because when he saw Eamonn coming, he went and hid behind one of the sets. We eventually managed to coax him out, and in the end I think he enjoyed the whole experience.

It didn't take much working out that sooner or later they would get around to me, if for no other reason than the fact that I had been in the show from the start and it seemed as though most of the others had already been done. At the time, of course, I wasn't aware of any moves being made to have me on the show, but I later found out that shortly before Edwina died, the producers of *This is Your Life* had been speaking to Sara in an attempt to arrange a show with me as the subject.

It was all pretty straightforward for them, having to deal with Sara, because she handled all my business affairs, so there were none of the cloak-and-dagger scenarios that sometimes occurred, with either a husband or wife having to concoct elaborate stories in order to keep their spouse in the dark about the show. It was all set to go ahead, but, of course, with the sudden death of Edwina, they postponed the programme. Sara assumed that would be it, but instead they asked whether they could go ahead some time later and a date was set for 1985.

There was a sort of drill involved whenever someone from the *Street* was on the programme, because they would be invited down to London on the pretence of something or other, and then the rest of us would be herded up, put on a train, taken to Thames Television studios in the capital and then hidden away until the appropriate time, when we would all walk on and greet whichever colleague happened to be the subject of the show. We would stay overnight in London and then travel back to Manchester on the train, ready to start work that day. However, the scenario was a bit different when they did me, and I have to admit that I really was taken by surprise.

I always thought I would have an idea if it was going to be

me, because of the routine I've described, but they changed their tactics. Instead of being asked to go to London, for some reason or other I was told that Thames were doing a telethon, and they needed a group of us from the *Street* to go on and say a few nice words and wish the event well. All I had to do was wait around until five o'clock one Wednesday afternoon and record the piece to camera at Granada Studios. So when rehearsals finished that day, I decided that it wasn't worth going home and instead hung around the studios, which I later learned really panicked some people, because they were busy preparing everything for the show that night, which, for once, was going to be done from Granada. I actually had to spin the time out and went for a cup of tea before sitting in my car and listening to the radio. Finally five o'clock arrived and I went inside to discover everyone else looking very smart, something I couldn't quite understand, because I was wearing a jumper and trousers. They assured me I looked fine and that we should just get on and record the piece we were supposed to be doing for the telethon. So we went to the back of one of the buildings to do our message, and just as I began to talk I heard somebody giggle. I looked up and saw Eamonn Andrews wearing an Arab headdress and leading a camel, while at the same time clutching the famous red *This is Your Life* book. He was dressed like that to remind me of my time in the army, and it was a truly unexpected moment for me. The shot at the start of the programme when the subject is confronted by Eamonn used to be one of the most popular of the show, and I can tell you that although I had half expected it would be me one day, for the reasons I have described, he really did take me by surprise. After the initial surprise introduction there was time for me to make use of the change of clothes Sara had brought for me, and then about an hour later I was onstage greeting a stream of people they had assembled from friends and family as they came on and said some very nice things, which was the format of the show. I enjoyed the experience of being on the show and receiving the famous red book, although it wasn't the one presented to you at the end of the show by Eamonn Andrews. You were sent a copy of the book a few weeks after doing the show, and it was more like a photo album, which was very nice and a lovely souvenir of a very enjoyable evening.

In 1985, much was made of the fact that *Coronation Street* was going to get a rival on the BBC in the shape of a programme called *EastEnders*. It was great for the press and the media in general, because they were able to start speculating about what this might mean for the *Street*. To all of us as actors, it really meant very little. We'd already been going for 25 years, and we all knew that we had our jobs to do. There was certainly no feeling that we were in competition, and that is still the case today. It didn't really affect us and would only have become a problem had there been a huge dip in our ratings, but that didn't happen, and it hasn't ever happened during the 25 years since *EastEnders* first made its debut.

I think *EastEnders* is a very good show, beautifully acted and beautifully written, but it's different to *Coronation Street*. It's set in a big city and in a part of London that has certain characteristics; we're essentially a little north-west backwater. That's how we started, and although the *Street* has moved on and evolved, there are certain characteristics and attitudes that will remain part of what we are and what we're about. The same is true of *EastEnders*. I jokingly used to say that if you got knocked down by a car in *EastEnders* someone would come along and steal your wallet, but if you got knocked down in *Coronation Street* someone would make you a nice cup of tea. I was just trying to say that although both shows are soaps, as we are now called, there is a lot of difference between the two, and that's a good thing. I think *EastEnders* is great and they do it very well. There's no actual rivalry, even though I know it's built up by the papers when there are the various soap awards. When we do meet, we all chat to each other and I think there is a mutual respect, because we're all actors trying to do our own work. In reality, the only rivals we have are whatever they put on at the same time as *Coronation Street* on other channels. There are an awful lot of soaps these days, but I think there is room for all of them, and as I have already mentioned it is the overall ratings that matter. There are other shows during the course of a year that might pull in huge audience figures, but they are only on our screens for a run of six or eight weeks. The *Street* is there five times a week, all year round, and if we maintain good ratings throughout a twelve-month period then it shows the programme is doing all right and is in a healthy state.

The 1980s saw a lot of changes in the *Street*, with many of the characters who had been in it from the '60s going and a whole new group of actors being introduced, while the decade ended with us moving to three episodes a week in 1989, heralding a very different era. We were about to celebrate our 30th anniversary as a programme, and I, of course, had been in it from the start. There was a lot of media interest in the fact that we had been around for so long, and I think we were all rightly proud of what had been achieved. So 1990 should have been a date I could look back on with great pleasure, but instead it turned out to be a year in which began a series of events that would go on to have nightmarish consequences for me.

13

SOME YOU WIN
AND SOME YOU LOSE

In 1990, *The Sun* newspaper published an article about me that I felt was libellous. I sued them and won my case, but lost close to £1 million in the process, and as a result became bankrupt and had to be hospitalised with an ulcer. These are the bare facts of a horrendous experience that began the year *Coronation Street* and I celebrated our 30th anniversary.

By this time the *Street*, just like all the other soaps, was big news amongst the tabloid newspapers. The programmes had become hugely popular, and with them so had the actors who played in them, and there seemed to be a great appetite for knowing more and more about them, as well as for any gossip associated with the shows. In the lead-up to the date of the anniversary, *The Sun* decided it was going to publish a series of features by a journalist called Ken Irwin. The articles were supposed to 'celebrate' the *Street*, but the first one that was published was about Julie Goodyear, who had become so popular since joining as Bet Lynch. However, the feature turned out to be quite nasty, and as I was due to be the subject of the next day's piece I grew a little concerned and bought a copy the following morning to see what had been written. When I read it I was both annoyed and devastated by what Ken Irwin had put in the piece. First let me say that I had not given him an interview and what was written seemed to be cobbled together. The tone was pretty unpleasant, and in the article he claimed that I was hated by the cast, had come close to being sacked more than any other actor in the show, that I was a joke for the writers and was carried by other members of the cast, giving as an example the famous Ken, Deirdre and Mike storyline. He also raked over some of the things I had got up to in the 1960s, which I did not dispute, but which were still highly embarrassing and had happened more than 20 years before. There was also the claim that I was as boring and smug as Ken Barlow. The 'boring Ken' line had come about during that heated scene with Deirdre and the tag had stuck with Ken, but it was the first time the label had been given to me as well.

I knew *The Sun* had a huge readership, and it was a horrible feeling to think that all over the country that morning there would be people picking up that paper and believing everything that was in the article. That year had seen the opening of the Studio One complex, which gave the programme a dedicated facility, including our own dressing-rooms, so when I reached the studio on the morning that article was published, I headed straight for my dressing-room. I knew that none of my colleagues actually did hate me, and, in fact, they would have been tremendously sympathetic. It was just that I couldn't face the prospect of seeing anyone, because I felt quite humiliated by the whole tone of the piece. I went to see the company secretary of Granada, Alistair Mutch, and he agreed the article was pretty horrendous and then suggested that I have a word with the lawyers used by the company, Goodman & Co. Once they had seen the piece, I spoke to them to see what they thought of it. They agreed that it was defamatory and that I could probably bring a libel case, but at the same time they recommended that I didn't do so, explaining that you were likely to suffer even more indignities during the course of such a case, it could attract adverse publicity and the fact that it would be a trial by jury meant that the outcome could always be uncertain and you could never be totally sure about winning your case.

Granada had a policy of not backing anyone in a libel case, and I think that was perfectly understandable, so it meant that if I was determined to go ahead with an action, I would be doing it on my own. The lawyer also explained that most cases never went to court because either the costs were too high, or the plaintiff was just too concerned about the sort of ordeal they would face in order to try to get justice. It was pretty depressing to hear all of this, but I felt so strongly about what had happened that I decided to go ahead anyway, determined to try to make sure that people couldn't get away with things like this. What had been written about me was untrue, and it was that that made me very annoyed. Looking back now I can clearly see that it was my pride and ego that were damaged, and I reacted in a certain way to that, which was a very dangerous thing.

I pressed ahead with my intention to bring an action and went to consult the country's leading libel lawyer, Peter Carter-Ruck, at his offices in London. What he told me gave me encouragement to go ahead with things, because he said that in his opinion I had a very good case that he thought had an 80 per cent chance of success, the highest percentage he gave to any libel action. It was what I wanted to hear, but once again, in hindsight, I know that although I was getting advice from an expert libel lawyer, the decision to go ahead with all of this was ultimately mine. I was so determined to right what I saw as a wrong, and in order to do that I believed I needed to go to court and win the case. I was very unhappy at the thought of some newspapers being able to write pretty much whatever they wanted about an individual, whether it was true or not. I was equally upset by the fact that it seemed the odds were so heavily stacked in favour of the newspaper, because the cost of a case and all the adverse publicity that might surround it proved to be too much of a deterrent to potential plaintiffs.

What I realise now is that I was not doing the right thing: it was my ego speaking. The whole case and my decision to go ahead with it was my last big ego trip. These days I hope that my ego is very much in second place, and I now try to obey my higher spiritual self. I'm convinced that pride was probably the ultimate motivation for what I did, and I ended up learning a great lesson from all of it, despite the fact that it turned out to be such a terrible time for me.

After meeting Peter Carter-Ruck, a very strange thing happened when I went to catch my train back to Manchester from Euston

Station. As I stood waiting for the gates to the platform to open, I heard a voice behind me say, 'Hello.' I turned around to see Ken Irwin standing there. It was incredible; I'd just gone to see the top libel lawyer in the country about taking action against the man who was now standing behind me in the queue, and here he was trying to make small talk. Looking back now it seems an amazing coincidence; it was almost as though I was being given a nudge to think again about going into the action I had decided on, but if it was, the meeting did nothing to deter me, and instead I told him how absolutely horrified I'd been by the article, and that I intended taking action.

My lawyers wrote to Kelvin MacKenzie, the editor of *The Sun* at that time, offering him the chance to apologise and pay our costs, but there was no reply. There was an awful lot of preparation to be done in the weeks and months that led up to the date of the trial, which was finally set for the end of October 1991, almost a year after the original article had been published.

In September *The Sun* paid £25,000 into court as part of a procedure that, up to that point, I was completely unaware of, so I asked what it meant. I was told that if I took the money that, in effect, would be an end to the whole thing. The defence would make an apology to me, the case would end there and I would get my costs. I was also told that having paid the money in, if I then decided to go ahead with the action and was awarded damages above £25,000, that would be OK, but if the verdict was that I should get that same figure or below, I would then have to pay both sides' costs from the time that money had been paid into court. This was yet another occasion where I could have stood back and thought long and hard before going on. It was another chance to stop and realise exactly what I was getting into, and the warning bells should have sounded a lot longer and more clearly than they did. Instead, I asked Peter Carter-Ruck what he thought and he said the sum wasn't good enough, so we carried on with the preparations for the case.

A month later *The Sun* paid another £25,000 into court, making a total of £50,000. Although this was more substantial than their first offer, I was advised that the odds of me winning were still in my favour, and the money paid in by *The Sun* was turned down. Once you start a legal action you are very much in the hands of your lawyers for the precise reason you have gone to them in the first place: namely the law is their profession and you regard them as experts. On the Friday before the case began, I had a meeting to discuss the offer and the strength of the case we had. The general feeling was that we should go on with it.

We were due to start the case on a Monday, but another case overran and that meant we couldn't begin until the Tuesday. My colleagues at Granada were wonderful and they were prepared to be called as witnesses: these included Johnny Briggs, Amanda Barrie, Michael Le Vell, Betty Driver and Bill Waddington, and also producer Mervyn Watson, writer Tom Elliott and director Brian Mills. It meant there was going to be some disruption to the schedules, but everyone was very supportive and happy to do whatever they could. Sara and I stayed at the Waldorf Hotel in the Strand, which was very near to the High Court, where the case was going to be heard, but as we quickly found out there was huge media interest and it meant that we had to take a taxi the few hundred yards, because the whole thing became such a scrum, with reporters and photographers vying to get into the best positions as we arrived.

I have to say that although I thought I was prepared for the events that unfolded in the days ahead, I very clearly wasn't. It had a huge impact on me, and I never realised just how big a story it would be. We seemed to be on the front pages of the papers throughout the trial, and there was always a posse of press people outside the court when we arrived each morning and then when we left each evening. We basically just used to go back to our hotel and lock ourselves away, but there was no escaping, because we were on the news programmes as well if we watched television.

On the first day in court, my *Coronation Street* colleagues were called and were wonderful. There was even a light-hearted moment in proceedings when Amanda Barrie tried to explain that her character, Alma, had had an affair with Ken. The judge was slightly bemused by all of this and at one point seemed to think that Amanda was having some sort of affair, but she quickly put him right.

I had to take the stand myself on the afternoon of the first day and then again the following morning, when reference was made to some of my activities during the 1960s. I wasn't even complaining about that part of the story, and as I have already mentioned, I am not proud of the way I behaved, but although the defence didn't actually pursue that line of questioning, they did ask that the court read that section of the piece. When the ordeal of having to be in the witness box was over I felt very distressed by the whole thing, and the worst part was that although I was the person making the complaint, I came away feeling as if it was me on trial.

I had to go back to Manchester that night to do a couple of scenes for the *Street*, which meant Sara had to face the hordes on her own the next morning, and the taxi driver she had refused to pull up at the steps of the High Court, so she had to run the gauntlet on foot with all of the press chasing after her. It was the only bad experience we had with taxis in London during the course of the case, because all the others we came into contact with were very supportive, even to the point of one of them shouting out, 'Good luck, Ken,' one day. As for Sara, she was magnificent. She was incredibly supportive and protective. Although the whole thing was certainly something we could have done without, she was determined not to be a shrinking violet in the face of all the publicity and public interest in the case. Each morning she strode proudly into court wearing a different outfit, and, in fact, one of the newspapers actually did a feature at the end of the week with pictures of her and pointing out that she wore a different outfit from Jaeger each day! It was one of the more humorous moments to come out of our time in London, but for the most part it was a very intense and draining experience for me and, I'm sure, for her, although she never once let me see that was the case and was like a lioness at my side as she realised the effect it was having on me.

The incident on the Wednesday in court when the whole '60s thing was brought up again proved to be just what the tabloids wanted, and it was all over the papers the next day. As the week drew to a close, the pressure was terrible and I found my pulse rate soaring, and it was to remain high for weeks after the trial.

Ken Irwin went into the witness box on the Friday and as part of his evidence said that I had given him an interview, but I simply could not remember this having taken place. Eventually he produced a transcript and also a cassette tape, which had me talking on it. I still couldn't remember having been interviewed by him, but then I realised what had happened.

As I have mentioned, as well as being our 30th anniversary, 1990 also saw the opening of the Studio One complex at Granada, which was a complex built especially for *Coronation Street*. The press were invited to the opening that day and there had been a question-and-answer session, and I was there to represent the cast. At one point I went off to the buffet and got some food before wandering around the room to talk to various people. One of them happened to be Ken Irwin, and we chatted as I was eating. I had no idea at the time, but he must have had a tape recorder hidden, and there was no way the conversation we had was an official interview. This was backed up by our press officer, who said that they would have had to have given permission for any kind of official interview. The Friday ended with the barristers summing up, but there wasn't time for the judge to sum up and give his directions to the jury, so the case was adjourned until the following Monday morning.

It meant that Sara and I went back to our hotel and stayed there over the weekend, not really bothering to go out, because there were so many photographers hanging around the place. It wasn't very pleasant, and just to add to the tense atmosphere, the Sunday newspapers really went to town on me and what had been happening. The Monday morning arrived and we trooped off to court once more, and there seemed to be even more attention, probably because they knew there was likely to be a verdict. The judge, Chief Justice Waterhouse, summed up the case and went through it all, and when he mentioned damages he said that they should not be punitive.

The jury was out for just under two hours and, if I'm honest, by that time I just wanted to get out of the High Court, leave our hotel and London behind and get back to some kind of normality. What I was very sure of was the fact that the whole thing had been much more of an ordeal than I could ever have imagined. I felt worn out and drained by the whole experience, but when the jury returned and the foreman said they had found in my favour, a wave of relief rushed through me. For a few moments I was able to enjoy the fact that I had won – it was a lovely feeling, the allegations that had been written about me were false and I had been libelled – but then came the sting in the tail. When the foreman was asked what damages the jury had awarded, the answer stunned me . . .

'Fifty thousand pounds,' he said.

It was absolutely amazing: that was the exact amount *The Sun* had paid into court, which in turn meant that I was now liable for all the costs. It was absolutely crushing, and it set in motion a series of events that would leave me in financial ruin. Initially what happened was that my counsel asked for me to be awarded costs even though the damages awarded matched the exact amount that had been paid into court by *The Sun*. The judge agreed and awarded me costs, but even this part of it had a twist, because the very next day many of the papers portrayed me as being out for all I could get. The whole thing was a nightmare, and rather than stopping there it seemed to just keep getting worse. The thing that got us off the front pages after the court case was the death of the media tycoon Robert Maxwell. Suddenly all the attention switched to him, and I had some understanding of how some politicians feel when they are at the centre of a storm and all the newspapers are focusing on them and then suddenly another big story breaks. You are no longer front-page news, and I have to admit that there was a sense of relief that the spotlight was no longer on me.

The Sun appealed the decision, but that appeal wasn't heard until 1992, a year after the original trial, and by that time I had developed an ulcer and had to be taken to hospital. The stress was intense and overwhelming, and it began to affect me physically, but at the same time I knew I had to carry on with my work and make sure that whatever might have been going on in my private life, it didn't start to have an impact on what I was doing as an actor on *Coronation Street*. Everyone on the *Street* was wonderful. The great thing was that nobody was judgemental, and that is still the case today; we are all very protective of each other. Everyone connected with the programme was, and is, very caring. I remember coming back after the trial and trying to thank everybody in the Green Room; I was shaking and on the verge of tears the whole time. I felt emotionally drained by the whole experience of the court case, and I was also overwhelmed at how kind and thoughtful all my colleagues had been throughout. I think I was physically on the verge of a breakdown, but I managed not to have one and kept working, which I'm sure helped me.

When the appeal was heard the panel decided that because the amount paid into court by *The Sun* had been the same as the amount awarded in damages, I should pay the costs. It was the law, and I was then liable to pay the original costs and the costs of the appeal as well. I was looking at having to pay something approaching £1 million, which was a financially ruinous situation for me.

The ulcer was only one of the consequences of what happened; I also used to wake up with the sweats, and I was worried sick about losing everything I'd worked for all my life: the house, not being able to pay for the kids' education, both things I was desperate to maintain. I had an overwhelming feeling of just not being in control. There was a creeping inevitability about all that was going on, and there seemed little I could do. Eventually I had to accept that bankruptcy was the only real option: there was no way out. I know that to many people it might not seem such an awful thing, given the circumstances of what brought me to it, but for people of my generation I think there is a certain stigma attached to the whole idea. In fact, once it was done it was OK. It was a chance to move on and rebuild. It wasn't quite the awful thing I thought it was going to be, and in the end it didn't affect our lifestyle at all. I kept thinking, 'When do I sit down with my plate and spoon, with all my furniture gone?', but it didn't happen. I won't say that it was a nice thing, and I certainly don't want to sound complacent or dismissive about the situation I found myself in, but it did not affect our lifestyle as a family.

I won't try to pretend I enjoyed the situation: it was awful, and some of the personal things were a bit unpleasant. I couldn't have any bank accounts, but I didn't want any. Sara paid all the bills, but she did all that sort of thing anyway. In many ways I was quite relieved to have to hand that sort of thing over, so she just gave me my pocket money and we got on with our lives. All of the savings went, and there were horrible moments when debt-collecting people were involved, which was pretty unpleasant, but we got through it. We went out for the same number of meals, bought the same amount of clothes and were still able to pay for the children's education. We also had the same house and the same cars. The cost financially was enormous, but in hindsight it was also a chance to start again.

Sara was absolutely magnificent throughout and so strong. In many ways that was her great moment; she was brilliant. She got us through the court case and then the aftermath. She certainly wouldn't stand any nonsense from anyone, and because she was so strong it certainly helped me. I was a quivering mess at times: I was upset, worried sick about the future and how we were going to pay for anything. I was just managing to focus on my work. Sara was the power of the family; she kept us all going. She was superb, and just as we had when Edwina died, we talked to each other a lot. Relationships are tested in moments like those we experienced, particularly where money is concerned, and we came through it together.

I would say to anyone, don't go to the law unless you really have to. My pride was injured by what had been written about me, and I allowed my ego to take over and take control. I could have gone to the Press Council, although they didn't really have any teeth in terms of what they could do, and there was also the other, obvious option of simply doing nothing. If I had done that I suspect the whole thing would have gone away and been forgotten in a couple of days, but instead, the fact that I went to court gave the situation fresh impetus. I was stubborn and wanted some form of justice, because I thought I had been wronged. Although that was true, I eventually ended up paying a heavy price for choosing the route I did in order to resolve the situation.

What I would say is that once I had gone to see the lawyers and taken the decision to use the courts, it became very difficult to pull back from what was happening. In a very short space of time I found that I had paid out thousands of pounds as the case was built and various lawyers were engaged to represent me. These people are experts in the law, and you feel very much as though you are in their hands. You write a cheque for £4,000 and then another for a few thousand pounds more, and pretty soon you are into the thing in a big way. You feel as though, having started the legal process, there is no way back. Do you effectively throw away the substantial amount of money you have already paid out, or do you go for it? Ultimately, of course, the decision is yours, but when you have people you regard as experts saying that you have a big case, you get caught in this net and you're not a free-thinking individual in the end. So you very quickly get caught up in this, and then you hear things that you haven't heard before, like the business with the defence lodging money with the court and what all of that could mean. I was also hit with a sort of 'customer care and attention' bill, which was something above the legal costs of the actual case. It was kind of like a builder building a house for £100,000 for you, and then saying he was going to charge another £100,000 for looking after you while he was building the house! The costs just seemed to go on and on; it was terrifying.

One of the great things that did help me during all of this time was the *Street*. It still had to be done, whatever I was feeling. I had to go into work, and I made myself do it. In a way it was a kind of saving grace, because it took me away from what was happening in my private life. It was something I could get hold of and become engrossed in, instead of sitting at home and worrying about all the things that had happened, and were still happening, because the repercussions went on for a long time. I had something to get on with, it was my work, and I know I was very fortunate to have it.

The management at *Coronation Street* were wonderful, and going into the studios was a sort of relief at the time; it really helped me through. I knew that once I came through the gates I was protected, and that has always been true for anyone who works on the programme. Even today, if you arrive at the gates and there are three or four photographers with long lenses waiting around, and you know that something might have happened to one of the cast and the press are interested, your immediate instinct is to get in and help them. We'll all tell the person concerned, 'We're with you, if there's anything we can do, just let us know.' It's almost an unspoken thing, but everyone knows it's there, and it makes you feel very comfortable and at home. If you want a shoulder to cry on, there are two or three of those around, and the management are always very caring as well.

From a purely professional point of view, no producer wants to have an actor working on the show who is a quaking mess, or on the point of a nervous breakdown, but the wonderful thing is that it's much more than just being professional. The producer and all the management people, as well as my acting colleagues, were just so nice and caring towards me, and that is the same for anyone else as well. If you have a problem, you can always go to see someone and you will be helped. I have to say that it's probably not in my nature to ask for help; I think it's something to do with my generation. I never want to feel as though I'm imposing my own problems on other people, and it's probably something that will always stay with me.

When I refer back to that time, there's a lot to reflect on. People have said to me, 'You were right,' but I wasn't. It was right in the sense that I think it was part of my destiny: it was planned and it was something I had to go through. It was a big teaching point for me, and a major test. There were all sorts of wrong bits of thinking in there when I made the decision to go to lawyers with regard to what had been written about me. It's so easy to kid yourself that you're doing the right thing, but having had time to reflect and think about all that went on in my life then, I can see the lessons I had to learn. By the time all of this happened I had been on my spiritual path for about 20 years, and I have already mentioned that it is a self-evolving process: it's ongoing, and you are learning all the time. Despite all that had happened, it didn't affect my spiritual beliefs; they were always there. I began to look at what had happened with the court case and also all that had gone on after it.

Life is about learning, and you learn more from the big things. I just had a feeling all the way through that there seemed to be a momentum to it all. I know now it was primarily about my pride and ego, but it was something I was meant to go through, and hopefully I've learned pretty well everything I was supposed to learn from it. Looking back, I think my instinct told me from the start that it was going to be bad, but I just got sucked into it. My spiritual side remained throughout it all, but it did become clouded. You start to wonder where it went wrong, but then come to the understanding that there's a reason for everything. Life won't try to give you a lesson unless you are going to be able to understand it, and I was able to understand something from all that had gone on.

Externally my life stayed the same, but what I needed to do was to rebuild things financially. As actors we don't get the same sort of money that big celebrities or singing stars earn, but we do get well paid, and it is a regular income from which I've been able to slowly rebuild. I'm quite convinced that it was part of my destiny to go through what I did, and the major impact was on me, from which I was given a lesson. There are no accidents in life. If you think you've been unfairly treated, just have a good old look at it and what it has meant to you. See what you have learned from the experience, because it will be a lesson and there will be a reason.

Since all of this happened, I have moved on in a practical sense but also with a better understanding. I hope that my ego is very much in second place now, because it's extremely liberating when you start to listen to your higher spiritual self.

14

BOXING DAY BLUES

In an ironic twist during 1992, at the time when the financial implications of my libel case were beginning to take hold, I found myself taking part in a storyline that had Ken Barlow being sued for slander by Mike Baldwin. Talk about art mirroring life! Of course, the other great irony was the fact that for quite a long time Ken himself was working as a journalist in his capacity as editor of the *Recorder*.

It was a shame that 1990 itself has such an unhappy memory attached to it, because of the publication of that *Sun* article, but away from my personal troubles, the *Street* carried on as it always has done, continuing to pull in great ratings and remaining one of the most popular programmes with the British public. Studio One had 30 dressing-rooms, which we could use as our own little retreat. I was given dressing-room one, which I still have to this day, and I have to say that I enjoy being able to use it and having a base for all of my things. It's not big, but it is perfectly fine for my needs, and I can go there to learn lines, read, answer mail or even have a snooze if I want to. Over the years I've personalised it with various bits and pieces, books and pictures. It's a nice, cosy little place, and I enjoy having it.

In the year we celebrated our 30th anniversary, we had a visit from Prime Minister Margaret Thatcher, who toured the site. I was asked to show her the *Street* set and we walked down to the Rovers together, where the rest of the cast were waiting. I think I was probably asked to show her around because of the fact that they knew I'd met her before and was also a Conservative supporter. A lot of people had been surprised by that fact when it emerged in 1983, probably for two main reasons. The first was that a lot of actors and people in the public eye prefer not to talk about their own politics for fear of isolating a part of their audience, and the second was because Ken Barlow was very much a socialist during the '60s and had always been portrayed as a left-leaning character when it came to his political views. It was a classic case of people associating the character with the actor who plays him, and it was understandable to some extent, but it seemed silly to be worried about letting people know exactly what I thought, and I've always felt you should be honest and straightforward about things like that. I did some appearances supporting various local prospective Conservative MPs during the run-up to the election that year, and also met Margaret Thatcher at a rally in Chester. Some time later Sara and I were invited to Downing Street and we were shown around by Mrs Thatcher herself, a tour that included a visit to the cabinet room as she chatted about some of the very difficult decisions she had made there during the Falklands conflict, which, at the time, hadn't long ended. We were lucky enough to be invited back a year later and once again had a fascinating and enjoyable evening with her. I was also fortunate enough to meet her successor, John Major, and found him to be a very likeable man. In 1992 we received an invitation to have lunch with him at Chequers, and the first thing he asked me was how I was after being hospitalised with the ulcer I had developed during all the stress of the libel case. He was genuinely concerned, and his wife, Norma, happened to be a big fan of the *Street*, so we chatted about the programme with her.

I liked both Margaret Thatcher and John Major, and I think that any prime minister, no matter what their political persuasion might be, has an incredibly hard job, and it's something I certainly would not want to have to do. From a personal point of view, it was very nice to be invited to places like Downing Street and Chequers and to get the opportunity to meet different prime ministers. Sara and I were also invited to Downing Street in more recent years in connection with some charity work we were involved in when Tony Blair was prime minister, and it just so happened that the day we went there was my birthday. I walked into one room, and there was Cherie Blair with a lovely chocolate cake for me and everyone sang 'Happy Birthday'. It was all very nice and, of course, she and Tony Blair knew I was of a different political persuasion, but they couldn't have been more kind. Of course, her own father, Tony Booth, had not only married Pat Phoenix, he had also appeared in the *Street*.

As I mentioned earlier, Ken did not end the 1980s or start the 1990s in the nicest of ways. Having been thrown out by Deirdre and then split up with Wendy Crozier, he was in a pretty bad state following that bust-up with Mike Baldwin in the Rovers. Once he had split from Wendy he knew he had made a terrible mistake in leaving Deirdre and messing up their marriage, but even when he begged to be taken back the answer was no. He became quite desperate in many ways and began to almost stalk Deirdre. She, on the other hand, was getting on with her life and even found herself another man in the form of amusement-arcade owner Phil Jennings. He was not the sort of man who Ken was going to like, especially as he was having an affair with his estranged wife. It got to a point in the storyline where Deirdre actually took out an injunction on Ken, while Phil Jennings decided to use threats against him in an effort to make sure he didn't pester Deirdre. By the time the year drew to a close, everything was set for what became something of a Barlow tradition over the years, namely a miserable Christmas, Boxing Day and New Year.

I used to joke that it always seemed to be the job of Ken to cheer the nation up by showing how miserable the holiday season was going to be for the Barlow family in one form or another, and New Year's Eve 1990 was a classic in that tradition. Ken was hoping that Deirdre would spend it with him and Tracy, but that didn't happen. Instead, Deirdre went off to Paris with Phil Jennings, and Ken ended up having a blazing row with Tracy. It was truly miserable for him and it produced a sad moment, which was great for me to have to play. As Ken sat at a table all alone, the realisation of what a mess he had made of his life began to dawn on him. He began to drink whisky and swallow some pills, feeling very emotional and sorry for himself. He tried to commit suicide, but was stopped when Bet Lynch walked in and began to talk some sense into him. It was a nice scene to play as an actor, and there were several more very good dramatic moments in Ken's life that seemed to pop up over the festive season.

A year before, there had been the very dramatic and emotional storyline of Deirdre confronting Ken just before Christmas and asking him whether he was having an affair with Wendy Crozier. Following the scene I described earlier, when Ken confessed he was and there were tears shed, he then decided that for the sake of Tracy the three of them should try to have a normal Christmas together. Of course, the whole idea made for some great television, and we got very good ratings for the Christmas edition of the show. The atmosphere in the Barlow household was tense to say the least, and both Anne and I felt the tension of the scenes we played as we tried to make out it was all 'happy families', even though Ken was having an affair and had given no indication to Deirdre that he was about to end it and come back to her.

Apart from the dreadful atmosphere of that year and the suicide attempt by Ken 12 months later, there have been other problems for him or members of the Barlow clan during the Christmas holiday season over the years, including Deirdre being held captive; her mother, Blanche, helping to ignite family rows over the Christmas dinner table; and Tracy threatening to kill someone. The unhappy family bit extended to Christmas 2009, with Ken getting angry with George Wilson after he offered alcoholic Peter a glass of wine, prompting Deirdre to congratulate him for ruining Christmas, as the Barlows looked forward to another miserable Boxing Day.

Scenes like that only serve to emphasise how dysfunctional all the various strands of the Barlow clan are. I've been asked what I think of the way Ken's relationships and family have turned out, and I have to say that I'm delighted. The fact that Ken has been married three times and had so many girlfriends, as well as having a son who is a bigamist and an alcoholic, an adopted daughter who is a murderer and other illegitimate offspring too, is absolutely wonderful if you are an actor in such a long-running show. The possibilities are endless, and one of the great things about the *Street* is that because it has been going for more than fifty years, it is able to draw on its own history for storylines. It's a great gift, and one the producers and writers have used to such good effect over the years.

Some people have quite literally grown up as part of *Coronation Street*. They have come into the show as youngsters and are now fully grown adults, with people like Simon Gregson, who plays Steve McDonald, Jack P. Shepherd, who plays David Platt, and Helen Flanagan, who plays Rosie Webster, developing from children or young teenagers into adults in front of millions of viewers. I think it's a real strength of the *Street* that they have come right through and become such a part of the fabric of the programme, and it is wonderful to see what fine actors they have become.

On the face of it, Ken probably isn't the sort of person you might have expected to be at the centre of such a dysfunctional family, but I think it is as a result of the way the programme has always been allowed to grow in a very natural way. A character does something, and whatever that is leads on to the possibility of another storyline being created, which in turn leads on to something else. It means the show has a very natural flow to it, and hopefully the viewer feels that nothing has been forced upon them. They can see where it all comes from and how certain characters have reacted to certain situations. Of course, it is a drama, and therefore the storylines have to have an impact and contain the sort of material that will engage and entertain the people watching the programme. Every so often the producer and writers might decide to turn a character on his head and see what comes out of it. It's doing the unexpected and giving a new dimension, which helps to add to the freshness of the programme for both the viewer and the actors who work on it.

Having had such a torrid time of it during 1990, I knew it would be interesting to see where the writers would take Ken's character. After the split from Deirdre, it meant that there were more possibilities open to them when it came to storylines for Ken. One thing was for sure: with his track record in the previous ten years, it seemed likely that three major themes would play strongly in whatever was written for him. The first was Deirdre, the second was Mike Baldwin and the third was the opportunity for him to forge relationships with other women. All three of these themes formed the core of what was to come in the next few years, and I have to say that I got some very enjoyable storylines, including a really unexpected one when Ken became a father once again.

The always-difficult relationship between Ken and Mike Baldwin took another twist, and once again women were involved, and it gave me the chance to play some scenes with the lovely Amanda Barrie. She was a wonderful actress and a really fun person to be around. She'd done some great work on stage and in films before coming into the *Street* in the early 1980s to play the character of Alma Sedgewick.

Towards the end of the decade Baldwin started to make a play for Alma, but as usual for him, he didn't exactly treat her well. As far as Alma was concerned, she knew Baldwin wasn't the nicest of men, but at the same time there was a sort of fatal attraction that she wasn't ever able to resist. As part of their on-off relationship, the writers decided it would be a good idea to introduce Ken into the equation. I thought it worked well, with her and Ken coming together as two pretty lonely people in need of some comfort, having both ended relationships with the people each of them cared a lot for. In Ken's case it was Deirdre, and in Alma's it was Mike. It was the sort of storyline writers can play around with, because as well as the dramatic and emotional moments that can be thrown into the plot, there is also room for humour, and there was one particular scene set in the Rovers that was good fun to play in.

The idea was that I would be going out with Alma, while Mike Baldwin was there with Deirdre. The underlying dislike the two men had for each other meant that the viewer knew something was likely to happen, especially when Mike began to try to goad Ken into some sort of reaction. In the past the whole thing might have ended with punches being thrown, or at the very least a heated verbal confrontation, but instead it was Deirdre who got upset with what she clearly saw as Mike's childish behaviour in trying to bait Ken, and she walked out of the pub, leaving Baldwin looking shocked and confused as the smugness drained from him. Needless to say, Ken enjoyed the moment hugely. The cameras then cut to an outside shot where Mike and Deirdre's taxi was waiting to take them to a restaurant, but she told Mike she had no intention of going out any more after what she had just witnessed, and Ken delighted in asking a crestfallen Mike if he could have the cab, because Baldwin and Deirdre clearly wouldn't be using it that night. It was a great example of how both drama and humour can be drawn out of one situation, and it is something the *Street* has been able to do throughout its time on Britain's screens.

Amanda was always good to play alongside and had those beautiful big eyes, which she used to good effect in another scene we had together, as Alma pretty much asked Ken to go to bed with her. It was all done in a very matter-of-fact way, with her taking the lead as the two of them decided to spend the night together: a very different scenario to the old days, when anything concerning sex was done with more of a nudge and a wink, leaving the rest to the viewers' imaginations, but a show like *Coronation Street* has to move with the times or otherwise it will lose its way. Over the years all sorts of themes have been introduced into the show, which have kept it up to date with what is going on in the real world and the way people act. It would be ridiculous not to do this, but at the same time it has to happen at the right moment and in the right context. There's no use introducing something about sex for the sake of it, because it just wouldn't work.

With Mike Baldwin lurking in the background, it was always likely any long-term relationship between Ken and Alma would be difficult, and so it proved. In the best Baldwin tradition, he decided to make sure Ken was out of the way for Christmas by convincing Tracy she should try to get her mum and dad back together. Ken then decided to spend Christmas with Deirdre and Tracy, which, unbeknown to him, left the way clear for Mike to worm his way into the affections of Alma once more and the two of them ended up in bed together. There was a lovely line in all of this from Mike after Alma later realised just how cunning and underhand Baldwin had been.

'I am what I am, a devious bloke – I tell lies,' he admitted. It was all wonderfully Mike Baldwin and helped to sum up his character, but at the same time it was said with a kind of pride, because he clearly admired those facets. In fact, he probably saw them as qualities, but Ken would have been appalled by them. It was a great way of illustrating what he was about and why he and Ken were never going to see eye to eye. They were opposites in so many ways, and that's what made their relationship so good to watch.

Alma eventually decided to say yes to Mike's proposal of marriage, but even that storyline had a twist, because he told her she was going to be cited as co-respondent by Jackie Ingram, who had briefly been married to Mike. However, Mike claimed he had paid thousands of pounds to keep Alma's name out of the proceedings, and so Alma agreed to the wedding. On the day of the wedding Alma found out that Mike had lied to her about her part in his divorce, but she still went through with the marriage, and there was a touching scene that she played with Ken just before she was due to go off to the ceremony, which was lovely to do. That same year also saw Ken and Deirdre divorce, but the writers were clearly keen to leave the door ajar on their relationship. All the anger and hurt of the initial break-up had disappeared and they had become friends once more, but at the same time there was an underlying feeling that both wished they were still together, even though they had moved on to rebuild their own lives. There was a nice touch to the way the divorce was marked, because it happened with them both together as Deirdre was nursing Ken after he had hurt his back.

The tangled web of relationships that is good for any soap surfaced again with Ken's next girlfriend. By this time he was teaching English at Weatherfield Comprehensive, and one of the pupils there was a boy called Mark Redman. Ken began to date the boy's mother, Maggie, who owned a florist's shop. Everything went well between the pair, and even Deirdre seemed to approve of the new woman in Ken's life, but I somehow knew all would not be well, and sure enough I didn't have to wait long for a storyline to develop that would throw the whole relationship into turmoil.

It was wonderful stuff, because Deirdre recognised Maggie as being an ex-girlfriend of Mike's, and, of course, Mark is his son. The great thing about all of this was that Ken found out about it through Tracy, who had been told by Deirdre. He was naturally stunned, but there was also the realisation that, yet again, Mike Baldwin had intruded on his personal happiness. Once the name of Baldwin is mentioned to Ken, all logic and reason disappear out of his head. As a result of all of this, Anne and I had another one of our heated scenes as Ken confronted Deirdre about telling Tracy the truth concerning Mark Redman. I also had to do a tense and dramatic scene with Jill Kerman, who played Maggie Redman, and that allowed me to really let rip, not so much at her but at the way I felt about Mike Baldwin.

In fact, the scene was very clever in that sense, because although it started off with Ken shouting at Maggie about why she hadn't told him Mike was the real father of her son, it soon became clear that the whole thing was now about his hatred of Baldwin, and I had a great line in the heat of it all just to illustrate this point.

'Mike Baldwin is not just somebody I don't like,' he told Maggie as his face twitched with anger and frustration. 'About ten years ago, he tried to take Deirdre away from me. Six years ago, he married my daughter, Susan. I hate him. I've wanted to kill him!'

Once Mike found out about who Maggie had been seeing, he had no hesitation in letting her know what he believed to be some home truths about Ken and his relationship with her.

'There's only one reason that slimy toad's hanging around and it's nothing to do with your pretty face,' he told her. 'It's me he's trying to get at. If you weren't my child's mother, he wouldn't look at you twice.'

Mike got a slap from Maggie after that, but it was really the beginning of the end of her relationship with Ken, and yet again the Ken–Mike dislike and hatred of each other overrode all else that was going on, rearing its ugly head as it was always likely to do from time to time. I think fans of the *Street* came to love the fact that the two of them were always going to come into conflict, and it was a question of sitting back and seeing what the pair would get up to next. Not surprisingly, the relationship between Ken and Maggie didn't last too much longer. In the fallout, Tracy told Mark who his real father was, and Maggie, in turn, spelled out some home truths of her own, letting Tracy know about Deirdre's affair with Mike.

There is no way you can play a character for as long as I have and not have a great deal of affection for him. Ken's views and actions are certainly not mine, but they are his and I have to respect that. There's no doubt that in many ways playing a character in the *Street* means you kind of live in a parallel world. It may be fictional, but you know your character better than anyone, and it's down to the writers and you to give him the life he leads on-screen. I know when I step on-set I am doing a job of work and acting out the part, but playing a character for more than 50 years is not like being in a long-running play. Any part you have in a play stays the same throughout the length of its run in a theatre, while playing a character in a soap means that there are always fresh scenes and stories being created for you. I think the freshness and variety of the work I was involved in during that period of the 1990s certainly helped me to stay focused on my work and provided a very welcome distraction to some of the problems I was having following the court case.

I always feel I'm very lucky to have a job that has been satisfying and in which I can immerse myself. I've always loved acting, and I've found acting on *Coronation Street* both enjoyable and satisfying, and to have been able to do it for so long has been a real pleasure. The twists and turns of the show are what keep it popular, and it's also something the cast look forward to. When you get a script and you see what is planned for you, it's always exciting. If it's a really big story that the producer and the writers want you to carry, then they will often call you up to see them and talk the plan through. It's nice to carry major storylines, and I was pleased to get another one in the mid-1990s when Ken became a dad once more.

After splitting up with Maggie Redman, his next major love interest came from hairdresser Denise Osbourne. It probably wasn't the sort of relationship most people who watched the *Street* would have thought of at the time, but it's twists like that that can often work and then lead on to other storylines. The fact that the two of them started seeing each other was one thing, but then Denise informed Ken that she was pregnant and he was faced with a whole new scenario. He clearly enjoyed seeing Denise, but at the same time he didn't particularly like the idea of being tied to her, and the idea of a baby made it all very complicated. With his track record as a father, Ken was clearly carrying some guilt about the way he had parcelled the twins off to Scotland all those years ago instead of taking on the role of a father.

Despite the fact that he is a basically decent guy, there is no doubt that over the years Ken has been pretty selfish on occasions, and one of them was certainly the way he allowed Peter and Susan to be looked after by their grandparents after Val's death. In truth, what he was really doing back then was allowing himself to become a single man again, without the day-to-day obligation of being a father. He liked the idea of being able to immerse himself in his work and at the same time date any women he took a shine to. There were a couple of occasions when he was clearly looking for a Val substitute, a woman he could marry and who would then be a housewife and a mother to his children. Yvonne Chappell virtually told him as much when she turned down his marriage proposal, and when he did find another wife, by marrying Janet Reid, she obviously had very different plans to his own, especially where the twins were concerned, and there was never any intention on her part to be a second mother to them.

When his son, Peter, told Ken a few home truths before Susan's wedding to Mike Baldwin, it clearly hit home hard, but at the same time I think he is one of these characters who sometimes finds it hard to admit their own wrongdoings and failings. It's a common fault with most human beings, but of course Ken has the problem of always striving to try to do the right thing, and when that doesn't happen, he often becomes frustrated with those around him and with himself. I think one of the different aspects that the writers were able to bring to the storyline featuring Denise and her pregnancy was the fact that Ken was no longer this young guy who, at one time, had been a fairly eligible bachelor. Instead he was a man in his mid-50s, whose days of being the father of a newborn child were long gone. It was a shock to his system and he was always going to have a problem dealing with it, whatever he chose to do.

Having a story like that is always good for the programme, and you will often find that after certain scenes or episodes have been broadcast, members of the public will identify with what has been going on. I have already mentioned the woman at my children's school who didn't want her own child to have anything to do with me at the time the whole Wendy Crozier storyline was playing out. Members of the public will often see something happening on the *Street* that is very close to home for them, and this can be a good thing. I know that when certain stories and situations are explored, they are done with great research and planning. It certainly isn't a case of just throwing a few scenes together and not thinking too much about what they mean and what will happen as a consequence.

There have been several big subjects tackled during the course of the 50 years the programme has been screened, and all of them have been well thought out, well written and well acted. *Coronation Street* is not real life, it's a drama, and as such much of what goes on has to be heightened to some extent, but the essence of the stories still have to have a sense of realism. Things like marriage, divorce, birth, death, sex and even murder have been dealt with over the years. It is all part of what life is about out there in the real world, and for a programme about pretty ordinary northern folk not to try to reflect some of those issues would be ridiculous. The secret is in doing it in the right way and making the whole thing engaging for the viewer. I think the fact that the *Street* is still around after 50 years shows that everyone involved in it must be doing something right on that front.

To make matters worse for Ken when he found out that he was to be a father, Deirdre returned after having been away looking after her mother, Blanche, and thought there might be the chance of a possible reconciliation. That notion was completely blown out of the water by what had been going on with Denise, and not only did they not get back together, but later that same year

Deirdre found herself besotted with a 21-year-old lover called Samir Rachid, whom she had met while on holiday in Morocco. Anne's storyline for this eventually saw Samir coming over to this country, and then Deirdre married him when the immigration services started closing in on him. So after being Deirdre Barlow for the past 13 years, she was now Deirdre Rachid.

I have to admit that it was a slightly strange experience for me to see Anne acting opposite this young guy who was now Deirdre's husband, especially after I'd had that role for so long! I think teaming her up with a young man was a bit of a departure, but at the same time it meant that both Ken and Deirdre now had these very new avenues to explore, and for any actor that is always an exciting prospect, waiting to see where the scripts will take the story, and with it your character. In Anne's case, her marriage to Samir proved very dramatic, with a twist that would eventually involve Tracy.

There was a lot of scepticism from Deirdre's friends regarding Samir, and clearly the immigration people seemed to think the same, as they began to regard it as a possible marriage of convenience on his part. She was very taken with Samir, and when he thought he might not be allowed to stay in this country, the pair decided to go and live in Morocco, selling number one to Mike Baldwin and using the proceeds to begin their new life together.

The following year saw big changes in the lives of both Ken and Deirdre, when she returned to the Street following news that Tracy had collapsed in a nightclub, having taken Ecstasy. She and Samir rushed back to England, while a horrified Ken waited to see if Tracy would come out of intensive care. This was in 1995, and once again the programme tackled a subject that was very relevant to what was actually going on in the real world, because the use of this form of drug by youngsters was becoming a worrying problem for many parents, and the long-term effects it might have were of equal concern.

In Tracy's case it was decided that after her collapse she would be left with kidney damage, bringing a whole new dilemma for Deirdre, which is exactly the sort of thing a soap is able to thrive on. It's a moment of high drama that then allows all sorts of possibilities to come into play. Tracy was not overly keen on the prospect of having to undergo dialysis for the rest of her life, which left the option of someone donating one of their own kidneys to her, but, of course, this can only be done if the tissue types match. Deirdre obviously wanted to donate her kidney, just as any mother would do in the circumstances, but Samir wasn't too happy about this, knowing that it would end any hope he had of having children with her. Ken was also willing to donate his kidney, but it turned out that neither he nor Deirdre was a suitable match. Samir then took the test and was found to be perfect, so he volunteered to have the operation.

In another twist to the whole plot, Samir was then attacked on his way to the hospital on the day the operation was due to take place, and was found unconscious. He was rushed to hospital but died on arrival, leaving Deirdre not only grief-stricken, but also with a very difficult decision to make. The kidney could still be used for the operation with Tracy, but Deirdre had to give her permission for it to happen. Anne played these scenes extremely well, as she balanced the shattering devastation of her new husband being killed with the knowledge that it would not have happened had he not been on the way to donate a kidney to her daughter. She clearly had problems reconciling the whole situation and did not want to talk to Tracy once she was out of hospital.

As for Ken, he had already become a father again before all the drama with Tracy played out. I had some very good scenes with Denise Black, who played Denise Osbourne, during the course of the relationship, leading up to the birth and subsequently after baby Daniel was born and all that went on then. In fact, there was even some drama leading up to the birth when she was told she had lost the baby, only to discover that she had been carrying twins and one of them had survived. I had a feeling that there was no way any story involving Ken having a son would be straightforward, and so it proved. There were lots of twists and turns, with Ken desperately keen to make sure he played a full part in his son's life, while Denise very much wanted to be an independent woman and had no intention of being tied down in any kind of domestic arrangement. She had intended to go it alone and not have Ken around, but he was there to see his son born, and in the end she was grateful that he was. The character created for Denise Black was quite a complicated one, and she was certainly someone who had her own issues to deal with. This often made her appear very vulnerable and, in turn, Ken found himself wanting to protect not only the new son she had given birth to, but also Denise herself.

At one point Denise left Coronation Street with the baby and went to live with her sister and brother-in-law, Alison and Brian, but she did return and even consented to moving in with Ken when he bought back number one from Mike Baldwin and set up home there, but, as ever, all was not what it seemed. Denise was having an affair with her brother-in-law and knew she needed to do something to stop it. Her solution was to propose to Ken, and having gone through all the ups and downs in the relationship with her, he was pleased to get the chance of the sort of permanency that he craved. The emotional scenes I had with Denise were some of the best I've done during my time on the *Street*. There was shouting, crying, rows, affection and physical violence, and I think it worked very well.

When Ken found out about Denise and Brian there was a huge row, just as you might expect. He punched Brian and, in a highly charged scene, threatened to kill Denise, telling her she was unfit to be a mother. The tearful and vulnerable Denise agreed, leaving Ken to look after Daniel and become the doting single parent he'd never quite managed to be with the twins. He employed one of his former pupils, Kelly Thomson, as a nanny, but although I enjoyed most of the storylines in this whole scenario there was one which I had a problem with, and to this day it is only the second time I have had that feeling with any of the scripts during more than fifty years on the programme.

The first time I had a problem with a script was the famous scene I had with Deirdre, which I have already discussed and in which I took it upon myself to change things when I slammed the door in Mike Baldwin's face. The writers write and we act.

The second occasion came along in 1997, and it was all part of the scenario concerning Denise and Daniel. Having made the effort to keep Daniel, the story had Ken doting on him and desperate to make sure he didn't make the same mistakes he had with Peter and Susan. The feeling was that he would fight tooth and nail to keep his son with him, but then suddenly I got a script that said that while Ken was out one evening, he would get a call from Kelly telling him that Denise had turned up and wanted to take his son away, ironically to Scotland, which was where Peter and Susan had ended up. Ken was naturally very angry at the news, but then in the space of one scene, he basically said, 'OK, take him.'

It just didn't ring true, and I actually had a word with the powers that be about it all, because I just felt it was wrong. Having built up this thing with Ken and Daniel, I couldn't believe that he would just meekly agree to him going. They apologised to me and agreed that it was all a bit sudden, but said that it needed to happen because of what was subsequently going to go on further down the line in other episodes, and there wasn't the time to try to rewrite or change anything. It was disappointing, but at the same time there simply wasn't anything that could really be done about it. By this time *Coronation Street* was being broadcast four times a week, and consequently the whole pattern of our work changed. So as an actor I had to ratchet up my emotions and feelings within the very short space of that one scene and try to convey why he was agreeing to Daniel being taken. The idea was that the law was more likely to side with the mother, and if Ken didn't cause a fuss then it might stand him in good stead when he went on to fight for custody, but the whole thing just didn't feel real. However, it is your job to make it work; there's no alternative. So in fifty years I've had just two instances of being unhappy with the script, which is not bad. In fact, I think it's pretty remarkable, really.

I might not have liked that one particular scene, but looked at as a whole, it means very little when you consider my time on the programme and the consistent quality of writing there has been over the space of five decades. I think it's an incredible achievement and I have been very happy to have had great scripts and great scenes written for me to act.

If there is one thing that can be relied on as an actor on the *Street*, it is the fact that some wonderful plots and storylines are always just around the corner. With some of them they don't just provide good entertainment, they also take on a whole new dimension of their own and really hit the pulse of the nation. It is one of the things that gives the show its strength and staying power.

15

STAYING POWER

When the whole Deirdre, Ken and Mike thing happened, that really hit the pulse of the nation in a big way. It went way beyond just being the latest big story in *Coronation Street*, it also became a talking point in the media, with all the column inches and discussions that went with it. In 1998, Anne was involved in another big story on the *Street* when she found herself in prison.

It was something that really gathered steam very quickly, with discussions and debates in newspapers and even Prime Minister Tony Blair getting involved. It was an idea that had been hatched during the time Brian Park was the producer, and although David Hanson was actually the man in charge when the whole prison scenario was played out, it most certainly had the hallmark of Brian, who made some of the most radical changes ever to hit the *Street* during his relatively short stay. In fact, Brian created his own notoriety while he was in charge by the way he went about things. Most producers will understandably want to leave their mark on the show in one way or another, otherwise there is really no point in them being there, but at the same time if they are going to be an effective producer they must have the good of the show at heart. I have always thought that the role of producer in *Coronation Street* is an incredibly important and difficult one, because there is so much they are responsible for. Brian may have made changes and was apparently dubbed 'the smiling axeman' by one TV critic, but he was a very dynamic guy who understood the *Street*, and I definitely think the programme thrived under him. He had good judgement and pushed through a lot in a short period of time.

From my own point of view I probably have him to thank for giving Ken some lighter moments in the programme, including the time he fell through the ceiling while crawling around in the loft and landed on a bed below containing one of his former pupils, Nick Tilsley, and Leanne Battersby. I also had a storyline during Brian's time as producer that saw Ken work as a male escort, when Alec Gilroy, who had married Bet Lynch and taken over the Rovers, decided to start a dating agency called the Golden Years Escort Agency. I remember having a conversation with Brian after he took over when he told me that he intended to make sure Ken had more fun, and I think that happened. I was certainly allowed to play more comedic scenes, which were a bit different to all the heavy stuff that I was more usually associated with. As much as I love good dramatic moments, I have also always loved comedy; it was just that Ken was always seen as a more serious character, and, let's face it, he was often involved in stories that had very little comedy in them. I remember once getting a letter from a fan in which the woman asked me for a signed picture and asked whether there was any sort of official fan club and at the bottom of the letter, 'Is there a Ken Barlow fun-pack?' A fun-pack was certainly not the sort of thing I could ever imagine being associated with a character like Ken!

Other characters in the *Street* did not thrive under Brian, with the likes of Percy Sugden, Derek Wilton and Don Brennan all leaving the show. Brian had a lot to do with the sort of storylines that were followed closely by the public, and, apart from Deirdre's brush with the law, that period also saw another story that had everyone talking when Hayley Patterson was introduced. She became involved with the meek and mild character of Roy Cropper, who took a shine to her, but it later transpired that Hayley was a transsexual whose real name was Harold. It was a very different sort of subject for the programme to tackle but, at the same time, exactly the sort of thing that keeps it going and gives it that staying power. If new ideas and directions can be brought to the programme, then it is able to maintain its vibrancy and, as a result, will flourish.

The role of the producer is crucial to the way the show functions, and we have been very lucky over the years to have had so many good ones who have cared for the programme and nurtured all that is good in it, while at the same time perhaps just tweaking things here and there, and seeing through some storylines that have been very popular and moved the show along, as should be the case. The only producer I really had a problem with was Tim Aspinall back in the 1960s. It wasn't just the fact that he seemed to want to get rid of some characters for the sake of it and put me on notice, as I described earlier; it was also because I didn't believe he had any real feel for the nature of the programme. He certainly shook the show up during his short stay, but I don't think it was better off because of it, and the axing of Lynne Carol was something I still consider to have been a big mistake. At the end of that particular period I think we were lucky to have someone like Harry Kershaw come back and take over the reins. The programme needed a safe pair of hands, someone who understood what was at the core of the *Street* and who could help the programme continue to grow and evolve. Quite early on in the show's history we had a producer called Derek Granger, who was in charge between 1961 and 1962. It was at the time when the programme had really taken off and its reputation was soaring. Derek knew that there were a lot of actors who saw the *Street* as real cutting-edge drama, which of course it was, because there hadn't been anything like it before and it had the sort of gritty feel to it that was very much in vogue at that time. Derek had the very ambitious idea of inviting Marlon Brando to be a guest on the programme. I don't know exactly how far down the line he got with the idea, or if any contact was actually made, but it certainly would have been interesting to have seen Brando using his method acting and trying to get to grips with a broad Lancashire accent.

Being able to move the programme on in new directions is an essential part of the job, because *Coronation Street* always needs to be moving forward. The decisions producers have to make are not easy ones. As a producer you can't afford to be too conservative, because then the show would very quickly fall behind in its approach to matters, but by the same token you can't jump too far forward in terms of the subject matter, because then you might offend a lot of viewers and they won't want to watch. They are big decisions to have to make, and I'm glad I don't have to make them.

It's a very demanding job, and one in which you really need to know about the programme. Nobody would be in the position of producing *Coronation Street* if they weren't really competent. They have total responsibility for everything you see on-screen, and it isn't just about the actual programme, because there are all the other things that he or she might have to deal with off-screen, such as sackings, private problems and illness, which can have a real effect on things like scheduling. The show also has an executive producer, and currently that is Kieran Roberts, who himself produced the programme for three years. He tends to leave the producer alone but is there if he's needed, and with his own experience he knows only too well what the job entails and is obviously a valuable person to have around. I think the job has become harder over the years, simply because the programme has grown and with it everything and everyone involved in it. *Coronation Street* is a big operation and the programme is shown five times a week: that doesn't leave too much room for error, and the professionalism shown by the producer is a big part of what the show is about.

When a new storyline is thought up, it doesn't just happen overnight. There has to be a lot of forward planning and structure put into it, and it is the producer who is at the helm when it comes to introducing a story or deciding on whether new characters should come into the programme or whether existing ones go, or taking a slightly different direction in what they are going to do in the *Street*. That is exactly what happened when Deirdre's brush with the law came about. It all started when she began seeing a guy called Jon Lindsay, who claimed to be an airline pilot. Ken had his suspicions about this and, in fact, was proved right when it was discovered that Lindsay's real connection with the aviation industry came in the form of him managing a shop at the airport. Undeterred by this, after confronting her new lover and getting him to admit the truth, Deirdre still went on seeing Lindsay and even lied to her friends about why he wasn't actually a pilot, saying he'd had to give up on medical grounds.

Just to make matters worse, she then agreed to give him £5,000 as a deposit on a house for the two of them in Didsbury. The web the writers were weaving for her began to get even more tangled as the storyline continued, and she found out that Jon was, in fact, married. It was too much for Deirdre, and she finally saw the light. Having split up from him, she then went and used a bank card he had given her to withdraw the £5,000 she had loaned him in the first place, and in doing so set in motion a train of events that would eventually lead to her being convicted of obtaining money and property by deception, with a judge sentencing her to 18 months in prison. The reason Deirdre was charged was that she had used the bank card that she believed was for their joint account, only to later find, when she was arrested, that it was in the name of a Captain Jenkins, an identity that, unbeknown to her, Lindsay had assumed in order to get the property. She tried to tell the police about Lindsay, but by this time he was long gone and they simply didn't believe her.

The great thing for me was that because of Ken's close ties to Deirdre in *Coronation Street*, pretty much anything she gets up to has an impact on him as well. It's the same for her, because if Ken is involved in something then you can bet your life it will have Deirdre in there somewhere along the line. It's only natural, really, because that is exactly what would happen if a couple had the same sort of connection and relationship in real life. What you do always affects others, particularly those people closest to you. In typical Ken fashion, he was very sceptical when Deirdre claimed she believed Lindsay had bought the house himself and, in turn, wasn't convinced of her innocence. Enter Mike Baldwin, who did stand by her, but cooked up a typically dodgy idea of getting her a false passport and a ticket to Spain. Ken stepped back into the picture to persuade her not to go ahead with the plan, but when Lindsay did eventually turn up and Deirdre called in the police, they believed his story of her being the one who planned the whole scam.

The writers did a great job when it came to telling the story of the trial, because Lindsay's lawyers called Ken as a witness against his ex-wife, and Ken admitted that Deirdre had lied to people concerning the reason why Jon Lindsay was not a pilot. Once more the writers were able to use the sort of character Ken was to help a storyline along. There was no way he could contemplate lying in the witness box and, at the same time, there was also a possible element of jealousy in there as well, because Ken still clearly had feelings for Deirdre and was unhappy about her going off with Lindsay. The upshot of all this was Deirdre being sent to jail, with the judge claiming she was a manipulative woman who had pushed Lindsay into lying in order to obtain a house for herself.

To gasps from all of her friends in the courthouse and a flood of tears from an emotional Deirdre, the judge passed the 18-month sentence on her, while Lindsay walked free from the court. It was a wonderful story, and I think everybody involved enjoyed playing their part in it, but there was no way any of us could have imagined the impact it would have, with the story going way beyond fans of the *Street*. It was reckoned that 19 million viewers watched the episode that saw Deirdre sentenced to prison, and while Emily Bishop and Mike Baldwin started a campaign in the Street to free her, it quickly went way beyond that.

Very soon people had T-shirts and car stickers sporting the 'Free Deirdre' slogan, and there were other ones as well, such as 'Justice for Deirdre' and a campaign to 'Free the Weatherfield One'. There were articles written in newspapers concerning the jailing of 'innocent Deirdre Rachid', and the crowning glory with regard to all of this was when Prime Minister Tony Blair stood up in Parliament and asked the Home Secretary to intervene in her case, all done with tongue very much in cheek, of course, but it just showed what an impact the whole story had. It was marvellous for the programme, and at the same time it showed just how popular the *Street* was and how much a part of British society it had become. It's quite thrilling in many ways to know so many people like what you do. We are there to entertain the public, and I think there is a great affinity between the people who appear on the show and the people who regularly tune in to watch us. Everyone connected with *Coronation Street* realises that without the public we wouldn't have a show, and at the same time it is always gratifying to know that the programmes we produce are liked by so many people.

Anne had some very dramatic and emotional scenes as Deirdre proclaimed her innocence to anyone who was within earshot while she was in prison. Her agony was finally ended after three weeks when another woman who had been tricked by Lindsay came forward to give evidence against him, and Deirdre was not only freed, but later also had her name cleared in the Court of Appeal.

The 1990s ended with Ken moving into a new and mellower phase of his life. In 1999, he celebrated his 60th birthday. By this time he had stopped teaching, having been made redundant from Weatherfield Comprehensive, but not before having a brief but meaningless relationship with the head teacher, Sue Jeffers, and he had taken a part-time job as an assistant at Freshco supermarket. He also had a pension, and I think it was a slightly different Ken Barlow who was preparing to welcome in the new millennium. It made perfect sense, because Ken had reached the point in his life where he was no longer the young, idealistic graduate who had it all before him: that had been 40 years earlier. He'd had marriages, affairs and children without ever quite achieving some of the things I'm sure he would have liked to have done, but, like so many people, he had started to accept his life and what the rest of it held for him. The one great constant for him for more than twenty years had been the love and affection he'd had for Deirdre. Their relationship had never been a smooth one, with both of them shouldering the blame for many of the things that had gone wrong between them, but there was always something there, and it was a theme the writers had exploited to such good effect.

The decade had begun with the two of them at war because of Ken's affair with Wendy Crozier, but it ended with them on much better terms. When Deirdre's mother, Blanche, arrived back on the Street, she made it her business to try to get Ken and Deirdre back together again. Blanche was played by the wonderful Maggie

Jones, and her character had always been very good whenever she had appeared on the programme, but she was to take on a whole new lease of life in the next ten years. Blanche became one of the best-loved characters in the programme, with her acerbic wit and constant put-downs for Ken in particular and anyone else who got within range. She was a great character, and the writers came up with some superb stories for her and, more importantly, some absolutely brilliant one-liners. Maggie Jones was a superb actress who brought Blanche to life like nobody else could have, and it was an absolute joy to work with her.

She desperately set about getting Ken and Deirdre back together in 1999 and even insisted on throwing a party for Ken's 60th, but, despite all of her efforts, it looked as though nothing would come of it. Instead it was Tracy who inadvertently began the process that some years later would see them not only reunited, but also remarried. That year she too arrived unexpectedly, having walked out on her husband, Robert Preston. Both Ken and Deirdre worked hard to convince their daughter not to throw her marriage away, and as a result the two of them grew closer, with Deirdre eventually consenting to move in with Ken. They weren't quite back together again and playing happy families, as several storylines over the next couple of years would show, but it was the first major step in getting them back together as a 'couple' for the *Street*, and both Anne and I then began acting opposite each other much more than we had for some time.

I think it was quite a clever idea to get the two of them together again over the next few years. It fitted perfectly with the characters' own history on the programme. I'm sure it must be a help to the writers to be able to look back on what has happened over so many years and use the history they have with certain individuals to devise new stories. It's all there for them, and the programme has an archive department that has a complete history of the show and all the episodes ever broadcast. It means that they can delve back into a character's history and be sure of exactly what went on in the past, what they said and what they did. It's a great asset to have, and one that is well used. It makes the *Street* the living thing that it is, because so many people in it have spent a long time in the show and therefore have that history. It's good for the viewers as well, because it makes the whole process better: they can see us all growing older in front of their own eyes, and it adds to the feel of the programme for them.

I know there are quite literally generations of people who have grown up watching the programme. I think it is the sort of show that is able to appeal to all sorts of ages. The *Street* has to be a multi-layered cake in order to do that, and obviously being around for as long as it has been helps it to be just that. There are different generations in the programme, and their exploits and lives, I'm sure, appeal to different sections of the public. The main thing is to make sure that when people tune in to watch the show, they can do so knowing there is something there that will engage and entertain them. A lot of hard work goes into making sure that is the case, but I think everyone connected to the show loves what they do and is proud of what we all manage to produce.

The *Street* has come a long way since those very early days of live episodes, and the way it is now put together and produced is light years away from those times in the 1960s. But as part of the celebrations for our 40th anniversary, in December 2000, it was decided to turn the clock back, in one sense, because once again *Coronation Street* was going to go out 'live', on 8 December, a day before the actual anniversary date. It was funny at the time, because I think quite a few people on the programme thought I'd be fine with it as I'd done those live broadcasts forty years earlier, but I don't think any of them realised quite how terrifying it can be, and I for one certainly prefer the way we do things now to the way we did it back then.

Of course, the technology and equipment we were going to be using was vastly different and the sets were so much better, but live television is live television, and it has a way of concentrating the mind like nothing else when you are acting. Nobody was forced to do the show, and it was made clear that if you didn't fancy doing it, that would be all right, but I'm sure it was always assumed I'd be OK about it because of my background and, having been there for the first-ever broadcast, I was hardly likely to not want to be involved in our 40th-anniversary edition.

The planning and logistics that went into the whole thing were huge, and it meant we had to have more detailed rehearsals than we would normally have, because it not only had to be word perfect, with the acting and movements during the scenes going like clockwork, we also had to take into account the way we were going to get from one set to another. In the old days this was all pretty simple, because everything was shot inside, so even if there was an 'exterior' scene showing the Street, it was all still done in a studio. The interior sets of the houses and things like the Rovers were all very close together and, as I mentioned earlier, if I sat in the Barlows' room I could quite literally lean across from a chair and my hand would be touching part of the set of the Rovers. In fact, I remember once having to make a dash from one scene to another and, although I had a suit on, my shirt was wet through because I'd just been having a bath in the other scene. It was all very basic, and that caused its own problems. For the episode in 2000, we had a lot more technology and the sets were certainly more realistic, but that also brought with it a different set of problems.

If someone wanted to get from the outside of their house to the inside, it would have meant a mad dash from the actual Street, around the back of the exterior set and then into the studios to whichever hallway or living room they were stepping into. So things like that had to be taken into account when the script was written, and it all had to be geared up into making it as easy as possible. There were different fixed units filming inside and outside, and we also had to be very careful about not making any noises off-camera, so when someone had to dash from one set to another there were people holding doors open so no unwanted sounds were heard during the broadcast. In the week leading up to the episode, nothing else happened; it was all about rehearsing over and over again.

Doing the live episode was very frightening, very interesting and very exciting. I'm glad we did it, and at the time I didn't think we would do anything like it again. There was one moment where I had a real panic, because I was convinced I'd gone to the wrong scene, but happily I hadn't. I think I was in quite a lot of the scenes, because one of the storylines running through the show was about the cobbles in the Street being tarmacked over.

Ken might have been mellowing slightly at that point, but there was still enough fire left in his belly for him to lead the residents in a protest as they tried to preserve the cobbles. He was even involved in helping to get a fake preservation order to stop it happening, and right at the end, when the people from the Street had won the day, Ken had to give quite a long speech, which involved him talking about tradition and the community and ended with him popping a cork on some champagne. It was very frightening to have to do the whole thing live, because with acting there's a rhythm and a formula that, if it gets broken, can leave you totally lost. The last thing I wanted to happen was to dry up during the middle of a long and important speech, but I got through it and the show was a big success.

We also had a rather special guest appearance from Prince Charles during the course of the episode, but he wasn't part of the live shoot. He had earlier come up to Granada to pay a visit to the set as part of our 40th-anniversary celebrations, meeting the cast and watching some of the filming being done. The story involving him was that he had been on an official visit to Weatherfield earlier in the day and had met Audrey Roberts, in her capacity as a local councillor, and that was edited to be used as part of the live episode. His visit was actually covered by the national media and several characters were seen watching the news report of the event, which also featured newsreader Trevor McDonald. When Prince Charles did visit the set, he was there for quite some time and was genuinely interested in what we were doing and what went on. I was lucky enough, along with some others, to have lunch with him that day, and it was an extremely enjoyable occasion for all of us. I think he is a good man, and his work with the Prince's Trust scheme has done some marvellous things over the years.

As nice as it was to do that episode, I think it only served to emphasise to me just how much things had changed during the 40 years I had been acting on the show. It may have been live as it was in the old days, but that was the only real similarity, because the show had moved on in so many ways since those days in the

1960s. It was a totally different animal, but at the same time it had shown its ability to change and adapt to the modern demands of television. It clearly had staying power, and that remains the case today. The show can only do that if it has good people working on it, and I'm not just talking about the actors. We may be the most visible part of the programme, but the great strength of *Coronation Street* is the colossal teamwork that goes into making it what it is.

I think that over the years the show has obviously had to adapt, and sometimes there has been a lurch here and there along the way when perhaps something hasn't worked so well, but that's bound to be the case. As I have already said, the producer is so crucial to the show and they have to love – and love is exactly the right word – *Coronation Street*. They have to understand its heart and where it has come from, that it was invented as this quiet little back street in the north-west of England, with people who were basically friendly and caring. The quality of the acting, writing and production has to be good, but I think that with all the changes that have happened during the course of the past 50 years, the programme is still basically about a caring community. It's maybe the most essential ingredient of the show, and providing that is remembered and maintained, I'm sure the *Street* can continue to be successful and adapt to any future changes and challenges that might come its way.

Of course, you sometimes get awful things happening as part of the storylines on different occasions, but at the end of the day I think the general feel of the programme is that it's the sort of place where people will put the kettle on and have a friendly cup of tea with you as they try to sort everything out. The biggest enemy would be if there was indifference towards or a lack of caring for the characters by the audience. The whole thing really is about the characters who are part of the *Street* and the fact that the public have to care about them. There have been times when there have been attempts to totally revamp the cast, but very quickly, when those processes started, they were reflected in the ratings. People like to see that core of continuity, the caring, amusing and entertaining characters. It's having those characters and introducing new people at the right time and in the right place that keep the programme going, and fresh and interesting.

I am often asked about the writers and the process the show goes through when it comes to scripts and stories. We are very lucky to have such good writers, and they have been consistently good right through the years. Those very early episodes were all written by Tony Warren, but everything on the show is now bigger and wider ranging than it was when I first appeared. We've gone from having a handful of writers in those early days to having 16 now, and they're all very good indeed.

The process that takes place in order to produce scripts of such high quality is a long one, and it is meticulously thought out. There are four script editors and they have their long-term conferences about every three months, in which they will all be involved. The script editors will then break down the stories into episodes and hand them to individual writers to pour in the dialogue, so that no one writer is being over-taxed at any one time. They have all been involved in the overall story, so they know where it's going to go, and it is then down to them to write the words for us, as actors, to deliver on-screen. In general, we will film episodes that the public will see on their screens some eight weeks later. We get the scripts about two or three weeks before we film the episodes, so they are actually produced about three months before they are shown, but the writers have been thinking about the long-term stories for a full three months before that.

All the actors on the *Street* have their own way of tackling the scripts they get; we all have our little routines that work for us. There is no right or wrong way of doing it; the main thing is to make sure that your method works for you and suits the way you like to learn your lines. I'm afraid that when I get a script I don't read my way right through it to see what everyone else is doing in the episode; instead, I'll look at the brief synopsis at the start of each scene, and then I take all of my scenes out of the script and put them in story order and read them, and then I put them in shooting order. I will then take them home, and each night I will make sure I know thoroughly what I've got to do the next day. If they are quite heavy scenes and there's a lot of dialogue,

I will work on them earlier than just the night before, because there's a lot to learn. In general terms I will be 'roughing' them, or, in other words, going over them to get into my head what I have to say and how I want to say it, but the night before a shoot is when I really brush up on what I am going to be doing the next day. I can only learn at night, so I will often do some of the preparation in my dressing-room at the studios and then do the actual learning at home. It has to be word perfect, whether it's just a matter of learning a few words or whether there are a lot of scenes with a lot of dialogue. Quite often if I know I'm going to have a heavy week with lots of scenes coming up, I will spend a lot of the weekend roughing it all and then learn the words the night before I actually do each scene.

I never tend to talk to anybody before I play the scenes. If there is a particularly long scene that Ken might be doing with Deirdre, I might be in the Green Room with Anne and suggest that we read through the words. We don't act; instead, we just quietly go through it. In the days when we were doing just two or three episodes a week, rehearsals were very much part of what we did. There was much more time to go through everything, and it was a very different way of working. These days, because the turnover is so great the process is not the same, and I have to say that I prefer the way we work today to the way we went about it years ago. I like the fact that I can step out of my dressing-room and onto the set, and then do the scene. I never actually act out the words of any scene before I go onto the set. That is the first time I speak them in the form they will go out in the programme. I think it adds a freshness to what I am doing, and I like that very much. If you have a shouting match to do, or a crying scene, you want to be able to let rip, and working in this way allows me to do just that, but at the same time you have to be word perfect, and learning the scripts in the way that I do works for me.

One of the other main reasons for the staying power of the show is the quality of the directors we have had working on it over the years, and the ones we have at the moment do a terrific job. Episodes are constantly being made, and the logistics involved in making sure there are five programmes screened each week are amazing. For one week of five episodes, a director will have five weeks to read the scripts, work out his or her camera angles, work on the scripts, film and shoot them, and then edit them. Each director has a five-week turnaround, so you could have five directors all working at roughly the same time, and each of them will probably do a three- or four-month stint. They will obviously need to know what has gone on before and what will happen after, but each director will work independently. A director will have their week of episodes, and the majority of those scenes will be done then, but some of the scenes will be shot before because they can't get them all done in one week, and that's called the pre-shoot. Some of the scenes will be shot after the main week, and that is called the post-shoot, so each section of five episodes is, in effect, shot over a period of three weeks. We can be working with three directors at the same time. One might be doing their pre-shoot, another doing their post-shoot and the third will be filming his or her episodes for that particular week, and they're all interlinked. I marvel at the logistics of it all, and don't quite know how they manage to do it.

I have to say that it can be a bit of a nightmare for the actors sometimes, because you could be working on scenes through something like 12 episodes. For example, let's just say there are a group of episodes, and we number them from one to twelve. I may be doing a scene from episode twelve, and then suddenly I have to do a scene from episode one, so that can mean what you will be doing doesn't follow the last scene you have played. When that happens and there is such a big gap between the scenes you are playing back to back, you have to have a word with the director and just ask him to fill you in on what has gone before so that you can judge the atmosphere and background of the scene you are about to play. Sometimes it can be a bit tricky, because you might have a script that has a big row in it but you have to shoot the scene after that row first. You don't really know how powerful that row is because you haven't actually done it at that point. The directors are there to make sure they get just what they want from each scene that he or she shoots, and the actors place great trust in them and their judgement, because the directors are the ones who decide how a scene should look on-screen.

Very occasionally the producer, who will look at everything that is shot, will say he is not happy with a particular scene, and if that happens the director will have to do it again, but that doesn't happen too often, and it is testament to the skill and professionalism of the directors we have that they are able to cope with a huge workload and at the same time help to produce what we all consider to be quality television drama.

In the last ten years since that live episode, I have had some lovely storylines to get my teeth into, and the writing for the programme just seems to get better and better. At the beginning of the decade Ken's life took a new twist when he discovered that he was a grandfather, and the irony of that story was that the father of his grandchild was Mike Baldwin. When we did the live episode it heralded the reappearance of Ken's son Peter, who turned up and declared that he had left the navy. He was played by Chris Gascoyne for the first time, who has gone on to do such a good job as Peter, particularly when he did some great scenes as the story of his battle with alcoholism played out to such great effect. Unusually for Ken, as part of the story when Peter returned he decided to lie to the police, claiming he, and not his son, had been the driver of a car that had been involved in an accident. This did Ken's relationship with him no good at all, and as part of a heated scene Peter told Ken that Susan had a son. It was the start of a typically tangled plot involving the Barlow family, with Susan admitting to her father that she had not had an abortion, as she had told Baldwin, but instead had given birth to a son who was called Adam, and then said she would never let Ken see his grandson if Mike Baldwin was ever told about what had happened. So the writers had, yet again, managed to get a new twist out of Ken and his family, while at the same time bringing Mike Baldwin into the equation. In the end, there was the usual mixture of anger and tragedy as Mike eventually found out that he had a son and demanded to see him, causing Susan to run away. In her panic, she had a car crash and died. Ken was desperate to keep Adam and wanted to marry Deirdre again, because he thought it would help his chances of getting custody, but in the end it was Mike Baldwin who was given the right to have custody, although he did agree in the end to let little Adam continue his education in Scotland.

Ken, meanwhile, gradually became closer to Deirdre during those first few years of the new decade. They had their usual little ups and downs, but, by 2005, there was only one way the relationship was heading, and in April of that year they were married for a second time, older and wiser, but with yet more family problems lurking just around the corner.

16

MY SECOND FAMILY

I was pleased when it was decided that Ken and Deirdre should not only get back together, but get married for a second time, too. It seemed to fit perfectly with the lives that had been created for them throughout their time in *Coronation Street*. They had both gone off and done very silly things and had had affairs with people, and yet their overriding need as they got older was for each other. They seemed more comfortable and suited to each other, and the affection and love that had always been there was finally recognised by the two of them. They knew they had faults and they knew they had a dysfunctional family, but they also knew they wanted to be together.

However, the decade started off badly for Ken with the death of his daughter Susan. He was also held captive, along with Mike Baldwin, at Freshco supermarket very early on in the new millennium. Marriage to Deirdre offered him some respite, but in the last few years he has not only battled to try to help bigamist and alcoholic Peter to overcome his drink problems, he and Deirdre also had to cope with the fact that their daughter Tracy was a murderer. I'm pleased to say that the strong and dramatic storylines never seemed to be too far away when it came to the Barlows, and long may it continue.

Apart from his own family causing him problems, there was also someone else in the *Street* lurking in the background who could be relied upon to provoke a response from Ken, and that was Mike Baldwin. When the two of them had been thrown together during the Freshco incident they had pretty much made their peace, but that seemed to be more because of their circumstances than anything else, and there was still an edge to their relationship once that was over. What did start to change things was the fact that Mike's mind began to deteriorate as the first signs of Alzheimer's disease started to take hold. Once again, it was a clever idea to have this once very smart and sharp businessman begin to crumble in front of the viewers' eyes, and although the *Street* is only fiction, I think it did highlight a disease that must be so awful for people to have to cope with and which must also be so distressing for those closest to the person who is afflicted. The story of Mike's deterioration was well handled by the writers, and so was the way in which they decided he should die.

It came almost a year to the day after Ken and Deirdre had got married for the second time, and it was one of the most memorable and talked-about moments in the history of the *Street*. There was a huge amount of publicity surrounding Mike Baldwin's departure, with a lot of press coverage, and even the *Radio Times* got in on the act when they mocked up a front cover featuring Mike lying on his deathbed with a selection of characters, including Ken, from the *Street* around his bedside, in a copy of the famous death scene of Admiral Nelson. Johnny Briggs had announced his intention to leave the programme the previous year, and when it became public knowledge, there was great interest in how he would end his days on the programme after 30 years. Johnny had been good for the show and, in turn, the character of Mike Baldwin and the relationship he had with Ken Barlow was wonderful for me. The number of great storylines and scenes that came out of their explosive pairing was incredible, and once that antagonistic relationship had been firmly established, I think we both benefited enormously as actors.

It was because Ken and Mike were such opposites that it worked so well, and although the spiky nature of what they thought of each other was always there, they had both mellowed slightly by the time Baldwin finally died; yet he had found time to mock Ken on his stag night, along with Dev Alahan and a terminally ill Ray Langton, who made a guest appearance in the episodes leading up to the wedding. All three of them had, of course, had a relationship with the woman Ken was about to marry. Neville Buswell's character only reappeared in the show until the wedding reception at the Rovers, when Ray Langton died while everyone else was dancing. I think it can be quite tricky when it comes to deciding how a character is going to be killed off. In Ray Langton's case it was always likely to happen quickly, because part of the story of his return was the fact that he was suffering from terminal cancer.

When it came to Mike Baldwin, his decline started to become obvious in the weeks leading up to his final appearance, but it was still important to get his ending right. As the disease took hold, Mike then contracted pneumonia and was taken to hospital, but that's not where he finally died. Instead it was decided that he would walk out of the hospital and be found wandering in his pyjamas outside the factory in *Coronation Street*. It was quite a touching moment as Ken put his jacket around Mike's shoulders and tried to comfort the man he had hated for so many years, keeping him warm as he phoned for an ambulance, but it all came to nothing when Mike suffered a massive heart attack and died in Ken's arms. It was a big scene and we did it in one take, going right the way through. I think it was very satisfying for both of us, but at the same time a bit sad, because it was the end of an era. No more fights, arguments, rows or squabbling over the same women. How could you not miss someone like that? Mike Baldwin was one of *Coronation Street*'s major characters, but, as Jean Alexander said when she left, it is the Street that is the star. We, as actors, are just part of it, and we all realise that. The show will always recover from the loss of a big character. It has proved to be the case on so many occasions, and its ability to do so is a tremendous strength.

One of the other major storylines to involve Ken came just a few years ago when Tracy was sent to prison for murdering her womanising boyfriend, Charlie Stubbs. It has to be said that Tracy had been trouble for some time for Ken and Deirdre. The writers had licence to turn her into a monster who could probably only be loved by her parents, and even they struggled at times. Both Ken and

Deirdre knew how bad Tracy could be, but even they were shocked when she was charged with murder. The fact that she'd had a baby girl called Amy and tried to trick poor Roy Cropper into believing it was his, even though Steve McDonald was in fact the father, was one thing, but murder was certainly something else. Both Ken and Deirdre struggled to come to terms with their daughter's guilt, and it was obviously very upsetting for them to see her sentenced to life, with a recommendation that she serve a minimum of 15 years, but there was no hesitation from the judge when she sent her down. At one point the woman playing the judge was told by the director to give Tracy a look that said, 'Don't mess with me,' which she duly did. I said at the time that I recognised that look, because I got it on a daily basis. The reason was that the woman playing the judge just happened to be my wife, Sara!

The producer of *Coronation Street* at the time was a guy called Steve Frost, and he had been the producer of *Emmerdale* at one stage in his career. Sara, who used to do bits of acting from time to time, had played a magistrate in one of the episodes of the show, and when it came to the *Street* having to have a court scene, he suggested that Sara might want to come in and play the part, which is exactly what she did. We filmed all of the courthouse scenes in Bradford, in a place that used to be a functioning court, and it was used again for scenes involving Tracy in 2010. We had 11 days of filming in 2007 when the original Tracy trial was taking place, and those involved in the scenes all decamped to a nice hotel in Bradford. Sara made our room a real little home from home for the time that we were there.

I think she really enjoyed playing the part, and it was certainly nice to have her there and working on the *Street*. Both my previous wife, Anna Cropper, and my son Linus had appeared in *Coronation Street*, and having Sara come in and be a part of it too was lovely. The storyline might not have been great for the Barlow household, but Bradford was very much a case of happy families for the Roaches during our stay there. It is an old cliché to say that you never know what is around the corner, and also that your life can change in an instant. That was certainly to be the case a year later, when my darling Sara passed away.

Death, whenever it comes and in whatever form, is always a shocking experience for those left behind. My spiritual beliefs have taught me that for the person who passes it is a very different matter and that they go on to a much better place, but that does not stop the shock the death of a loved one can cause or the utter sense of grief and helplessness that fills you when it happens.

One Saturday in February 2009, Sara and I were spending a relaxing morning chatting to each other in bed. Our daughter Verity had been staying with us and had been feeling under the weather. Sara had gone to the doctor's with her the previous day, and he had prescribed some medicine for her. I went to get the medicine from another room and came back to the bedroom to check with Sara that I had got the right stuff. She was sitting up in bed, and I sat down beside her and we started chatting again. All of a sudden I heard Sara give out a little sigh, and then she slumped to the side. I immediately asked her if she was all right and went around to the other side of the bed to see what was wrong. She was gone, totally out. I tried to revive her and bring her round, but then the thought kicked in that I should get on the phone right away and call the paramedics. The person on the other end of the phone told me what I should do while I waited for them: things like making sure Sara was lying in the right position and didn't have any clothing on that was at all restrictive. They were at the house within five or ten minutes and immediately got to work; they tried all sorts of things to try to revive her, but nothing seemed to be working. They kept saying that they couldn't get a pulse as I looked on in shock and horror at what was happening. The decision was quickly made to transfer her to hospital. I told them I would follow on, having made sure Verity was OK. The poor girl had witnessed all the trauma of Edwina being found unconscious, but this time, perhaps because of the medication, she was still asleep.

By the time I got to the hospital there were two men in suits waiting to meet me outside, and then one of them spoke.

'I'm sorry: it's bad news, Mr Roache. We're trying to do everything, but I don't think there's much hope,' he said.

My head was spinning at this point and I was probably functioning on autopilot. I didn't really have time to think and take everything in; I was just reacting as best I could. It wasn't long before a doctor came to see me.

'We might have to make a decision,' he told me. 'Do you want to be involved in that decision?'

It's a mark of just how dazed and confused I was at the time that at first I said, 'No,' and then quickly corrected myself and said, 'Yes, of course I do,' but very soon after that brief conversation he returned to give me the shattering news.

'I'm afraid there's no decision to make,' he explained.

I don't think she ever did come around; she went at that moment when she sighed and fell on her side. She hadn't had a massive heart attack and felt terrible pain before passing out; she had simply sighed and then passed out, and she never recovered from that moment. It took nine months before the pathologists could come up with an explanation for what had happened. I received a letter from the coroner asking me to go to the inquest. It wasn't something I particularly wanted to do, but he insisted that I should attend and so that's what I did. I went to the Coroner's Court, not realising that it was all so formal. The coroner came out in all his regalia and bowed to me; I bowed back, and then he sat down. I was the only person there apart from the clerk of the court, and then the coroner took off his ceremonial wig and was really kind to me. Even now when I think of that moment it makes me want to cry, because he wasn't this cold sort of figure that you might have expected; he was very much the opposite and could not have been nicer.

'I'm sorry about all of this,' he apologised, 'but we have to go through it.'

He then went on to tell me that he'd called me there without any of the press knowing and then apologised for all the delay there had been and explained that it had been a very difficult case for the pathologists to explain, but finally they had found out what the cause of death was. Sara had suffered a non-structural arrhythmogenic heart failure. Put simply, it meant that the electrical impulses to the heart had stopped. There was no ailment, no stroke, no heart attack or blood clot, nothing like that. There was no structural failure, no disease, nothing wrong anywhere, other than the fact that the electrical impulse to the heart had stopped and they didn't know why. She just went.

When I first found out she had died, I was in a strange state; I just began doing all that I had to do. I was sort of numb; I couldn't feel anything. The police phoned on the night she died and said that in the case of sudden death they had to investigate. I asked them not to go to the house, and so they met me at the hospital. They then asked me to identify Sara in front of them, and one of them was watching me the whole time. I was aware of this process, because a similar thing had happened when Edwina died. I went into the room and they asked if it was my wife, and I confirmed that it was. She was lying there looking very serene and calm, and they were just watching me the whole time and then asked me some questions, before explaining that they would have to come back to the house at some point to go through certain things, which they did. They wanted to know what the different pills were next to the bed and various things like that. I realised they were just doing their job, but it wasn't a particularly pleasant experience. The officer who came at a later date was especially trained for just the sort of situation I found myself in, and he was very good and very kind, but it just took so long for them to find out exactly what had happened.

I rang my son Will, who was in London, and told him that it wasn't good news and that his mother had had a heart attack. By this time Sara was already dead, but the last thing I wanted was Will trying to drive up while he was crying. As soon as he walked through the door, I hugged him and told him what had happened. He later said that he thought something more had happened, but he'd pushed it to the back of his mind while he drove up. It was an awful time for him, and then together we had to tell Verity.

It's strange, but from the moment Sara died I started to plan things. I thought to myself, 'The top priorities are making sure Verity and Will are OK; nothing else matters.' I didn't want to think about anything else; I just wanted them to be all right. Everyone was very good to me when they found out about Sara, and I realised it was a huge shock to anyone who had known her. People were very kind, and Stuart Hall, the TV and radio presenter, who is a good friend, was wonderful and helped me a lot. I decided that I didn't want a funeral as such; I wanted a memorial service. I wanted it to be a celebration of Sara's life, something she would have liked and something that those who had known her could enjoy, which I think was what happened. As for me, I had to start learning to cope with all the things she used to do. Sara was magnificent, and as well as being my wife, she also used to manage me. She did everything for me, and it was such a strange feeling not having her there. It had all been so sudden, and in a way I am grateful for that. There was no illness, no lingering pain. It was instant, as it had been with Edwina, and although it doesn't stop the initial grief, there is a comfort in knowing there was no pain attached to the way Sara died. So really the method of her going was the best there could be, in many ways.

Although we had to wait nine months to find out what had actually happened, we were at least issued with an interim death certificate, so the memorial service could go ahead. It was touch and go for a while, but they eventually issued the certificate, which was a blessing, because some people have to wait until the actual report is filed. Sara was always so vital, so sort of in-your-face about everything, so positive about life. She had lovely big blue eyes and was a beautiful woman; it was so hard to believe it had happened. That she had died. One consolation was the fact that I know she would have wanted to go that way. She didn't like the idea of old age or of being ill, but it was a huge shock to have her go so suddenly.

As always, everyone who worked on *Coronation Street* was enormously sympathetic towards me, as they are for any of their colleagues who are having a tough time of it. They were very much like a second family, just as they had been when Edwina died. Many of them had come to the memorial service, and the producer, Kim Crowther, could not have been kinder. She rang me after I'd been off for about two weeks to see how I was, but also to tell me that I could take as long as I wanted to come back. However, obviously I knew that she needed to have some sort of date, because having someone off for a long period of time can cause a scheduling nightmare. That was the last thing I wanted, and also I thought I should get back to work: something inside me said that I should.

'Just give me one more week and I'll be back,' I told her.

Once more she told me that I didn't have to come back until I felt comfortable and ready, but I made the decision and a week later I turned up for work, which I have to admit was a bit of a mistake. I should have given myself a little longer, but I didn't realise that at the time and it wasn't easy.

I probably wasn't quite ready, but then I don't think I was ever going to be ready. I think it was just something that's in me; it's my training as an actor. You turn up, no matter what, and get on with your work. I wasn't able to objectively think the thing through; maybe someone else would have said they wanted another two weeks. It probably didn't help that the storyline I was involved in straight away saw Ken lapsing back into his bad old ways and embarking on an affair with the glamorous Martha Fraser, played by the wonderful Stephanie Beacham. Stephanie was very warm and lovely, as well as being very professional. We were doing all of our filming on location that week, because our scenes were set on the canal boat that Martha had. I found it quite difficult to get back into the swing of things, and one of the problems was that I hadn't realised just how emotionally drained I was. As actors we are the instruments of our work, and when we act one of the tools we use is the emotion we have within us. I was empty; it had all gone, used up in the previous three weeks as I'd tried to come to terms with what had happened and at the same time get on with all the practical issues of day-to-day living.

One of the hardest things to happen to me once I began to go to work again was coming home and seeing Sara's car sitting in the drive. The house wasn't empty when I got home each day, because I have three noisy and very lively Jack Russells, but at the same time there was nobody else there. The person that I had loved and shared my life with was gone, and the realisation of that was hard to take to begin with, but at the same time my spiritual beliefs told me that because she was now in a better place, I should be happy for her. I also knew that having me grieving did her no good at all. I had to slowly but surely start to rebuild and remodel my life.

Will and Verity were good and stayed with me for some considerable time, but they also had to get on with their lives. I know Will became particularly frustrated with the hold-up there was in getting a verdict on what had been the cause of death; he just couldn't understand what was taking them so long. Although I wanted to know too, I think I was able to push it away slightly, and my main concern had been to make sure that we had the memorial service. If that had been delayed, I think it would have been truly awful.

I tried to get on and lead a normal life as best I could following that first week back at work, and I have to say that when I actually got back to Granada and Studio One, I began to feel more comfortable and relaxed. I had my little dressing-room, which may be a bit of a monk-like cell in a way, but I really like it and was able to retreat there whenever I wanted to. My colleagues were absolutely wonderful to me, and I shall always remember their kindness and the way in which they made me feel so much better. It truly was like coming back to a family once I drove through the front gates. Everyone, and I do mean everyone, was just so kind. I was also aware, having experienced what it was like after the death of Edwina, that it is not an easy time for those around you, because some people are not quite sure how to react, but once I'd got over that initial week when we were filming on location, things began to get better and I started to get my routine going.

I had lots of friends who were there for me, and who would phone or call in to see how I was doing. Something that did hit me one day was coming home and looking at a pile of washing that was in the basket. There was a whole heap of shirts that I'd taken off and just thrown in there and, of course, when I used to do that Sara took care of them. As well as all the other things she had done for me, she also took care of all the washing and ironing. In fact, ironing was like therapy to her; she used to love doing it. Even if we stayed in some grand hotel, she would ask for an ironing board and start ironing in our room. Seeing all the dirty shirts piled up made me realise that I had to do something, and my good friend Stuart Hall came to the rescue, suggesting I ask Jenny, the woman who cleaned for him, if she would work for me too, which I did. Happily she agreed to pop in a couple of times a week, and she has been marvellous: she cleans, does the washing and the ironing, and is great with the dogs, which is not an easy thing to accomplish, because they can be a bit lively and quite a handful on occasions.

Sara also bought all my clothes for me; I never bought any for myself, and I'm still wearing the ones she got me, although I suppose I'm going to have to go out and get some new stuff at some stage, which I'm not looking forward to. I also had to do very basic things like going shopping in a supermarket, which, once again, was something I'd never really done. I am, though, quite good with my own company. I don't feel the need to be surrounded by people all the time, and I think the fact that I have such an all-consuming job has helped as well.

Friends were very supportive when they heard what had happened to Sara. I had lovely flowers and messages from people like Paul O'Grady and Cliff Richard, and the response I got from the public was amazing. I literally had sackfuls of mail passing on their sympathy, and it was wonderful to know that there was so much love and affection out there. I will always be grateful for their thoughts, and it really was overwhelming.

There is no doubt that since Sara's passing my work on *Coronation Street* has helped me to settle back into a routine and get some kind of normality into my life. I realise that at the age of 78 I am very lucky to be involved in a job that I absolutely love and enjoy so much. The *Street* is like a second family for me and, I suspect, for everyone who works on it. We all spend so much time involved with it in one form or another, and the friendliness of the place is something that people always remark on. It's a very happy environment, and I'm pleased that I have been a part of it for more than 50 years.

Having some strong storylines and plots to immerse myself in after I returned to work was wonderful, because the work was interesting and stimulating. As ever, the writers came up with some great stuff, and it was lovely to have that twist with Ken getting involved with Martha. The character of Ken may be seven years younger than me, but, at the age of almost seventy when he embarked on his affair with her, he probably should have known better. He was quite taken with her and the fact that she seemed to love the arts, but at the same time he never told her that he was a married man. Ken might have mellowed, but his weakness for women was still there, and it was only when a near disaster occurred, when alcoholic Peter was almost killed in a fire at his flat with his son, Simon, that Ken began to be jolted to his senses. Martha wasn't exactly pleased to discover Ken was married, but it looked as though he would actually leave Deirdre for her at one point. However, he had a last-minute change of heart and decided he couldn't. The twist in all of this was that he'd already written a letter telling Deirdre he was off, but Peter had found out about the affair and came to his father's rescue by finding the letter and tearing it up. In true Ken tradition, even though he had embarked on an affair and got away with it, he began to feel guilty and felt he had to tell Deirdre what had happened. It's the sort of thing Ken has been doing all of his life when it comes to women. He succumbs to temptation, but in the end his honesty will not allow him to go the way many other men might.

It wasn't the only time he got into trouble with another woman, because after Tracy's murder charge he and Deirdre had a real set-to, which saw Ken walk out. In fairness to Ken, it was a desire to see his son Daniel that was the main motivating factor, but Denise Osbourne was also around and made a play for Ken. For once nothing happened, and he returned to Deirdre. When Ken told Deirdre about Martha she was understandably upset, but the great thing about their relationship now is that it is much more forgiving. Ken had done the same with Deirdre when she had strayed with Dev Alahan. They each know the other is not perfect and they have a lot of history between them, but they get on with things. They are older and wiser, despite the lapses on occasions, and they are also far more forgiving. They have also worked as a team during an assortment of family crises, and I always know that another one of those storylines is just around the corner, because of the sort of family the Barlows are.

Peter's alcohol problems offered a new slant to the Barlow family late on in 2009, when he wanted to open a wine bar with his girlfriend, Leanne Battersby. Ken was against it for obvious reasons, but Peter assured him that he was on the wagon and could cope with being so close to a load of booze on a regular basis. So immediately there was the conflict between Ken and his son, which was nothing unusual. I sat back and waited for the scripts to arrive in anticipation of some nice meaty conflict scenes involving Ken and Peter. I got really excited one day when I was getting my scripts sorted out and saw that as part of one scene Ken drives a JCB through Peter's bar. I thought it was a wonderful idea. The thought of a slightly deranged Ken demolishing Peter's dream of a wine bar seemed fantastic, and I actually thought that I should probably start taking some sort of lessons in order to learn how to drive one of the things properly. I'd had enough trouble with a motorbike back in the '60s when I'd had to come thundering down the outside set of the *Street* in one take to know that when mechanical things were involved, you really had to plan things meticulously. The strange thing was that nothing was said to me about this whole idea, and I began to wonder when they wanted me to get involved in the stunt. Curiosity got the better of me and I decided to ask when the big day would arrive, only to be told that the phrase 'Ken drives a JCB through Peter's bar' was meant in a metaphorical sense relating to the whole idea of the scheme, and I'd taken it literally!

It was silly, really, because if I had thought it through I would have realised that even if they had intended for that particular piece of machinery to be used, it would have been a stuntman involved in driving it and not me. The old days of hanging by a rope from the top of a roof, as I had done in the 1960s when I was involved in talking Christine Hardman out of her suicide bid, were long gone. Stuntmen have played an important part in the show for many years now, and the health and safety regulations involved for anyone on-set these days means that stunt professionals take over when it comes to things like planning fight scenes through to fires and crashes. I remember chatting to the guy who was going to be crashing a car that was supposed to be driven by Don

Brennan during a scene from a 1997 episode. The plot called for a deranged Don, who had been trying to kill Mike Baldwin, to jump into Alma's car and then go crashing into a wall, with all the flames and debris there would be from such an incident. The stuntman explained that a series of different objects were going to be placed in front of the car at strategic stages, and they in turn would actually take the impact and slow it down, so that by the time he reached the wall he had virtually stopped anyway. The effect, when it was shown, was quite spectacular, and it made you realise how professional these guys are and how meticulous the planning of any stunt has to be in order for it to work, be safe and look authentic.

I even had a stunt double in that episode when I had to fall through a ceiling and land on a bed with Nick Tilsley and Leanne Battersby. The stuntman did all the hard work and came crashing down onto the bed below. Once that had been shot the scene was cut, and I then had to get on the bed in a crouched position and the cameras started rolling again, making it look as though it was one continuous take.

Getting things like that right and making it all look good has always been an important part of the way the programme is put together. A lot of time, trouble and effort goes into every episode of *Coronation Street*, and the trick is to make sure the viewer is carried through it without anything getting in the way of their enjoyment. So not only do the scripts have to be good and of a high standard, along with the acting and direction, there also has to be great attention to detail. It's no use having a scene outside the Rovers with the reflection of a boom mike visible in the window, and, likewise, you can't have a scene in somebody's house where you hear the sound of a camera moving. Even a very simple scene involving two people on opposite sides of the Street will involve shots from one side then the other, and then perhaps close-up shots of the actors involved. This whole thing might only last for seconds on the screen when it is shown, but the actual mechanics of it have taken a lot longer.

I once had a scene with Tracy, who was played by Dawn Acton at the time, which involved me talking to her in the flat I occupied above the corner shop, her running down the stairs, the two of us running down the Street and then the scene finally ending in the Barlows' house. The whole thing lasted no more than two minutes when it was shown, but it actually took four days to put together. We shot the bit in the flat on a Monday, and the part with her running downstairs was done on the Wednesday, because although it looked as though there was a flat above the shop, there wasn't, and so the stairs were just a separate prop in the studio. We then did the outside stuff running down the Street on the Thursday and finished with the interior part in the Barlows' on the Friday.

It is also incredibly important to get continuity throughout the programme, with both what we say and what we do. When it comes to dialogue there is a record of every word ever spoken on the show, which means it can be referred to for historical purposes when it comes to future scripts, and also in case anyone queries anything that has been said. The other really important continuity is in the way we look on-screen. If I am walking down the Street and into my house, it's important that I look the same when I walk through the front door as I did when the outside shot showed me opening the door. As the houses on the *Street*'s exterior have no insides to them, this means that you will go in through the door and then the scene is cut. The interior shot will then take place in the studio, but you have to look the same as you step into the house. Every time something like this happens, a digital picture is taken of you and then wardrobe and make-up will make sure that you do look as you should do, although I managed to make a bit of a mess of this some years ago. We shot a scene with me going into the Barlows' house that was done on the Monday, but the next part of the scene wasn't done until a few days later, by which time I'd had a haircut. There was nothing that could be done, so they had to make the best of it, and it was only a quick shot, but if you saw it you must have thought that I'd managed to have the quickest haircut in history! I'm also often guilty of forgetting to put my wedding ring on during scenes, and I will often hear someone saying, 'Bill, have you got your ring on?' It's a little thing, I know, but that sort of attention to detail is so important to the show.

One of the great joys of working on *Coronation Street* has been the fact that over the years we've had some lovely guest appearances from some wonderful actors. Most recently, apart from Stephanie Beacham, we've had the likes of Nigel Havers, June Whitfield and Anthony Valentine. I enjoyed having Anthony in the show, and I think he enjoyed his time with us. He appeared as little Simon's other grandfather, and the fact that he had plenty of money and didn't mind letting anyone know about it was always going to make him the sort of person Ken would take a dislike to. The fact that Ken also felt that Anthony's character, George Wilson, was trying to buy Simon's affection did not sit well, and things were always likely to end in tears.

The one thing Ken and George were united on was the need to make sure Peter straightened himself out and got off the booze, but when George decided Simon needed protecting from his own father and kept his grandson away from Peter, things got a bit out of hand. George took Simon for a trip to Blackpool and the youngster went missing, setting the scene for everyone having to decamp to Blackpool as we all searched for the youngster. It meant that we had to spend time in Blackpool, which would have been lovely but for the fact that we had to do all the filming in freezing conditions and it was shot during the early hours of the morning. We were all given nice rooms in a hotel for us to rest in while we waited to be called for the various scenes, and I also managed to persuade the guy who was in charge of some of the amusements to open up and let me play on one of the motor-racing games they had there. When you are filming at odd times like that and in cold conditions, there is a lot of dead time and you need to make sure you keep yourself amused. Anthony came up with this wonderful nonsense verse while we were filming in the rain on one occasion and, just like a bunch of giggling kids, we all started to recite it. This was how it went:

> Not a mutter did he utter as he slid into the gutter.
> A pig come by and lay down by his side.
> A lady what was passing was quietly heard to say,
> 'You can tell a man what boozes by the company he chooses.'
> At which the pig got up and slowly walked away.

It was all beautifully delivered in a very broad Lancastrian accent by Anthony, and very soon that was it: we were all muttering the verse as well. It's strange the sort of things that can amuse you at that time in the morning.

Another lovely guest appearance we've had was Sir Ian McKellen, an actor who absolutely adored the *Street* and was genuinely thrilled to join the cast in 2005. He even bought us all little chairs with canvas backs that had our names on. I know Nigel Havers has enjoyed playing the suave escort Lewis Archer, while June Whitfield was an absolute delight when she came in to play Blanche's friend May Penn. It was lovely to have June on the show; she is such a superb actress and a lovely person, but there was a bittersweet tinge to her appearance, because she came in as part of the episodes that showed Blanche's funeral, earlier this year.

That particular storyline was difficult for all of us, because not only had the character of Blanche passed away in *Coronation Street*, our dear friend and colleague who played her so beautifully, Maggie Jones, had actually died months before.

17

THE STREET COMES FIRST

Maggie Jones held a special place in the affections of everyone she worked with during her time in *Coronation Street*. She was a delightful person and a great actress who played the role of Blanche to perfection. The character was marvellous, and whenever there was a scene in which she featured you knew there were going to be some great lines, but it was the way Maggie managed to deliver them that made it all so special. Her timing was absolutely brilliant and couldn't be faulted. Anne and I used to love playing in scenes with her, even though Ken was often the victim of her cutting one-liners. Typical of the sort of thing she did was this deadpan observation to Deirdre one day:

'Good looks are a curse,' Blanche told her daughter. 'You and Ken should count yourselves lucky.'

It was marvellous stuff and just the sort of thing everyone came to expect from Blanche. Maggie actually died in December 2009, and by that time she was very frail. All of us who knew and worked with her were extremely sad when we heard the news. I think it was particularly upsetting for Anne, because Maggie had been her on-screen mum for so long. Although Maggie passed away in December, her *Street* death and funeral didn't take place until some months later, and we did all the filming for it in March 2010. I am often asked whether I get confused between who I am and the character I play. The answer is that I don't. Ken may physically do things the way I do them, but he does different things to me and thinks differently to me. His mannerisms and appearance are my mannerisms and appearance, but that's as far as it goes. So I don't have any identity problems with him; I'm just his caretaker.

After Maggie died her character had to be written out of the show, so just months after the actress had actually died, we were shooting scenes concerning the death of Blanche, who was supposed to have died while in Portugal. Right in the middle of doing all of these scenes we then had a memorial service for Maggie, which pretty much everyone connected with *Coronation Street* went to. So we were suddenly playing the death of a character and then we were dealing with the death of the actor. For the first time that I can remember in all of my time on the programme, the complexity of it all did have me confused in the sense that I was very emotional about it all and so, too, was Annie. We weren't quite sure what we were crying at, because there was this intermixing, the like of which I've never known, for the two of us. We were incredibly fond of Maggie Jones as a person and of what she had made Blanche in the show. It was a very strange situation. As actors we were doing a performance about a character, and then as individuals we were going along to the memorial for Maggie. In the end, I think doing the scenes for the programme helped both Anne and me, because what came out of them was a lot of humour, simply because they were all about Blanche.

As part of everything that went on for her, Ken had to make a speech in the Rovers. I've done speeches on the show before, some of them quite tricky, though none of them had really presented a problem, but this time that was not the case. It was about a page and a half long when I saw the script, and I didn't really think anything of it at first, but when it came to learning the words it was suddenly a different matter. Some things are easy to learn, some things are not, and this certainly fell into the latter category. I just couldn't get it right. I was trying to rough it and run through the lines in my head the night before I was due to do it, but it just wouldn't happen.

When we got on-set, I still felt that it wasn't there and I couldn't do it. The whole thing was a horrible experience, because in my own mind I thought, 'This is it. They're all going to be watching me, saying, "What's happened to Bill?"' However, as soon as we went for the take it was there. I did it right through, the director was delighted and there was a round of applause from everyone who was on the set. I think what happened to begin with was that I had allowed all the emotion of the situation to creep into my thoughts, and it was getting in the way. In the end, I took my time and it just flowed. At one stage I thought the whole thing was going to be a disaster, but in the end it worked and it was very satisfying.

It is moments like that that make acting on the programme so special, and it is why I have enjoyed my time in *Coronation Street* so much. I have always felt fortunate to be a part of such a wonderful show and appreciated the fact that as an actor I have been continuously employed for such a long period of time. In a profession such as mine, I know how lucky I have been to be able to do that. I suppose it also means that to still be around in such a show means I must be doing something right, and I am acutely aware that it is the public who play such a big part in the continuing success of *Coronation Street*. If viewers did not tune in and the ratings fell, I know the programme would be in trouble, but hopefully that will never happen, and the *Street* happily shows no signs of losing its popularity.

Fans play a big part in what we do, and I have always thought it nice that they appreciate what we do. They have been extremely kind to me over the years, and I have always got on well with them. Whether they like Ken or Bill Roache, or perhaps a mixture of the two, I don't know. I regularly receive a lot of post and always try to reply to the letters, but have to admit that I began to fall behind after Sara's death and I still don't seem to have caught up with a lot of the mail. The vast majority of the correspondence I receive is very nice; I rarely get any nasty letters, and since writing a book a few years ago about my spiritual beliefs, I have started to get a whole new section of correspondence from people who are also interested in the subject.

I suspect a lot of the people who write to me are fans who have grown old with me; they might have watched the show from the very early days and grown up with the *Street* as part of their lives. I'm lucky in as much as I don't seem to attract fans who are perhaps a little too enthusiastic, although in the very early days I did get the occasional letter that contained a pair of knickers when I opened it. I also had a slightly uncomfortable feeling about another fan a few years ago, when I attended some sort of local event in Manchester, and someone who was very obviously a *Coronation Street* fanatic began to talk to me. I was there with Sara, but we'd gone in separate cars, so when it was time to leave I asked this guy where he had to get back to. When he told me I realised that I passed through it on my way home, so I offered to give him a lift and thought no more about it. As I drove along he kept saying, 'I can't believe it, I can't believe it. Ken Barlow's giving me a lift home!' I suddenly began to feel slightly uncomfortable, because there was definitely something strange about the way he was carrying on, and although I waved him off with a smile when we got to where he wanted to be dropped off, I have to say that I was quite pleased Sara was following on behind me. One of the nicest things about my life and what I do is the fact that by signing a simple autograph or having a chat with someone, it can really make their day. Some of the older women who come up to me are absolutely charming, and stopping to have a chat with them is always something I enjoy doing. They walk off smiling, and it leaves a really nice feeling to know that by doing something as simple as talking I have actually made them happy.

Being in the programme has given me a platform to do all sorts of other things, from chat shows and programmes like *Stars in Their Eyes* and the *Paul O'Grady Show* and appearing with Anne Kirkbride in the video that accompanied Peter Kay and Tony Christie's 'Is This the Way to Amarillo' hit record to playing in things like pro-celebrity golf matches with some of the greatest players the game has seen, like Gary Player, Tony Jacklin and Nick Faldo. It's lovely to be asked to do all sorts of things and I've had some wonderful moments away from the *Street*, but, of course, it is because of the programme that some of those moments have occurred. I had two wonderful years where I did a reading at the Albert Hall for the memorial service that is held there each year. It is a magnificent building, and for an occasion like that it is packed full with an audience you would never experience anywhere else. You have the Queen and Prince Philip and a lot of the royal family in attendance, as well as the prime minister and the heads of all the strands of the armed forces; in fact, just about anybody who is anybody goes to it. I was asked to do a Bible reading, and I have to admit that it was quite a daunting experience, but at the same time very enjoyable as well. The next year I was asked to read a couple of very emotive poems concerning the Battle of Britain, and once again I was very nervous, but it was a tremendous experience and one that I will always remember.

I have been fortunate enough to meet the Queen on about eight occasions, going right back to my days in the army, and one of the most memorable and enjoyable occasions occurred during 1992, when she visited Preston as part of its celebrations at having been granted the status of a city. At the Guild Hall there was going to be something that was effectively a private piece of entertainment for the Queen and Prince Philip, which would go on for about 20 minutes and include a choir singing. I was asked to contribute a four-minute 'something' during this, but I really didn't have a clue what I could do, so I rang up a guy called John Stevenson, who was a writer on the programme, and asked if he had any ideas. About ten minutes after having the conversation with him, John rang back and said he was going to write a piece for me that was going to be about the fact that a certain part of Lancashire had managed to produce more well-known comedians than anywhere else in Britain. I did the piece, and it went really well as I listed and talked about some great names who had come out of the area over the years, including the likes of Les Dawson.

After all of this had been done Prince Philip chatted to me about the talk I'd given, and he clearly seemed to like comedy and comedians. He told me that he had once had a conversation with Les Dawson in which the two of them had somehow got onto the subject of black puddings. Apparently Prince Philip had said that they should be grilled, but Les insisted they should be fried. About ten years after this conversation, Les took part in a Royal Variety Performance, and as Prince Philip went down the line after the show, shaking hands with the performers, as soon as the two men set eyes on each other, Prince Philip immediately said 'grilled', and Les replied 'fried'!

Later that same day at Preston, I asked an equerry whether it would be possible for the Queen to meet John, and both she and Prince Philip came and talked to him and his wife, as well as Sara and me, for about five minutes. It was all very relaxed and a lovely moment that, once again, I will always remember.

I have also enjoyed being able to do charity work over the years, but rather than spread myself thinly, as I might have done in the past, I now intend to concentrate my energies on the work that will be done by the Sara Roache Foundation. It is a charitable trust that has been set up to concentrate on the sort of charities that I know would have been close to Sara's heart. I won't have anything to do with the actual administration of it – that will be left to my daughter Verity and other trustees – but I will be out there as the sort of public face, if you like, and the foundation will be initially supporting about four or five separate charities.

I like to get involved with things that mean something to me and which I feel I can help with. That happened earlier this year when I talked about my deafness. It was amazing how many people were unaware of my condition, and the whole thing got quite a lot of publicity. The 50 per cent hearing I have in each ear has never affected my work, and acting must be one of the best professions to be in for someone like me. After all, actors tend to talk loudly and they speak clearly. I do have trouble picking things up if there is background noise or if somebody is speaking very softly and quickly, but big, loud sounds are fine, and I don't really find I have a problem.

Mind you, I prefer not to take any chances when it comes to waking up in the mornings in order to get into the studio on time. When Sara was alive it wasn't a problem, because she would always wake me up, but now I use a good old-fashioned alarm clock with two bells and a big hammer that rattles against them when it goes off. It's essential for me and part of my morning routine. When that alarm goes off I have to sit bolt upright, otherwise I know I'll go off to sleep again, and then I always make sure I give myself plenty of time before setting off for the drive into

Manchester. It is strange to think that I have been turning up at Granada Studios to work on *Coronation Street* for more than 50 years, because it simply doesn't seem that long, probably because I have enjoyed it all so much.

The programme has given me an awful lot, and I hope, in return, that I have played my part in its success. I always made it a rule that, with the exception of my family, the *Street* comes first; it has to if I am going to do my job properly. I have learned to build my world around working on *Coronation Street*. That doesn't mean it dominates my life, but it does mean that lots of other social things have to be geared around it, particularly these days, when so many episodes are being made. There are periods where I might have a very heavy workload, with a lot of scenes over two weeks. When that happens, I always say that it is like entering a dark tunnel, because it can be pretty unrelenting. You learn your lines, you do your scenes the next day and then you go home to learn more scenes in preparation for the following day's shooting. We all have those periods where you hardly have time to come up for air, but then you might get a week where you have very little to do, and other weeks where you have time off. Your life is pretty much governed by the board near the front of the studios that shows the schedule for the coming two weeks. I always tell anyone new who comes into the show that if they can master that and the coffee machine, everything will be fine. Once you know what your personal workload and schedule are, it means you can plan things around them.

I have already mentioned the family atmosphere that I feel exists within *Coronation Street*, and it is a way of life to everyone who works there. I'm sure the friendliness of the place helps everyone on the show, and although the actors can have some tough days and a heavy working schedule, the pace really is unrelenting for the technical staff and other people who work there, and who are used to working very long hours, often in very tough conditions. The family atmosphere took on a new meaning last year when it was decided to hatch a storyline that would fit in perfectly with both the show's anniversary and Ken's 50 years on the *Street*. The great thing was that it was not only going to involve me, but also my two sons, Linus and Will. I was absolutely delighted when I heard about the idea, and although the story was actually seen in September, the filming for it had to be done at the beginning of July, because that was the only time Linus could get away from his busy schedule playing Michael Cutter in the *Law and Order* TV series in the USA. He lives in New York now and has had tremendous success with the series out there. Will is also a very fine actor, although he now calls himself James Roache in order to avoid confusion with me. In fact, I once got listed as having taken part in work he'd done, so I think he decided it was better to use James, which is his second name anyway.

I am extremely proud of all my children and love them dearly. The fact that two of them have chosen to become actors had nothing to do with me, and I don't think they were at all impressed by what I did when they were growing up. Having a father who happened to be on television regularly never really meant anything; it was all rather taken for granted. They just had very ordinary childhoods, and that was the way we wanted it. Of course, they didn't mind the little perks that sometimes went with having a dad who was quite well known, like the time we went to the Tower of London and ended up being ushered to the front of a queue and then given what amounted to a private tour. I also recall one occasion when I'd taken Verity over to the comedian Les Dawson's house to play with his daughter. I had to laugh when Les's little girl asked Verity what it was like to have a famous dad!

The idea of getting Linus and Will to be part of the show was wonderful for me, and the storyline of a letter being found from Ken's first girlfriend shot the whole show back 50 years to the very first episode, in which Susan Cunningham appeared. The fact that he found out Susan wanted to see him because she was pregnant opened up a whole new plot. Ken discovered that he had another illegitimate son, and using Linus for that part gave it a lovely twist. Just to add to things, Ken also discovered that he had another grandson, who was played by Will. The idea of Linus and Will playing father and son was just great. It was also fun to see Linus back on the set of *Coronation Street* thirty-five years after he last appeared, playing nine-year-old Peter.

The whole thing was very exciting for me, and the producer, Phil Collinson, was very keen on it. The limiting factor was that Linus could only give two weeks of his time because of other work commitments, and for any major story in the *Street* that is really not enough, but we got on with it and I thought it worked very well. As usual, the writing was superb, and it was wonderful to have my two sons working with me. They stayed at my house, and we would have a meal in the evening and then go into the conservatory, which we nicknamed 'the Actors' Workshop', to go through the scripts.

Linus has been involved in some very big things on stage, screen and TV, and I remember saying to him early on that if he had any notes with regard to the way we should play things, then he ought to let me know. 'Look, Pa,' he said (Linus always calls me 'Pa'), 'we're in your world here – you've been doing this for 50 years. If you've got notes, you give them to me!' Will nodded his agreement, but there were never any notes, we just got on and did it. There were little discussions about the script here and there, about what we thought the meaning of this scene or that scene should be, but that was all. The whole experience was a very happy and relaxed one.

As often happens, the scenes were shot out of sequence, and I remember that one of the first we did involved me talking quite deeply about the relationship between a father and son. Although it was Ken talking, I think both Linus and I felt a lot of the script was rather pertinent to our own relationship, because all those years ago when I had been divorced there had been a period when I really hadn't had contact with him. It was touching, and Linus said that he felt the parallels quite strongly at one point.

While we were shooting our scenes, we would all use my dressing-room. We'd travel in together, go into make-up and wait to be called on set. The first time we were called, we had a quiet word run just to check things, did a little run for the cameras so that they knew what to expect when we started shooting the scene and then it was a case of cue and – bang! – we did the scene straight off. No retakes, no pick-ups, and we were off and walking back to the dressing-room. 'I don't believe it,' said Linus when we got back. 'I don't believe the speed you work at here.'

In fairness, we had done a lot of the groundwork at home, but the fact of the matter is that's how the system works on *Coronation Street*. It's not dissimilar to the way a major film would work, except we do in ten minutes what they would probably take all day to do.

Scenes like these with Linus and Will made me realise just how central to my life the character of Ken Barlow has been: I have enjoyed playing him immensely, and I hope the public have enjoyed having him around for the past 50 years. I have no intention of retiring; I'm happy to carry on, because I love what I do. I also realise I'm lucky to be doing it. There isn't a day goes by where I am not grateful to have a job, and to have a job that I love so much. I like the discipline of it; I like the joy of hitting my lines right; I like the lovely family set-up that is the *Street*; and, as long as they want me, I can't envisage a time when I wouldn't want to do it.

I feel great physically, and I think I'm lucky when it comes to the way I look, because I don't do things like exercise and I don't eat particularly well. I think it must be in the genes. I'm seventy-eight and Ken is seven years my junior, but I hope people still think he looks young for his age. I'm sure the key to staying young is to stay active, and I love having a job that is both challenging and demanding. There are many things I still want to do, and at the moment I am trying to write some children's books, but all the things I want to do, I'd like to do while I am here working on the *Street*. I am thrilled to be a part of the programme and excited by what the future holds. The show has shown the ability to adapt and flourish in the past, and it will continue to do so in the future.

After more than 50 years on the *Street* I am often asked what the secret of Ken's staying power has been. I'm not sure there is any one thing, but I do know the public clearly like him, and for that I am extremely grateful.

I just feel that I've learned my lines and turned up on time.

18

BEHIND THE NET CURTAIN

By the time 9 December 2010 came around, I had appeared in 3,940 episodes and been part of the show for 50 years. During that time, I had seen and experienced an awful lot, but I can honestly say that my 3,941st appearance on *Coronation Street* was one of the most nerve-racking and exciting of my entire time on the programme, because it was broadcast live as part of a week-long celebration of the show's anniversary.

Having been in the historic first episode of the programme in 1960, still being part of *Coronation Street* 50 years later was something I was very proud of. As I have already mentioned, the show's anniversary was also a very personal landmark for me, and in the end the year 2010 was one of the most enjoyable, stimulating and exhausting that I can ever remember. The highlight was undoubtedly that week in December with all the episodes devoted to a huge storyline that would see a tram crash in the Street, causing death, devastation and moments of high drama. The centrepiece of the week was an hour-long live episode that was broadcast on 9 December, exactly 50 years after the very first programme went out.

I think we all knew that something special would be planned for the anniversary celebration, but I don't think any of us working on the *Street* could have envisaged the sort of thing that producer Phil Collinson had in mind. Phil joined the show in July, taking over from Kim Crowther, who had done a wonderful job during her time in charge. I have already described the role of the producer and just how important it is to the show, particularly in terms of moving the programme forward. The producer must also love the show and understand *Coronation Street* if he or she is going to be successful in the role. It was clear that Phil Collinson was first and foremost a great fan of the programme, but he also had to be someone with the experience, drive, ideas and enthusiasm to oversee one of the most important periods in the show's history. The storyline was his baby, and he took a lot on. I think he was amazed at the speed with which the management agreed to it all. The whole thing was going to need a big budget, with the kind of special effects that had never been seen on the programme before.

When it was announced soon after Phil arrived that there would be a series of episodes that would involve a tram crash, I think we were all very excited, but none of us really had any idea exactly what would be involved. The sheer hard work and logistical nightmares that such a project would produce was something I had never experienced during all my time on the *Street*, but when it was all over I can honestly say that it proved to be one of the most wonderful moments of my life as an actor. The whole thing required a team effort from every single person involved in *Coronation Street*, and it was a privilege to be part of it all.

On the face of it, having five episodes during that week sounded clear-cut enough, but even if every one of them had been pre-recorded it would have involved a huge operation on all fronts; when you threw in the fact that we were going to go live on the fourth day, it meant that a whole set of new problems would have to be surmounted if the thing was going to come together as a seamless piece of work. In short, although one episode was going to be live, it had to fit perfectly between the two that would sit either side of it on the Wednesday and the Friday. Because any episode is filmed roughly two months before it is actually seen on the screen, four of the five episodes were going to have to be shot in October ready for the December transmission; the exception, obviously, was going to be the live broadcast.

Once again, the writers were brilliant, and the great thing was that although the tram crash would be this huge moment, it wasn't just about the disaster of that event; there were several other storylines running right through the week, and those would continue to evolve and move on in the weeks and months that followed the crash.

When the whole process for the filming of the episodes began, it was pretty clear that we were all going to be involved in something very special. For a start, the security involved was on a level I had never seen before. Obviously, nobody wanted the details of what was going on leaked. The broad outline was already known, and we as actors knew that there were going to be some characters killed off as part of what was going to take place, but even we didn't know exactly what was going to happen and who would go. The scripts were broken down so that you were only ever given your own bits, and there was a watermark through every one of your pages with your name on it. So if a page of my script had been found somewhere, marked with the name 'William Roache', I would have been in trouble! You had to shred all your old scripts, and although we talked to each other I never really knew what was happening with other people.

I think the whole security thing only served to make it more exciting and special for all of us. There was a bit of conjecture as to what might happen, and there was a theory that went around amongst the cast that there would be a surprise, that somebody would be killed off and we wouldn't be aware of it until the last moment. Rumour was rife that it might be one of the principal cast members who would be killed off, but none of us knew who it would be. At one point, somebody's name was mentioned as a possible candidate to go, but I pointed out that they had already been involved in shooting scenes that would be shown after the crash, only to be told that those scenes might have been done in a way that they could be easily removed at a later date! It was all good fun, and the cloak-and-dagger atmosphere just added to the whole experience.

The actual filming for the recorded episodes was physically very hard. It took four weeks, and because the crash was going to take place at night, it meant heavy schedules for everyone. We filmed from seven in the evening until five the following morning, five days a week. It was cold and wet during all of the outdoor scenes, and then the work also involved lots of other scenes that were done in the studios. But despite the gruelling schedule, I think that all of us – producer, director, writers, the crew and the actors – felt it was going to be something special.

It turned out that there was going to be an explosion in The Joinery, a bar that was about to be opened by Nick Tilsley, and the damage caused would take out a chunk of the viaduct, leading to a passing tram coming crashing off the rails and into the Street. That, in a nutshell, was what was going to happen, but in order for it all to come to fruition a huge amount of planning and organisation had to be put in place. The Street had to be turned into a scene of devastation for the duration of the shooting, and because we work so far in advance all the knock-on effects had to be taken into account. There was quite an unreal feel to the place when we came into work and saw all the things that were happening.

It was incredible to see all of this start to take shape, with bits of houses taken apart and rubble strewn all over the place, not to mention the tram that had been specially constructed, as well as other bits of it that would be used in some of the indoor shots. There were going to be lots of explosions and fires burning everywhere as the full horror of the crash and the consequences of it unfolded through the episodes. As you might expect with all that sort of thing going on, there were lots of stunt people involved. When it came to the time for them to set up the explosion in The Joinery, we were all told that we had to clear the main area of the Street, but that if we wanted to watch we could do so on monitors that were going to be set up at the far end, where the medical centre was. When I heard this, I felt a little bit cheated, because I really wanted to see the explosion happen.

'I want to see this!' I thought to myself. 'I don't want to miss out.' So when everyone went off the Street to take cover, I, like some naughty schoolboy, sneaked into the Barlows' house. It has a little bay window at the front, and from my position in there I could see straight into where the explosion was going to take place. If the stunt coordinator had known I was in there, he'd have come and got me out, and it was all quite exciting as I anticipated the arrival of the dramatic moment. However, my excitement turned to mild concern as I stood waiting for the big bang. They cleared the Street, a sort of countdown began, and I suddenly realised that I felt like someone standing on their own before an atomic bomb went off. The thing might be quite powerful, I suddenly realised, and the window I was standing behind might get blown out, shattering me with glass. I saw that the window had some net curtain hanging down. I gripped the bottom of it, hoping that it would act as a kind of shield should things go wrong, and so, sheltering behind the net curtain, I waited for the big moment to arrive and – whoosh! – the thing went up and I could feel the force of it and hear the bang. I loved it, I wouldn't have missed it for the world, and I know that I got the best view of anyone.

I had a bad fall on the first day of filming, in a scene in which I was supposed to be running towards the tram. I got to the edge of the kerb and then slipped and fell heavily on my right side. The long nights were tough physically, because a lot of what we did was in reaction to the explosion and the crash. There was one shot involving Jane Danson, who plays Leanne, and me where we had to run towards the tram crash and then, as we were doing that, we were thrown back by the explosion. The two of us had stunt doubles for the first bit, but we still had to keep falling back onto the cold, wet cobbles, and we lost count of how many times we did that. When the episode was shown, that particular shot was over in seconds, and if you'd blinked you would have missed the moment. But it was things like that that were so necessary for the overall look of the story.

There were lots of fires going on, and these were created with gas chutes that blew flames into the air. I actually liked them because they warmed the place up a bit, and when you're filming in damp and cold conditions, it's quite nice to have a burst of warmth every now and again. The crew were brilliant and brought round things like hand warmers and warm coats in between takes. It was such a huge effort from everyone to make sure it got done in the way that it should. Two directors, Graeme Harper and Tony Prescott, did the episodes, with Tony directing the live episode and the two either side of it. Both of them were superb and deserve a lot of credit for what went on and how the whole thing turned out.

It was quite an experience to spend that much time on night shoots. We sometimes do them in the *Street* during the course of a year, as I had in Blackpool about twelve months earlier, but to do it for four weeks was very different. I got a taste of how shift workers must feel, because there's no doubt you have to get used to a completely new way of operating each day. I'd get home after filming and try to get some sleep, but it was very strange, and at first you have to readjust. The good thing was that there was no filming at weekends, so that was quite a nice break. It wasn't easy, but everyone was enjoying the excitement of it all so much that there was always a lovely atmosphere.

Once all the filming for the recorded episodes had been completed, we returned to filming for what was to follow, and once again we were back into the routine of acting in episodes that were going to be seen about eight weeks later. The amazing thing was how the Street was put back together again. Over a period of a weekend, they managed to get everything looking pretty normal once more. The tram was put into storage, ready to be used again for the live episode, and the rubble and debris that had become the normal backdrop were taken away as houses and roofs were reconstructed. Once more, it was a tremendous effort from those involved, and we, as actors, came back in to see everything pretty much restored to normal, an amazing feat, really, and all part of the huge logistical operation that was needed to make sure the story worked.

Continuity was also a big concern, and all of our clothes had to be stored, with garments that were dirty or damaged kept in exactly the same state, so that they could be brought out and used on the night of the live episode. I had a little bit of dirt on one of my shoes, and even that had to look exactly the same when I put them on again. But I have to admit that there was one thing that wasn't quite the same about my appearance when it came to the live broadcast – and that was my hair. It had grown very long at the back and felt a bit untidy, so I'd had it cut. This sort of thing has happened over the years, and since that infamous moment

I described earlier in the book, when I'd had a haircut between shooting outdoor and indoor scenes, I'd become quite conscious of the need for continuity when there was a gap in filming. I usually managed to get around the problem by explaining to my hairdresser that I could have only the merest of trims on these occasions, but unfortunately, after filming the tram crash scenes, I had a little bit too much taken off just before the live episode, and if anyone looked really closely they would have seen that my hair was longer on the night before we went live and also on the night after, because those were the ones that had been recorded some weeks earlier.

Nobody was forced into appearing in the live episode. As had happened before, there was always the chance to opt out. But I think it was just kind of assumed that I would agree to do it, and although I knew the whole experience would be stomach churning, there was no way I was not going to do it. After all, I'd been there at the start when we did the live broadcasts all those years ago, and I had also done the live episode ten years earlier, so I certainly wanted to be part of the 50th anniversary celebrations. Although I could remember how nervous doing live episodes makes you, I still wanted to do it. I have to admit, though, that the tram crash live episode seemed much worse than any of the others, mainly because it was here and now, and it was going to be such a big thing for the programme because of the special anniversary. I actually had more to do in the episode that went out in 2000, because of the speech I had to give, but this one involved a lot of waiting around for the cameras to cut to the scenes I was in, and the wait in between each of them seemed to go on for ever.

We had about ten days in which to rehearse for the live episode, and they began with a read-through for everyone. We sat around a huge square table that had been set up in one of the studios and started to familiarise ourselves with the script. In the days that followed, we had to rehearse all the scenes that would be shot on the night, some inside and some outside. My scenes were going to take place in the hospital as Ken anxiously waited on the outcome of injuries his son Peter had sustained when he was trapped in The Joinery in the immediate aftermath of the explosion.

All the rubble and damage had to be put back, as well as having the tram placed in exactly the same position it had occupied before the Street was cleaned up after filming the other episodes. It was incredible to see it all looking as it had done several weeks before, and the attention to detail was superb.

On the day of the broadcast, we came in quite late and then had a dress rehearsal. Time just seemed to disappear, and before you knew it we were going live. I have to admit that you have a feeling of horror waiting for it all to happen. Nerves are an amazing thing. But we all knew we were in the same boat, and it was one massive team effort, because we were all relying on each other. It was a full, complicated episode, written by Jan McVerry, and they had decided not to go for the easy option. A lot of it was filmed outside on the night, and the director went for some very difficult shots, with lots of people moving around. It's quite a small site, but in all I think there was something like 375 people involved on the night, and 26 cameras were used. Different units were set up in all the places that would be filmed.

In my case, I just had to wait quietly until action was called for the hospital scene. You wait and wait and wait, and suddenly you have to do your bit. You hear a voice saying, 'Right! Twenty seconds, studio . . . ten seconds . . . cue!' So then you do your bit and after it they cut to a different scene. You then have to wait and wait all over again before the same process takes place. It's a frightening feeling when you know that fourteen million people are watching, and you certainly don't want to be the one who messes up!

Whenever we film, there's a box where the director will be, and there will be several camera shots that they will be looking at. He will call out the shot he wants at any particular time. It is then up to the vision mixer to press the right button to bring up the particular shot that has been asked for. Because the live episode was such a complicated exercise, with things going on in the studio and outside, they flew in this huge control centre, and the panel that the vision mixer had to use was about ten feet long. She was called Linda Kelly, and she was a real star on the night, because she literally had to run up and down this thing playing it like some huge organ to get the smoothness and transition from scene to scene spot-on.

When it was over, a huge cheer went up, and there were hugs and kisses all round. The best thing about doing an episode like that is the feeling of relief when it's all finished and you know it has gone well. There was a bit of a party after the episode had finished, and we got feedback from people who had been watching it and who said it had looked great. People made speeches, and there were more hugs and kisses and congratulations. There was a feeling of joy and great satisfaction that we had all been involved in a very special night – one of many special nights the programme has enjoyed during more than 50 years on our television screens.

After all the excitement of the live episode, it was back to normal a few days later when we returned to work to start filming for future shows. It epitomised what *Coronation Street* is about and why I believe it can keep going from strength to strength. The programme always has to move on. Celebrating our 50th anniversary was wonderful for the show and for me, but the programme is really about the here and now and what will happen in the future.